CREATING
MANDALAS

D0763455

CREATING MANDALAS

For Insight, Healing, and Self-Expression

SUSANNE F. FINCHER

Foreword by Robert A. Johnson

REVISED EDITION

SHAMBHALA • *Boston & London* • 2010

Dedicated to the memory of my mother Ada Wre Handlin Foster

SHAMBHALA PUBLICATIONS, INC.
Horticultural Hall
300 Massachusetts Avenue
Boston, Massachusetts 02115
www.shambhala.com

© 1991, 2010 by Susanne F. Fincher
Please visit www.creatingmandalas.com
for more information on mandalas.

9 8 7 6 5 4

Revised edition
Printed in the United States of America

⊗This edition is printed on acid-free paper that meets the American National Standards Institute Z39.48 Standard.
♻This book is printed on 30% postconsumer recycled paper. For more information please visit www.shambhala.com.
Distributed in the United States by Penguin Random House LLC and in Canada by Random House of Canada Ltd

Library of Congress Cataloging-in-Publication Data

Fincher, Susanne F., 1941–
Creating mandalas: for insight, healing, and self-expression / Susanne F. Fincher; foreword by Robert A. Johnson.—Rev.
p. cm.
Previously published: 1991.
Includes bibliographical references and index.
ISBN 978-1-59030-805-9 (pbk.: alk. paper)
1. Mandala. I. Title.
BL604.M36F56 2010
203'.7—dc22
2009047906

CONTENTS

FOREWORD

NEVER BEFORE HAS MANKIND been in such need of the healing power of the mandala as at present. Our fractured, disintegrating world cries for that cohesive force which is the great power of mandala.

Someone asked Dr. Jung what the prevailing archetype of mankind would be at present. He replied instantly and vehemently, "Disintegration!"

This disintegration which we suffer—one has only to look at modern painting or hear the chaotic sounds of contemporary music—is certainly the greatest danger which faces us in the modern world. The psyche offers up the specific healing element, the mandala, when it is most needed, and we will be wise to hear its timely structure. Never have we needed it more.

Susanne Fincher's book is warm, direct, easily comprehended in its healing mission. She writes as an artist but makes a wonderful synthesis of this art with fine scholarship. This book is a mandala in its own right, and it is healing simply to read it.

Robert A. Johnson
Encinitas, California

PREFACE TO THE 2010 EDITION

THE YEARS SINCE *Creating Mandalas* was published have been busy, productive ones for me. My three children are grown and now I have four wonderful grandchildren who have shown me again that mandala-making skills come naturally to young ones. I have had the privilege of meeting people from all over the world who have shared their personal mandala stories with me. My travels have taken me to places where mandalas were sacred among ancient peoples: Korea, Turkey, Denmark, England, Ireland, and the southwestern United States. Curiosity has led me to explore mandalas that are danced, walked, and sung as well as drawn and painted.

I have listened and learned from the teachers at Drepung Loseling, a Tibetan Buddhist monastery in Atlanta. I have attended the construction of a number of the monks' sand mandalas, marveling at their patience. Being present for the ceremonial deconstruction of their mandalas has made me aware of my Western assumptions about art and its purposes. Now, when I must purge a pile of artwork left by people who cannot or will not take it, I make a ceremony of remembering them as I shred their drawings for the recycling bin.

Joan Kellogg, one of my most important teachers, died in 2004. She was a resource and support for me during the writing of *Creating Mandalas*. I continue to explore her ideas, delving into some of her sources: Eastern religions and Jungian psychology. Ms. Kellogg's original formulation of the Archetypal Stages of the Great Round of Mandala as twelve stages in a cycle of growth aligns her theory with ancient ideas about twelve as a number of wholeness: the signs of the zodiac, months of the year, hours in a day and a night, Biblical tribes of Israel, apostles of Jesus, and the number of deities in several mythologies. Her work has now passed into the hands of others who emphasize her Mandala Assessment and Research Institute (MARI) mandala card assessment, which is based on thirteen stages. My own interests follow a different path: creating mandalas as a meaningful practice for personal growth, and so I embrace the Great Round as a mandala of twelve stages whose center is Jung's archetypal Self (inspired by the *atman* of Hinduism).

I have guided groups creating mandalas at numerous workshops, conferences, and retreats. Especially memorable have been those at the Jung Institute in Zurich, Switzerland; the mandala classes for teachers in Sarajevo, Bosnia and Herzegovina; the workshops with complementary health practitioners in Seoul, South Korea; the presentations at conferences of the American Art Therapy Association; and the week-long Mandala Intensives first held in Asheville and Black Mountain, North Carolina, and now at my Plum Blossom Studio in Atlanta.

I enjoy teaching people about mandalas. My books have been written in response to needs expressed by people I meet. Over time several individuals who were especially shy about making a mark on paper asked me, "Is there a coloring book you can recommend? I find it soothing just to color." For these people and others like them I created the Coloring Mandalas series, with the hope that the books might be a stepping stone to more self-directed creative expression. Inspired by my friend Elizabeth Rucker who held a yearlong medicine wheel group, I invited some friends to join me for a twelve-month Great Round mandala group. Writings, activities, and art from this group of women have found their way into *The Mandala Workbook*, a guide for exploring mandalas in depth.

When my publisher asked me to update *Creating Mandalas*, I took a look at it and was pleased to find that the book has stood the test of time and needs little revision. Based on my experiences since the writing of *Creating Mandalas*, it seems appropriate to add a chapter on "Mandalas and Groups." May the new edition of *Creating Mandalas* be a useful resource for your insight, healing, and self-expression.

Susanne F. Fincher
Decatur, Georgia
September 2009

PREFACE TO THE FIRST EDITION

IN 1976 I WAS SUFFERING through the death of a child and a painful divorce. Night after night I brooded in my study after sleepwalking through the day's activities. My misery was so intense that I withdrew and had a hard time reaching out to share the depth of my pain and sorrow. I cannot remember exactly when, but I felt compelled to take up drawing, an activity I had enjoyed as a child.

I bought myself a set of felt-tipped markers and a pad of paper. I began to draw designs, just letting my hand go where it would. I did not try to draw anything from the reality "out there" because I did not have the energy to concentrate on looking. One day, I felt the urge to draw a circular design. It was very simple, just some concentric circles of various colors. After completing it, I noticed that I felt a little better.

I began looking forward to my evenings alone when I could get out my drawing materials and go to work. I knew that the drawing was helping me heal my wounds in some way. I began to think that art might be healing for others as well. After some searching, I discovered that art was used for psychological healing by mental health professionals called art therapists.

Discovering art therapy gave direction to my life. I pursued the necessary training and became a registered art therapist. I began working with individuals and groups using art. The imagery of clients' art served as a medium of communication that brought rich symbolism into the therapy relationship.

My interest in the circular drawings I did was pushed to the background until I read about the work of an art therapist named Joan Kellogg. Kellogg uses drawings in a circle as a guide for understanding the personality of the individual who creates them. She bases her theories on the work of Carl Jung, who had earlier identified such drawings as "mandalas." I became fascinated with the possibilities opened up by Kellogg's insights. After studying with her, I began to use mandalas with individuals and groups in art therapy. As my knowledge grew, I began to teach classes about the mandala, to lecture on the subject, and to offer mandala workshops at conferences. As of this writing I have seen thousands of mandalas, and assisted hundreds of individuals in understanding their mandala symbols.

My fascination with the mandala has continued during the fifteen years that I have created mandalas with paint, markers, paper, leather, clay, wood, and stones. I have sought to expand my awareness through study of the mandalas of other cultures, especially those of Tibetan Buddhism. I have also been privileged to meet and learn from elders of several Native American traditions.

The mandala is a living presence in my life. I draw, study, and learn from my mandalas and the mandalas of those who share their personal growth with me. Mandalas have been an anchor for me at times of darkness, pain, and confusion. Through mandalas I have reached a deeper understanding of myself and my place in the cosmos. They have been a gentle—and sometimes not so gentle—reminder that life goes on, and that the greatest celebration of life is wholehearted living. In this book I share what I know about mandalas. May this knowledge prove as useful for you as it has for me.

Susanne Foster Fincher
Conyers, Georgia
September 1990

ACKNOWLEDGMENTS

MANY THANKS TO Marilyn Clark, Laurie Downs, Nita Sue Kent, and Debbie Lincoln for sharing their mandalas and telling their stories. Thanks to Maureen Ritchie for her poem. I am indebted to Jim and Annette Culipher, organizers of the Journey into Wholeness conferences, where my ideas about the mandala evolved. Thanks also to Robert A. Johnson, whose support helped bring this book to completion. Finally, thanks to Joan Kellogg, who opened the door into the world of mandalas.

1 MANDALA: A REFLECTION OF THE SELF

A PERSIAN SHEPHERD GAZES at the night sky and sees a swirling spiral pattern in the stars. An American child selects a crayon and joyfully scribbles on a piece of paper, over and over again moving hand and arm in a circular motion. A Scandinavian priest of the sun god steps onto wet sand and traces a circle round his feet. An Indian pilgrim reverently circles the monument marking Buddha's enlightenment. A Tibetan monk takes brush in hand to begin his morning meditation: painting a traditional circular design. A German nun experiences a vision of God as a fiery wheel. What do these very different human beings have in common? They are all participating in the compelling human fascination with the circle.

Why has the circle been such an important part of human culture since ancient times? Why do people of all cultures, times, and places find the circular motif such a satisfying and meaningful form of expression? Here is one man's description of his insight into the meaning of the circle, which he calls a "mandala."

> I sketched every morning in a notebook a small circular drawing, a mandala, which seemed to correspond to my inner situation at the time. . . . Only gradually did I discover what the mandala really is: . . . the Self, the wholeness of the personality, which if all goes well is harmonious. (Jung, 1965: 195–196)

Carl Gustav Jung, a Swiss psychiatrist, adopted the Sanskrit word *mandala* to describe the circle drawings he and his patients did. *Mandala* means center, circumference, or magic circle. Jung associated the mandala with the Self, the center of the total personality. He suggested that the mandala shows the natural urge to live out our potential, to fulfill the pattern of our whole personality.

Growth toward wholeness is a natural process that brings to light one's uniqueness and individuality. For this reason Jung called the process individuation. He advocated respectful attention to the symbols of the unconscious as a way to enhance personal growth. Jung saw the spontaneous appearance of mandalas in dreams, imagination, and artwork as evidence that individuation is taking place. The result of individuation is a harmonious unity of the personality with the Self serving as the central unifying principle. Jung wrote that the basic motif of the mandala

> is the premonition of a centre of personality, a kind of central point within the psyche, to which everything is related, by which everything is arranged, and which is itself a source of energy. The energy of the central point is manifested in the almost irresistible compulsion and urge to *become what one is,* just as every organism is driven to assume the form that is characteristic of its nature, no matter what the circumstances. This centre is not felt or thought of as the ego but, if one may so express it, as the *self.* (1973b:73)

Where did the idea of the mandala originate? The motif of the circle appears very early in human history. Ancient rock carvings in Africa, Europe, and North America make use of the circle, spiral, and similar designs. The purpose of these designs is a mystery, but we know they were important because so many were created. What do we know about human beings that can help explain their choice of the circle as a meaningful design?

Let us turn first to natural history for an answer. Consider for a moment where we all originate. We grow from a tiny round egg, supported in the womb of our mother. In her womb we are encircled and firmly held within a spherical space. When it is time to be born, we are pushed by a series of circular muscles down through the tubular birth canal and out through a circular opening into the world.

Once born, we find ourselves on a planet that is itself circular, moving in a circular orbit around the sun. We are anchored to the earth by gravity so that we are not conscious of our spinning. Yet our bodies know. If we look even deeper to the level of the atoms that comprise our bodies, we find yet another universe where elements whirl in curving patterns. The subliminal experience of circular movement, like the memory of our mother's womb, is encoded in our bodies. Thus we are predisposed to respond to the circle. We share these facts of human life with all human beings both ancient and modern.

By considering what life was like for our ancestors living on this planet long ago, we can discover more reasons for the importance of the circle. Ancient peoples lived close to nature. The natural rhythms of the heavens and the earth were dramatic forces that dictated the way people lived their lives. Hunting and gathering were done by the light of the sun. When night came our ancestors retired to sleep. Clustered around a fire, they quite naturally gathered in a circle turned toward the light, warmth, and movement of the fire in the center.

If we define consciousness in the simplest terms as being awake, then lack of consciousness would be sleep. During the day while the sun shines, human beings are awake, conscious, and active. When night falls, human beings sleep and consciousness, like the sun, disappears in darkness. With a new day the person awakes again to consciousness. The alternation of sleeping and waking is regulated by the light of the sun. Therefore, the sun is an apt symbol for the wakefulness of consciousness which it stimulates in human beings.

Imagining ourselves back to the time of our first ancestors, we can understand how the sun, stars, and moon would have fascinated us. An interest in these natural elements is revealed by the fact that some of the world's earliest ritual practices apparently revolved around the sun. Ancient mandalas carved in many places around the world suggest an awe of the sun and the moon. These circular heavenly bodies could have served our ancestors as natural symbols, shaping consciousness and assisting human beings to develop their thinking beyond purely instinctive levels. In Denmark there are ancient carvings that suggest the step from instinctive group mind to individual consciousness of self.

Near the sea, neolithic carvings of ships are found. Mandala sun symbols in the vicinity support the conjecture that these ships are associated with rituals of sun worship, possibly invoking blessings for a safe voyage. Occasionally one sees footprints superimposed above the outline of a ship. Sometimes footprints are suggested by a circle apparently traced around the feet of a person. A line bisects the circle indicating the separation between the feet. A second line is placed horizontally to the first so that the whole design appears to be a cross within a circle.

This design seems to have been used as a symbol for the sun by ancient peoples. Thousands of years later the same design is produced spontaneously by young children during the process of developing their sense of personal identity. The step from participation in group mind to a sense of individuality had to be taken at some point in human evolution. The shift in consciousness that is naturally achieved by modern children might have been made first by a few remarkable individuals. Could it be that the foot tracing mandalas in Denmark provide a clue about how this step was taken?

It could have happened something like this. Priests were individuals singled out by the group to perform rituals. They may have even functioned as a human stand-in for the sun god in ceremonies. A priest, by tracing around his feet at the place he stood while representing the sun, could leave a visible sign of the presence of the sun deity at an event. Perhaps a priest enacting the sun might, at some point, have had a transfiguring experience that enabled him to make a leap in thinking.

The mental process by which the change took place might have been as follows. A priest accustomed to saying, while tracing around his feet during a ritual, "That which occupies this space is the sun," might instead have had the thought, "That which occupies

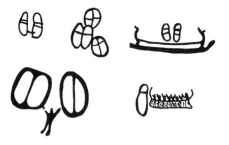

In Nordic rock carvings dating from before the Bronze Age, footprints and foot tracings appear above the outlines of ships. The footprints probably symbolize the presence of a priest of the sun god at the blessing of the ship.

this space is *I*." We have no way of knowing for sure, but it is possible that some of the first persons to experience themselves as individuals were priests like the ones in Denmark. By enacting the sun, perhaps they came to know themselves as individuals, separate and apart from the group. Out of such experiences, mediated by symbolic interaction with the circular form of the sun, consciousness of self may have been born.

The mysterious, ever-changing moon could have influenced the thinking of human beings as well. Legends of the Maori people of the South Pacific suggest some intriguing possibilities for how this could be so. There are many stories that have as their hero Maui, a sort of everyman. In the stories he is involved with a woman named Hina. Maui is always the same irrepressible character in different tales. However, Hina takes many forms. Sometimes she is Maui's ancestress, at another time his mother, his sister, or another relative. It is difficult to understand why a character with the same name should be so variable. We may begin to understand the identity of this changeable woman when we learn that *Hina* translates as "moon." Her many guises reflect the various phases of the moon: now new (young), now full (mature), now waning (aging).

Susanne Langer suggests that the Maori legends make use of the moon as a natural symbol for woman and womankind. She writes: "The moon expresses the whole mystery of womankind, not only in its phases but in the complicated time-cycle of its complete withdrawal. Women in tribal society have elaborate schedules of taboo and ritual of which a man cannot keep track" (1976:191). Through time and the process of condensation, which allows for more and more layers of meaning to be associated with an image, the moon became an ever-richer symbol that said something about life itself. Langer continues:

> . . . just as life grows to completeness with every waxing phase, so in the waning period one can see the old moon take possession gradually of the brilliant parts. Life is swallowed by death in a graphic process and the swallowing monster was ancestor to the light that died. The significance of the moon is irresistible. Ages of repetition hold the picture of life and death before our eyes. No wonder if men learn to contemplate it, to form their notions of an individual life on the model of that cycle and conceive death as a work of ghostly forbears, the same who gave life, and that notions

of resurrection or reincarnation should arise from such contemplation. (191–192)

Experiences with their bodies, fire circles, and the easily studied examples of the sun and the moon, placed before our ancestors the form of the circle. It should not be surprising that they adopted the circle as a symbol for consciousness, and for life, death, and rebirth. Most probably as an outgrowth of these ideas, the circle was incorporated into the creation myths of many cultures. These legends seek to answer the question "Where did I come from?"

Egyptian mythology describes the cosmos as a seamless round before time began. Within this circle Nut, goddess of the sky, and Geb, god of earth, were tightly bound to one another. With the loosening of this circle, the world parents separated and set in motion time, creativity, and consciousness. In the Upanishads, ancient religious literature of India, we find this account:

> The sun is brahma—this is the teaching. Here is the explanation: In the beginning, this world was nonbeing. This nonbeing became being. It developed. It turned into an egg. It lay there for a year. It burst asunder. One part of the eggshell was of silver, the other part was of gold. The silver part is the earth, the golden part is the sky. . . .
>
> What was born of it, is yonder sun. When it was born there were shouts and hurrahs, all beings and all desires rose up to greet it. Therefore at its rising and at its every return, there are shouts and hurrahs, all beings and all desires rise up to greet it. (Cited in Neumann, 1973:107)

Creation myths based on the idea of the circle are found in the traditions of Europe, Africa, and the South Pacific as well as India. Clearly, this motif resonates with deeply felt human intuitions. In our own Western culture the circle as the beginning of all things has appeared in the writings of Plato. He has given us this account of creation:

> . . . he established the universe a sphere revolving in a circle, one and solitary, yet by reason of its excellence able to bear itself company, and needing no other friendship or acquaintance. (Cited in Kaufman, 1961:331)

The alternation of day and night, the ever-changing moon, and the rhythms of the seasons became the foundation of a world view based on circles. This point of view, important to peoples still living close to nature, is eloquently expressed by Black Elk, the Dakota elder:

> Everything the Power of the World does is done in a circle. The sky is round, and I have heard that the earth is round like a ball, and so are all the stars. The wind, in its greatest power, whirls. Birds make their nests in circles, for theirs is the same religion as ours. The sun comes forth and goes down again in a circle. The moon does the same, and both are round. Even the seasons form a great circle in their changing, and always come back again to where they were. The life of a man is a circle from childhood to childhood, and so it is in everything where power moves. (Cited in Neihardt, 1961:32–33)

Viewing the world as a circle had some very practical applications as our ancestors took to the high ground for a clear view. They saw that the horizon line appears to be a circle. Human beings, in an effort to move safely about in large land areas, devised ways to orient themselves within this vast circle. In developing schemes for finding their bearings, it would have been natural to begin with the space they knew best: that occupied by their own body. Let us consider the body, with its arrangement of limbs and organs, as a focal point for organizing the space within the circle of the horizon.

The bilateral arrangement of the body creates a right and left side. With arms outstretched in opposite directions away from the body, one might imagine lines extending beyond the outstretched arms to the horizon. This establishes two opposite directions in the circle. The placement of the eyes in front of the head naturally suggests the line of sight as another direction, and implies its opposite as a continuation of this line extending behind. Thus we can imagine the classic mandala pattern consisting of the horizon line (circle) and four lines converging at the body in the center.

This scheme for dividing up space was utilized by Etruscan soothsayers. They interpreted events according to where within this imaginary mandala design the happenings took place. The use of the body to establish directions is also suggested by the Native American custom of including the center point of the self as another direction in their system of orientation. Native Americans also add the directions up and down, suggested by the vertical stance of the body, giving a total of seven directions.

When the imaginary mandala of the body and its four directions is oriented with reference to the constant position of the northern polestar, one has established the four cardinal directions. With this scheme our ancestors could have plotted a straight path from one place to another. They could maintain their direction even when obstacles required a temporary diversion from the desired path. This would have been important for survival. Being able to plan one's travel would have made possible return visits to water and sources of food. The usefulness of the classic mandala form as a reference establishing orientation in physical space no doubt added to its potency as a symbol.

Knowing the position of the polestar was crucial to the orienteering described above. Eons of observation affirmed its unmoving position in the sky. Our ancestors also studied with interest what appeared to be the cyclical movements of other stars. They identified constellations and gave them names such as the Bull (Egypt), the Crab (Persia), and the Ram (India). The moon and planets were thought of as deities. The Chinese imagined the moon as a goddess, stopping each night in the star palace of a different warrior-lover.

The night sky appears to be a huge circular bowl filled with points of light. The movements of heavenly bodies within this round suggested a wheel to ancient observers. Among the Celts, the heavens were called the Silver Wheel of Arianrhod. It was here that blessed souls found their home.

Stonehenge is an earthly reflection of this celestial wheel. It is thought that this structure was developed by early British peoples to mark the progress of the sun through a year. The careful placement of stones causes an alignment to occur at sunrise on the day of the summer solstice. This stone circle was undoubtedly a center for rituals celebrating deified heavenly bodies.

Thousands of years of astronomical observation resulted in the development of the zodiac, a wheel with twelve segments. Each of the twelve parts of the circle, also known as houses, is assigned the name of a different constellation. The zodiac shows the positions of the sun with regard to the moon, stars, and planets during a year's time. Astrologers believe that they can predict future events based on the relationships established by the zodiac. We have here

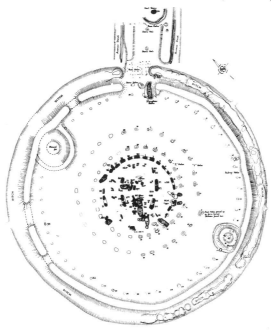

Stonehenge was established as a sacred observatory. It mirrors the circular disk of the night sky.

another example of the use of the circle for orienting oneself in the world.

We can see how the circle has been useful in efforts to explain how things began, to find one's bearings in the world, and to symbolize the wonders of nature. It is not surprising that the circle has also been part of rituals that attempt to induce, channel, contain, or invite experiences of the sacred. Many religious rituals begin with the establishment of a sacred circle. Voodoo priestesses, for example, trace a circle on the ground to issue an invitation to the gods. Native American shieldmakers begin their sacred work with a circle dance and chants that beseech the guidance of the Creator. Some ceremonies use circular movement to create an ecstatic state of mind. Eskimos incise a circle in stone with repetitive, rhythmic movements for long periods of time in order to bring about a trance. Dervishes spin to participate in the sacredness of the circle as a manifestation of celestial harmonies. The dramatic climax of the sun dance ceremony of the Plains Indians comes when participants swing suspended by ropes, revolving in a slow circle around a central pole.

The space within the ritual circle is changed from ordinary to sacred space. For peoples who perceive in the circle a reflection of the essence of life, creating a circle is a sacred action. It may also be an attempt to achieve resonance with the divine harmonies of the universe manifested in the circular paths of the sun and moon. By synchronizing one's actions with the divine plan, it is thought goodness will result. It is for this reason that contact with the sacred realities defined by the circle is thought to be healing in cultures such as that of the Navahos.

The Navaho peoples of the Southwest live a quiet life ruled by traditional ideas about nature, life, and health. Illness is thought to be the result of a disruption in natural harmonies. When a Navaho healer is asked to help a sick person, he goes through ritual activities that restore the natural balance. He smooths a circular area on the ground and creates a mandala with colored sand. The sand painting is made in a traditional design selected by the healer to address the needs of the situation. Once completed, the patient is placed at the center of the sand painting. The sacred order in the mandala design is thought to restore harmony and invite helpful deities, therefore bringing about the restoration of health.

Places existing in nature can also take the form of the circle. Caves and mountains are notable examples. Ancient peoples often identified impressive natural places as sacred without the need for human rituals to make them so. Deep, dark caves were held in awe as places to contact the ancestors. Lofty mountains, where one could command a farseeing view, were felt to be closer to the spirit world of the sky. Rituals at holy sites sanctified them even more.

The celebrated Mount Fujiyama in Japan is an example of a natural sacred site. Mount Fujiyama is a volcano seventy miles southwest of Tokyo. It is the tallest mountain in Japan, rising to over 12,000 feet above a flat plain near sea level. Legend has it that the volcano formed in a single night in 285 B.C. It has been quiescent since the 1700s.

Fujiyama is an isolated peak that can be seen for miles. It is a favorite subject for artists and poets. As Japan's sacred mountain it is visited annually by thousands from all over the country. A spiraling pathway carries pilgrims from its base near the ocean to its snowcapped peak. They stop at numerous shrines and temples located along the sloping climb for refreshment, meditation, and the pleasure of a fine view of the water and surrounding countryside.

People establishing civilization began building structures for ritual purposes with reference to sacred caves and mountains, perhaps hoping to incorporate something of the power of natural sites. The kivas of the Pueblo Indians are built like caves underground. They are round because "the sky where it meets the Earth is a circle" (Williamson, 1978:82). Perhaps aspiring to draw closer to the sky deities, people constructed forms that suggest the shape of a mountain. Some of the earliest known man-made sacred mountains were built in Mesopotamia more than five thousand years ago. These structures are called ziggurats.

Ziggurats were built according to plans based on numbers and proportions gleaned from careful study of the moon, stars, and planets. Each consisted of a square, truncated pyramid ascended by a prescribed number of steps. The top of the ziggurat was considered most holy. A sacred tree was often planted there, and it served as a platform for astronomical observations. Climbing to the top of the ziggurat moved one to the center of the sacred precinct. As sacred space this point also symbolized the Center, the primal source of all creation. The ziggurat functioned as a model of the cosmos, and the story of creation was encoded in its structure.

The tradition of the ziggurat continues in sacred places of the East, such as Borobudur in Java, Indonesia, and Sanchi in India. Sanchi is revered as the site of the Buddha's enlightenment. The structure consists of a massive dome fifty feet high in which resides a sacred relic of the Buddha. The dome is circled by a walkway. Outside the walkway four walls form a square entered through elaborately carved stone gates.

The Buddhist shrine at Sanchi is the setting for ritualized circular movements as well. Pilgrims enter the shrine through the east gate, mount the walkway, and circumambulate the shrine in a clockwise direction. As the devotee enters the gate and moves closer to the relic, he is caught up in a powerful psychological state (Craven, n.d.:72). Being in the presence of a relic of the Buddha is thought to have beneficent effects. The circular pilgrimage around the stupa

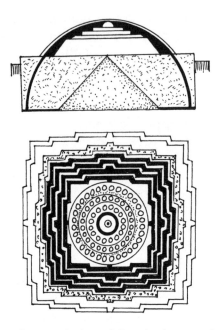

The elevation and ground plan of Borobudur temple in Indonesia illustrates the mandala pattern.

serves to heighten the intensity of the experience. This site has been the focus of continuous devotions for over two thousand years.

If we imagine ourselves above the shrine at Sanchi looking down upon it, its three dimensions would appear to be reduced to a flat design of two dimensions. We would then find a close resemblance between the patterns of Sanchi and those of the intricate mandalas of Tibet. Tibetan mandalas, also known as thangkas, incorporate the forms of the circle and square along with an array of other figures, symbols, and motifs. One can discern in the squares the basic structure of a walled fortress entered by four gates. The symbol of a deity is placed in the center circle. We can see how the Tibetan mandala reiterates the pattern of Sanchi with its circular dome and square-walled precinct.

There is another similarity. Devotees also circumambulate the thangkas. They do so not with their feet, however, but with their eyes. They trace the mandala design according to customary procedures. Each gate is guarded by a fierce deity that represents an aspect of self that must be confronted before moving nearer the center: attachment, greed, fear. The mandala serves as a map of inner reality that guides and supports the psychological development of those wishing to advance in spiritual awareness.

The Tibetan mandala serves as a visual aid to meditation. Mandalas may also be attempts to illustrate a particular spiritual realization. Jung (1974) suggests that this is the way ritual mandalas were first created. Tucci agrees that mandalas were first discovered through experiences of introspection driven by "some intrinsic necessity of the human spirit" (1961:27). Only later were they put to use in order to retrace a pathway to states of mind that originally inspired the mandala. Tucci writes:

> The mandala born, thus, of an interior impulse became, in its turn, a support for meditation, an external instrument to provoke and

Tibetan mandalas resemble the floorplan of a temple. The sacred center is protected by a wall with four gates, each guarded by a demon.

procure such visions in quiet concentration and meditation. The intuitions which, at first, shone capricious and unpredictable are projected outside the mystic who, by concentrating his mind upon them, rediscovers the way to reach his secret reality. (1961:37)

The mandala as a visual aid to attain desirable mental states is also known in Europe. There are wonderful examples in Gothic cathedrals, in the rose windows that invite the eye and dazzle the viewer into a sense of harmony, awe, and exultation. Medieval European churches often incorporate a circular labyrinth designed in floor tiles near the entrance. This mandala is a representation of the pilgrimage to the Holy City of Jerusalem. Pilgrims pray as they move on their knees from outside the labyrinth, slowly progressing inward toward the center and the New Jerusalem. Performing this symbolic journey, it is felt, helps the devout Christian move closer to the mythic Jerusalem, which is a metaphor for union with God.

The desire to share her experiences, to teach and guide others to the same realizations, inspired Hildegard of Bingen to create mandalas. Through her mandalas, Hildegard sought to communicate an understanding of God received in mystical visions. This eleventh-century Christian saint described an image of God as

a royal throne with a circle around it on which there was sitting a certain living person full of light of wondrous glory. . . . And from this person so full of light sitting on the throne there extended out a great circle of gold color as from the rising sun. I could see no end to it. (Cited in Fox, 1985:40)

The labyrinth in Chartres Cathedral.

In another vision she reported seeing a wheel centered like a womb in the chest of a towering figure. She writes: "Just as the wheel encloses within itself what lies hidden within it, so also does the Holy Godhead enclose everything within itself without limitation, and it exceeds everything" (cited in Fox, 1985:40).

The mystical experiences of Hildegard compelled her to begin creative work in writing and illustration. It seems that this activity was for her a celebration of what she had seen, a way to provide a container for the numinous experiences, and an attempt to bring information to others in a form they could understand and find useful. The creation of mandalas was healing for Hildegard. She began her work much burdened by illness. When she expressed her creativity in writing and illustration, her symptoms disappeared.

Another European mystic, Jakob Boehme, created mandalas symbolizing Christian cosmology. He envisioned two great realities of spirit and matter (nature) turning together as wheels within the larger circle of the Godhead. He wrote:

> The wheel of nature turns in upon itself from without; for God dwells within himself and has such a figure, not that it can be painted, it being only a natural likeness, the same as when God paints himself in the figure of this world; for God is everywhere, and so dwells in himself. Mark: the outer wheel is the zodiac with the stars, and after it come the seven planets. (Cited in Jung, 1974:239)

Boehme would make of his cosmic vision a mandala for meditation. He writes that "we could make a fine drawing of it on a great circle for the meditation of those of less understanding" (cited in Jung, 1974:239).

Boehme was much concerned with opposites. His ideas were influenced by the traditions of alchemy that prescribe the separation of base matter into opposing elements preceding refinement and distillation into a valuable substance. His work was controversial because he suggested that all things consist of a dark and light aspect, even God. His mandalas appear to be divided into two parts subsumed by the greater wholeness of the circle. We can see in his work a reliance on the form of the circle to contain and organize disparate elements in a harmonious whole. This reflects his mystical vision that all things are contained within the larger reality of God.

Giordano Bruno, an Italian living during the Renaissance, created a series of mandalas he believed would bring about positive changes in individuals who used them. His designs represented perfect forms purported to exist in an ideal plane. He encouraged the use of his mandalas in visualization exercises. Bruno believed that by taking the images into memory, the imagination would become imprinted with ideal forms. This, in turn, could result in a personal transformation for the better, more in keeping with the harmony depicted in his mandalas.

From this discussion it is clear what a rich and meaningful tradition the mandala has for human beings as a method of orientation, a spiritual practice, and a connection to the cosmic rhythms of the universe. In order to bring this information to a more personal level, I will describe in some detail a typical mandala ritual as practiced in the East. A most intricate and detailed liturgy of the mandala has been developed by Tibetan Buddhism. In order to understand the procedures of mandala practice, it is necessary to know something of the beliefs upon which it is based.

Early Buddhists established the belief that there are two planes of existence, two absolutely different worlds, between which there is no communication. As Tucci explains, one world is our familiar reality, in which karma operates, and which is forever dying and being born again. The other world is nirvana, which is reached by a qualitative leap when karma, and the force which drives it or derives from it, is stopped or suppressed. This is accomplished when, through cognition and living experience, it is realized that the universe is "solely a becoming and a flux" (Tucci, 1961:3). This arrests the momentum of the karmic process, and makes possible the leap into nirvana.

The plane of nirvana has come to be defined as the Absolute, the true essence of all that appears to exist in the world as we know it. The Absolute is imagined as light. The devotee experiences it with the mind's eye when attention is removed from sensing external appearances and focused within. It is colorless dazzling light. A traditional text explains the experience of realization as follows:

> Now to thee will appear the light of the Pure Absolute. Thou must recognize it, O son of noble family. At this moment thy intellect, by its immaculate essence, pure and without shadow of substance or quality, is the Absolute. (Cited in Tucci, 1961:6)

To attain enlightenment, one must exert oneself to see through the illusion of the separateness of things so as to experience the unity of the Absolute. This calls for the restructuring of the beliefs of the ego. Consequently, the work to attain enlightenment is inner work, even though it may be supported by outer practices of ritual, meditation, or other activities.

Tucci notes that the devotee wishing initiation to the way of the mandala must be well along on his inner work in order to be accepted for training. Work with the mandala is undertaken with the tutelage of a guru who judges the readiness of the devotee and instructs him in the techniques at a propitious time and place. The mandala tradition to which the aspirant is initiated depends upon the knowledge of the guru, his judgment of the needs of his pupil, and the signs or auguries of the occasion.

A space on the ground is cleared in a secluded place. A proper attitude is induced in the pupil through ritual cleansing, meditation, fasting, and chanting. The pupil is given colored threads and instructed in the procedures for laying out a circle divided in four equal sections. The mandala is created using paints, inks, or colored sand. Traditional designs and colors are used, yet there is opportunity for some individual variation within the standards. Materials, such as lapis lazuli ground for blue pigment, contribute their own symbolic meaning in the ritual.

Once the colorful stylized form of the Tibetan mandala is completed, the devotee is guided through steps of meditation. These are designed to move him through encounters with aspects of himself that hamper his full realization of pure consciousness. Part of the technique requires deepening his understanding of the traditional symbols in the mandala through personal experience. This inner work is facilitated by visualization based on the mandala. The devotee calls up a mental image of figures in the mandala. In his mind's eye he concentrates on these images, moving them through prescribed changes in relationship to himself. In order to intensify the experience, the guru reminds him that the images are not real, but simply the projection of his own imagination.

> O son of noble family, these paradises also are not situated elsewhere, they are disposed in the centre and at the four cardinal points of thy heart, and coming forth from it they appear before thee.

> These shapes come from no other place; they are solely the fabric of
> thy mind. As such thou must recognize them. (Cited in Tucci,
> 1961:27)

Through training and repeated practice the devotee learns to call
to mind a vivid image of the mandala, and dwell on this as a means
of bringing about his return from the world of separateness to the
realm of unity where he is in communion with pure consciousness.
Thus, the mandala serves Tibetan devotees as a pathway to and
from various states of consciousness.

Mandalas have traditionally served as instruments of meditation
to intensify one's concentration on the inner self in order to achieve
meaningful experiences. At the same time they produce an inner
order. Mandalas symbolize "a safe refuge of inner reconciliation
and wholeness" (Jung, 1973:100). Mandalas give meaning in the
psychological sense, as important for a feeling of aliveness as the
need to be oriented in physical reality is for survival. In the next
chapter we will focus on how the mandala can be of use to
contemporary persons of the West in our own search for meaning,
personal growth, and spiritual experience.

2 CREATING AND INTERPRETING A MANDALA

JUNG INTRODUCED THE IDEA of the mandala to modern psychology. His discovery grew out of his own inner quest. At age thirty-eight Jung had quit a university post because the academic life had become stale. He devoted himself to his inner life and kept a journal of his dreams, thoughts, and drawings. Each morning in his journal he sketched circular designs, simply following his inner impulse to do such drawings.

Jung observed that his drawings changed as a reflection of his state of mind. One day he received an irritating letter from a friend, and the next day the circle he sketched had a rupture in the boundary. Jung felt sure that his change in mood had resulted in a variation in his drawing. With the aid of his drawings, Jung observed his psychic transformation from day to day.

Jung learned that a circular design such as his was called a *mandala,* a word that means both center and circumference in Indian traditions. The mandala of India is a microcosm of the ideal reality with which devotees of Eastern religious seek contact. Jung realized that mandalas had special meaning for Westerners as well. Their significance derived from their role as a symbol of the Self. Jung wrote: "The self, I thought, was like the monad which I am, and which is my world. The mandala represents this monad, and corresponds to the microcosmic nature of the psyche" (1965:196). Jung's insight was affirmed in a dream some years later (ibid., 198). He dreamed that he was with a group of people with whom he had nothing in common. They were walking through a dark, damp, ugly city. It was a traditional European city laid out in a neat pattern with all streets converging toward the center. Off in the distance the group spotted a square at the city center.

Inside the square was a circular body of water, and surrounded by the water was an island. Upon the island grew a magnolia tree covered with red blossoms. The tree stood in bright golden sunlight. It appeared to Jung that the tree both emanated and reflected light. He was dazzled by the sight.

The group with the dreamer Jung remarked that they did not know why anyone would want to live in such a place. Jung thought to himself, as he looked on this light-bathed tree, that he knew very well why one would want to live there for the tree radiated a serene, spiritual calm. The vision of the tree as a lighted center in darkness to which all paths lead added weight to his conviction that the pattern of psychological development is not a neat, linear progression. Development consists instead of the return again and again to the center of the psyche, the Self. With the experience of the dream he had discovered the archetype of the Self, that aspect of the human psyche that creates pattern, orientation, and meaning. He wrote that "the goal of psychic development is the self. There is no linear evolution; there is only a circumambulation of the self" (1965:196). Jung reports that this insight gave him a feeling of stability, and brought the return of inner peace. He was encouraged to continue during a difficult time in his life.

As it was with Jung, so it is with you. The Self generates a pattern within your inner life. Your mandalas reveal the dynamics of the Self as it creates a matrix where your unique identity unfolds. The mandala circle mirrors the Self as the container for the psyche's striving toward self-realization or wholeness. Within the mandala motifs from the shared past of all human beings and symbols of individual experience find expression.

The mandala suggests mysteries that may make it seem exotic, confusing, or difficult. It is really as easy as child's play. In fact, as children we all discovered the mandala for ourselves. At age three or four the pleasure of scribbling gives way to the mastery of form. As Kellogg (1970) has shown, the art of children from all over the world contains mandala forms: circles, crosses inside circles, suns, circles with faces, and so on.

The drawing of mandalas is spontaneous, untaught, and performed in much the same way by children from varied cultures. It rarely continues with such intensity past age five. From these facts we can conclude that drawing mandalas is part of an orderly natural pattern of psychological maturation. This activity appears to accompany the process by which children learn consciousness of self.

It is fascinating to note that the mandalas drawn by children replicate those created by human beings thousands of years ago. Why should these patterns in children's art be so similar to those created by human beings long ago? Perhaps it is because children are taking the same steps toward consciousness that the ancients took. That which was hard won by adults thousands of years ago is repeated by modern children who quickly recapitulate the historic development of human consciousness on their way to maturity.

Neumann (1973) suggests that the mandalas children draw help them establish their identity. It is part of an inborn process of orientation which allows the child to establish a sense of self as one existing in the real world of time, space, and location. This urge for orientation apparently inspires the creation of mandalas as well. Perhaps modern children respond to the same inner promptings as did their ancestors when they created mandalas. Neumann attributes this impulse to the archetype of the Self.

The conscious identity of an individual, that which we know about ourselves, is called the ego. The ego forms early in life from within the structure of the Self, which functions as if it were a web supporting the individual identity. The ego exists always in relationship to the Self. Edinger (1972) suggests that there is in this relationship a lifelong rhythm of ego-Self separation and ego-Self union which governs psychic life. The rhythms of this dance, as the ego seemingly moves closer, then away, from the pattern of the Self, are reflected in the forms of the mandala.

All of us will have an encounter with the Self sooner or later. We may experience a desire for meaning in our lives, a wound to the pride of the ego, or a confrontation with what seems like disaster. We may fall in love with an unsuitable person, become ill, or receive a vivid dream. Wholeness demands that we establish a relationship with this mysterious center within us.

A woman once told me of a dream in which she was instructed to "make a circle of the four winds." She was given specific directions that she could follow in this visitation by the Self. For

Motifs from ancient stone carvings from northern Europe display the same patterns as children's art.

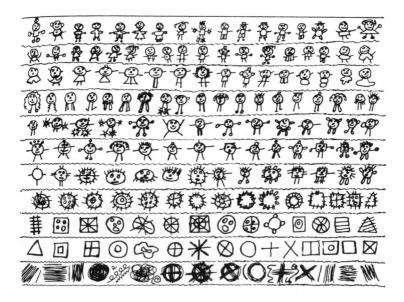

The mandalas of modern children.

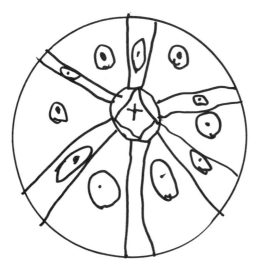

A mandala drawn by a four-year-old girl.

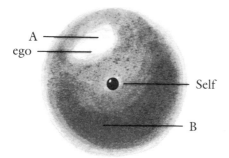

The psyche can be compared to a sphere with a bright field (A) on its surface, representing conciousness. The ego is the field's center. The Self is at once the nucleus and the whole sphere (B). (After Jung, 1964: 161)

most of us the voice of the Self is not always so clear. Once we decide to open ourselves to the relationship with the Self, how do we go about doing it?

The unconscious where the dynamism of the Self resides is that part of our psyche that is by definition unknowable. How can we allow the unconscious expression in order to establish such a relationship? Perhaps another way to phrase this thought is: How can we create a sacred space into which we can invite the Self? We can attend to the language of the unconscious and we can honor and cultivate our relationship with the Self by creating mandalas. Mandalas contain and organize archetypal energies from the unconscious in a form that can be assimilated by consciousness.

Jung discovered that drawing, painting, and dreaming mandalas is a natural part of the individuation process. He encouraged his analysands to give free rein to their imagination and create mandalas spontaneously, without a predetermined pattern in mind. His theory of the mandala has been carried forward in the work of Joan Kellogg. Kellogg is an art therapist who engaged in research with Stanislas Grof at the Maryland Psychiatric Research Center during the 1970s.

Kellogg finds that we modern Americans, like our ancient forbears, must center ourselves at times of transition. The need for orientation to a new reality causes us to focus inward on ourselves temporarily. The mandala helps us draw on unconscious reservoirs of strength that make possible a reorientation to the external world. Kellogg considers this use of the mandala as comparable to that of cultures where mandalas are created in religious rituals. However, she maintains that mandalas need not be limited to religious or therapeutic uses. The mandala

> can be used as a valid path in its own right, as a vehicle for self-discovery. The grasping of the Ariadne thread can launch one on the journey to the Self, with no guarantee of arrival, only the hope of eternal transformation. (1978:12)

When we create a mandala, we make a personal symbol that reveals who we are at that moment. The circle we draw contains—even invites—conflicting parts of our nature to appear. Yet even when conflict surfaces, there is an undeniable release of tension when making a mandala. Perhaps this is because the form of the circle recalls the safe closeness of the womb. The calming effect of drawing a circle might also be caused by its capacity to serve as a symbol of the space occupied by our bodies. Drawing a circle may be something like drawing a protective line around the physical and psychological space that we each identify as ourself.

The mandala invokes the influence of the Self, the underlying pattern of order and wholeness, the web of life that supports and sustains us. By making a mandala we create our own sacred space, a place of protection, a focus for the concentration of our energies.

When we express our inner conflicts in the symbolic form of the mandala, we project them outside ourselves. A sense of unity may be achieved merely from the act of drawing within the circle. Jung wrote of the mandala:

> The fact that images of this kind have under certain circumstances a considerable therapeutic effect on their authors is empirically proved and also readily understandable, in that they often represent very bold attempts to see and put together apparently irreconcilable opposites and bridge over apparently hopeless splits. Even the mere attempt in this direction usually has a healing effect. . . . (1973b:5)

The way of the mandala described in this book is an active meditation for the purposes of personal growth and spiritual enrichment. It is based on mandala traditions from around the world, the insights of Jung and Kellogg, and personal experience with the mandala. This mandala work is best performed in solitude, with an attitude of reverence for the eternal patterns of the Self and respect for the truth of the moment. Healing, self-discovery, and personal growth are invited when we make a spontaneous creation of color and form within a circle. With care and attention we can learn the symbolic language of the mandala and go deeper into the meaning of who we really are.

This book gives step-by-step instructions for the creation of mandalas. It offers suggestions for ways to interpret mandalas for greater self-understanding. The creation of mandalas is a rewarding activity that enriches the lives of those who take the time to master a few simple procedures. As Jung wrote, "When the self finds expression in such drawings, the unconscious reacts by enforcing an attitude of devotion to life" (1983:24). When we work with the mandala we may know moments of clarity when the opposites are poised in consciousness and we experience a reality of harmony, peace, and meaningfulness.

How do you begin mandala work? First, select your materials. Mandalas can be made with clay, stone, paint, pencil, flowers, sand, leather, wood, or cloth. The possibilities are limitless. Mandalas can be created by individuals, couples, or groups. For the remainder of this book, however, I will focus on the drawing or painting of mandalas by individuals. (Instructions for drawing mandalas are adapted from Kellogg, 1978.) Materials suggested for creating mandalas are the following.

> white or black drawing paper, 12 x 18 inches
>
> oil pastels, colored chalks, markers, or paints
>
> 10-inch paper plate
>
> notebook and pen or pencil
>
> ruler and compass (optional)

A substantial white drawing paper works well. Black construction paper is an alternative choice. When using black paper, I find that chalks give the brightest colors. Ordinary hair spray is an adequate fixative for chalk drawings.

Loose paper seems better for drawing. Drawing pads may influence the choice of forms because the binding on one side of the paper makes it different from the other sides. Determining the top of the mandala is also more difficult in bound paper pads. Drawings on loose paper can be collected and stored in artist's portfolios designed for keeping art work.

Mandalas can be done on larger paper, although storage is more of a problem. Mandalas on smaller paper tend to appear a bit constricted. This, of course, is a matter of individual choice. You should use the paper you feel comfortable with.

The preferred setting for creating mandalas is a private space where you will not be interrupted for at least an hour. You will need a flat work surface for drawing. Abundant light will help you see clearly, the better to do your work. Silence or pleasant music are conducive to a productive atmosphere. Lighting a candle or burning incense may heighten your ability to concentrate on this as a time apart from your regular routine.

After placing your materials on the work surface before you, seat yourself comfortably and begin to relax your mental state to enhance creativity. While working on your mandala, you will get better results if you are able to suspend judging and thinking as much as possible. There is no right or wrong mandala. Each is simply a reflection of the person you are at that moment in time. In order to give expression to the unconscious, let instinct guide your choices of colors and forms.

Before you begin drawing, it may be helpful to take a few extra moments to relax. Inhale deeply, and imagine tension leaving the body with each exhalation. A few stretches may loosen up some knots of tension here and there. Try to clear your mind of the concerns of the day. Allow yourself a break from responsibility, just for this time apart, with the acknowledgment that you will resume your duties at the end of your mandala meditation.

Once relaxed, you may want to close your eyes and begin to focus attention inward. You may notice forms, colors, and shapes dancing before your mind's eye. Using as little thought as possible, select a color, form, or feeling from your inner vision as the starting point for your mandala. If nothing appears to you, simply go on to the next step.

Next, open your eyes and look at the colors before you. Guided by your inner vision, or simply responding to the colors themselves, choose a color to begin your mandala. You may almost feel that the color chooses you. Next, draw a circle. You can use the paper plate as a guide, or you may choose to draw the circle freehand.

Continuing to use as little thought as possible, begin to fill in the circle with color and form. You may begin in the center or around the edge of the circle. You may have a pattern in mind, or you may have none. There is no right or wrong way to create a mandala. Work on until you feel the mandala is completed.

The next step is to identify the proper position of your mandala. To do this, turn the drawing, looking at it from all angles. Try to disregard the edges of the paper and look only at the design itself. One way to know if the mandala is properly oriented is by your sense of balance, or a feeling of relaxation that is your inner voice saying, "this is right." When the proper orientation is found, mark the top of your mandala with a small *t*. You will benefit from going through these steps, even if you think you already know where the top is.

Dating your mandalas is helpful for future reference. Include the month, day, and year. Even though each mandala is unique, remembering their sequence in time can be difficult without dates. Knowing the sequence in which certain forms and colors appear can help you to establish their meaning.

Sometimes drawing one mandala is not enough. If you are left with an unfinished feeling, you may want to draw more. You can use the same procedure to focus your thoughts within, select colors, and make your drawing. When you do more than one mandala on the same day, you may find it helpful to number each one in sequence, 1 for the first, 2 for the second, and so on.

Now, place your mandala before you so that the small *t* is at the top. It is best to look at your mandalas from at least arm's-length distance away. Perhaps prop it up a few feet from where you are sitting. You may want to pin it up on the wall for a good view. Your mandala might even be placed in some sacred space set apart from your living quarters where you can look at it often.

You may end your mandala meditation here, if you like. Many feel an ineffable satisfaction upon completing a mandala. Some people feel reluctant to shift the focus of their mandala experience away from this feeling. Simply by concentrating on your mandala, by drinking in the forms and colors with your eyes, you give yourself valuable visual feedback.

Your experience with the mandala might be varied by imagining yourself very small and pretending that you are walking in your mandala as if it were a room. Then ask yourself how it feels to be in your mandala-room, where you are most/least comfortable, and what your symbols look like from this perspective. If you choose to go further into the meaning of your design, you may use some of the techniques described below and in the following chapters on color, number, and form.

Up to this point you have made use of visual imagery and feelings in your mandala work. Next you can begin to put into action verbal and rational modes of thinking. You can make use of words, association, and amplification to clarify information in your mandalas. This may help you understand the messages of the unconscious encoded in your symbols. You will need a notebook and something with which to write.

First, give your mandala a title. Let this come to mind with as little thought as possible. The title should sum up your first impression of the mandala as you look at it from a little distance. You may want to enter the title in your notebook. You can also record the date of your mandala and its series number if you are working with more than one mandala from the same day. When working with a series, it seems best to work with each mandala separately before trying to see the meaning of the series.

Next, list by name the colors in your mandala. Taking each color in turn, beginning with the predominant color, work through to the least-shown color. You may want to make a special note of the color with which you drew your circle. Also include the color of empty space where paper shows through. After each entry write your associations: the words, feelings, images, or memories that come to mind as you look at that color.

As you compile your list of associations to colors you will begin to identify your individual vocabulary of color. You will not only discover which colors you like and dislike, you will also begin to learn what people, ideas, and feelings you associate with certain colors. You may even find that certain times in your life are associated with colors. Your unique life experiences will have shaped your opinions about colors. This personal set of meanings will provide important clues for arriving at the meaning of your mandala.

Next, list the numbers and shapes in your mandala. Numbers will usually be discovered by counting objects in your mandalas, such as the number of "raindrops." Vague shapes may need a phrase of description, such as "bottom squiggle," "pink splash," or "jagged wave." Other shapes will be easily described as "star," "fetus," "horse," and so forth. You may want to concentrate on each shape in turn, becoming aware of words, feelings, and memories that come to mind. Make a note of these as they occur. Your associations do not have to make sense. At this stage you are gathering raw material. Meaning will become more clear later in the process.

Once your list of associations is complete, read back through it, referring to the title you assigned your mandala. You may begin to notice a pattern of meaning in the words you have written down. Perhaps your list of associations will suggest a theme. Next, attempt to express the central theme of your mandala, derived from its title and your associations, in a few sentences. You may choose to record these sentences in your journal. They will be a valuable reference for future mandala work.

When working with your mandalas you may find that the color with which you draw a shape can change the meaning of the shape. For example, consider the meaning of a mandala that is dominated by a white cross in the center. The associations to "cross" might be "crusade, stepping forth, taking a stand." Associations to the color white may be "anemic, unseen, otherworldly." The fact that the cross is white makes it a less powerful statement of resolve in the symbolic language of the artist. It is as if the desire to stand firm is there, but the energy to do so may be lacking at this time.

When you take the time to follow the steps outlined above, symbols contained in your mandala can be translated from visual to verbal. This allows you to process the information more completely by using both visual/spatial and verbal capabilities of your brain. These steps can bring to your awareness the meaning of symbols, so that added information about yourself becomes available. With this technique you can chew and digest the nourishment contained in this rich, personal reflection of who you are: your mandala.

Now let us see how these techniques are used in deciphering the meaning of a mandala created by an art therapist. She is a middle-aged married woman, mother of three. She entitled it *Sea Flower* (See Plate 1, following page 80). Her associations to the colors, numbers, and shapes in her mandala are as follows:

> Dark blue: deep, abyss, mama, ocean, dark, death, hidden, nighttime
>
> Light blue: tender, Blue Boy, satin, Virgin, sky, bright, comfort
>
> Hot pink: vivid, lively, fun, fiesta, sexy, loud, noticeable, hot
>
> Pale pink: tender, soft, vulnerable, baby, rose, flower, feminine, inner, fluffy
>
> Medium pink: caustic, prissy, candy, gum, private, stark
>
> Purple: regal, serious, dignified, heavy
>
> Four: balanced, paired opposites, four functions, Self, four directions
>
> Eight: four pairs, ate, a group, one day past a week, hate, late, bait
>
> Flower: beautiful, growing, alive, feminine, gift, natural
>
> Small pink flower: vibrant, alive, off-center, short-armed, energetic, explosive, expanding, powerful
>
> Blue flower: serene, maternal, beautiful, poised, balanced, contoured
>
> Light pink flower: brash, young, floppy, large, tropical, carrion-scented
>
> Dark pink flower (behind): strong, mature, holding, supporting, protecting, withering, sinewy
>
> Flower petal: heart, opening, cap (hat), pointing or moving outward, expanding
>
> Dots: mysterious, new, unknown, fecund
>
> Eggs: potential, twins, family, jewels, healing stones, royal jewels, numinous, satiny, velvet, eggs

Pink "birds": predatory, invasive, sheltering, rising
Purple line: protection, small, cut short, broken

Note how the same pink form suggested two shapes to the woman: pink "birds" and "dark pink flower (behind)." She discovered the numbers four and eight by counting the petals of the flowers. Her associations to "pale pink" are at odds with her associations to "light pink flower." The woman summarized the meaning of her mandala as follows:

> My noble, serene, spiritual, egocentric inner balance (small pink, blue, and light pink flowers with purple outline) is threatened by an invasion of caustic, self-critical thoughts (pink "birds"). These are a reminder of my humanness. At one and the same time being human brings the thought of death (dark blue, carrion-scented light pink flower), and the reassurance of the natural wisdom of the flesh, inherited from countless generations of ancestors (dark pink flower behind). A little of the dark goddess mystery (dark blue) is carried to the very center of my being (dots) where its presence generates a vibrant burst of energy, creativity, and power (small pink flower). This flower helps me *see* the process of being human, and that is why its title is *Sea* (see) *Flower*.

Understanding this mandala helped the woman become aware of her tendency to overidentify with spirituality. Knowing this helped her accept the disruption of that ego position as necessary for grounding rather than as an unwelcome threat. Her realization of the mystery of death resulted in an enhanced appreciation of her aliveness. The dynamics of the Self brought her down to earth through this mandala.

Making your own list of associations to colors, shapes, and numbers is an important step in working with your mandalas. Each person will have a unique vocabulary of meanings. Some meanings will stay the same, while others will change with time. Your associations are a reflection of who you are.

Once your personal associations are listed, it can sometimes be helpful to turn to other sources of symbolism for additional information. The decision as to whether this new information is appropriate for your mandala can sometimes be judged by your spontaneous reaction. When reading about your symbol do you experience a feeling of excitement, perhaps a silent "Ah-hah!"

within? If you do, then chances are that the information is relevant for you at this time.

Your reactions to amplification will not always be so easily understood, however. You may experience a total lack of response, or even revulsion, to symbolic meanings which may be valuable for amplifying symbols in your mandalas. The real test of validity is whether your inner work is fed with the addition of this information. If you feel the urge to draw more mandalas, the amplification may be considered successful.

You can never delve to the absolute bottom of the meaning of a mandala. The colors and forms you use reflect a living process. Just as a natural spring may bubble up at unexpected places and defy efforts to contain it, so the psyche can never be neatly categorized and completely understood. Coming back to the same mandala a month or a year later may bring fresh insights that are equally true. You will probably encounter some mysterious forms that are never understood even though they appear, disappear, and reappear regularly in your mandalas.

With experience drawing and studying mandalas, it is possible to identify typical forms and colors and see them evolve as you grow and change. Learning what these forms symbolize gives you insight into who you are. Deciphering the meanings of forms in your mandalas can give you added knowledge of the pattern of the Self within your life. The best indicator that you have made a successful interpretation of your mandala is that your personal growth process is deepened, enhanced, and energized.

The creation of mandalas helps you cooperate with the process of individuation. Creating mandalas supports the integrity of the ego. At the same time it gives you an overview of the larger context of the Self within which the ego exists. Drawing mandalas can serve as a centering device to bring clarity out of confusion. Mandalas can give you contact with the deeper wisdom within and help you live out who you are truly meant to be. The way of the mandala can become a celebration of the gift of life itself: an opportunity to grow, to love, and to be.

3 COLOR IN MANDALAS

As a young child I was fascinated by the colored lights on Christmas trees. One hectic holiday season, soon after the arrival of a baby brother, a blue light on the tree branch down low caught my attention. The color attracted me almost against my will, and I was drawn nearer. Soon I found myself cuddled up under the tree, gazing intently at the blue light, almost touching it with the tip of my nose. My body began to relax, and feelings of calmness and serenity came over me. I learned then that the effect of color is direct, visceral, and emotional.

Color in mandalas expresses your innermost thoughts, feelings, intuitions, even your physical sensations. Analyzing the meaning of colors in your mandalas helps you understand the messages being sent by your unconscious. The meanings of some colors may be obvious and easy to understand. Other colors may defy insight. Sometimes colors may have several layers of meaning, each one telling you something different. A color may mean something different each time you use it. Consulting a list of colors with their traditional associations can open up new possibilities, or enrich and clarify what the colors in your mandalas mean.

While meanings for colors are not always and everywhere the same, there do seem to be more commonalities based on the shared experiences of many generations. For example, the sun has warmed and nurtured growing things since time began. Yellow, the color of the sun, has come to symbolize light, warmth, nourishment, insight, and, of course, the sun itself to peoples the world over. So it is with all colors.

The color associations in this chapter are given only to stimulate your thinking about the colors in your mandalas. These are not the "right" meanings. This is an array of possible meanings, sometimes even overlapping or contradictory. There are no hard and fast rules for determining which meaning fits your mandala. It is best to begin afresh with each mandala and its associations.

Read through the information presented in this chapter for each color in your mandala. As you read, some words and ideas will seem full of energy. Others will seem dull or lifeless. Add the lively associations to your journal alongside your personal associations to colors.

I have drawn much of the color information given here from the literature, art, religion, and philosophy of Europe and America. Some color symbolism from other cultures is included, though gaps and oversights are inevitable. The references given are meant to demonstrate the rich history of color symbolism and to stimulate the imagination of the reader working with mandalas.

Color information has also come from individuals drawing mandalas in art therapy, as well as the observations of clinicians who use the mandala as a projective personality indicator. And finally, I have incorporated the findings of a survey exploring the color associations of several hundred individuals attending conferences on religion and psychology. All these sources add to our understanding of the living tradition of shared color meanings.

Before turning to the color descriptions, a few guidelines about color placement in mandalas may be helpful. When looking at your mandala, notice the color placed in the center. This color symbolizes what is most important to you at this time. Does one color predominate in your mandala? If so, this color highlights that which has your full attention for the moment. The use of a variety of colors shows that your energy is more evenly distributed among several areas of attention.

Look at the color with which you drew your original circle. This will be a clue to that aspect of yourself you are presenting to the world. As a rule, this circle represents your ego boundaries. If you chose red, for example, you might be showing the world your energy or anger (depending on what red means to you). If you used green, your nurturing abilities may be prominent in your relationship with your surroundings.

Colors placed in the top half of your mandala most often relate to conscious processes. These in the bottom half tend to show what is going on in your unconscious. Looking at your mandala as if it were a clock face, that which appears at twelve is available to your conscious awareness. That placed at six is furthest from consciousness. Colors placed at three and nine represent ideas moving across the threshold between conscious and unconscious.

Look for areas in your mandala that show especially heavy or light use of color. Color applied heavily underscores the message conveyed by the color symbolism. Heavy color also reveals powerful emotions related to whatever is symbolized by that color. Color applied with a light touch shows a tentative approach that may be caused by fatigue, self-doubt, or even sadness.

Those of a less analytical nature will benefit from simply looking at the colors appearing in their mandalas. Color choices are largely guided by the unconscious. Even when you carefully choose the colors in your mandalas in an attempt to control what is shown, unconscious dynamics greatly influence the final results. It is safe to say that the colors you use are a direct expression of inner states that are usually beyond conscious awareness.

When you study your mandalas, unconscious symbolism expressed in colors is seen by "you," your conscious self or ego. This experience communicates information from unconscious to con-

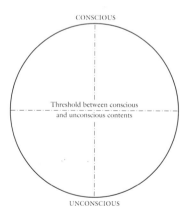

The placement of colors and forms in mandalas can indicate whether what is symbolized is close to conscious awareness, far from awareness, or moving over the threshold of awareness.

scious levels of personality. Even without delving into the meaning of colors, communication takes place. This serves to expand consciousness in the service of individuation. However, taking the time to bring your understanding to full consciousness through keeping a journal is profoundly nourishing to the psyche.

When studying your mandalas, try to keep in mind that there are no good or bad mandalas. Just as you would not condemn a flower that grew in an unexpected color, so you are obliged to accept and appreciate what comes in your mandalas. In your series of mandalas look for the natural flow of color and form that reflects your unique life process. So long as you see variety and movement of color, be assured that life is unfolding within you, even though the pattern may surprise you from time to time.

BLACK

Black is the color of darkness, evil, death, and mystery. It speaks of emptiness, the womb, and the lively chaos of beginnings. Von Franz describes black as "belonging to what cannot be consciously known" (1974:254). Black as a symbol for darkness balances its opposite, white, a symbol of light. Creation stories of many cultures are rich in the imagery of darkness and light. The Bible begins with this poetic statement:

> In the beginning God created the heaven and the earth.
> And the earth was without form, and void; and darkness was upon
>   the face of the deep.
> And the Spirit of God moved upon the face of the waters
>   (Gen. 1:1–2)

A Maori creation myth continues the theme of original darkness:

> Rangi and Papa, the heaven and the earth, were regarded as the source from which all things, gods, and men originated. There was darkness, for these two still clung together, not yet having been rent apart; and the children begotten by them were ever thinking what the difference between darkness and light might be. (Cited in Neumann, 1973:102)

The darkness and obscurity of mythic beginnings is comparable to the dark, formless substance with which alchemists began their work. Alchemists looked for the blackening of this dark material as a sign that the process of transformation had begun. This phase they called the *nigredo*. It was a time of profound change when important developments were taking place unseen.

Black may symbolize the murky beginnings of any process. It also suggests the original, abundant, inexhaustible source of energy that initiates the process. Cirlot suggests that

> the dualism of light/darkness does not arise as a symbolic formula of morality until primordial darkness has been split up into light and dark. Hence, the pure concept of darkness is not, in symbolic tradition, identified with gloom—on the contrary, it corresponds to primigenial chaos. (1962:73)

A connection to this source of primal abundance is signified by the black doves, swans, and other creatures that appear in European fairy tales and, perhaps, in your mandalas as well.

The mystery of the womb, where new life originates and comes into being, is another dimension of the meaning of black. The similarity between woman's generativity and the hidden closeness of the earth that grows new plants may explain our ancestors' choice of dark, earthy sites for the celebration of fertility. Ancient goddesses of caves, grottoes, and other dark womb-like sanctuaries presided over the secrets of birth. Perhaps reminiscent of the earthy goddesses who came before her, the Greek Diana of Ephesus was depicted with black hands and face.

Dark goddesses mediated the passage from nothingness to birth as a human being. So it is that their color (black) may also represent, in a more general sense, the descent of spirit into matter, into time. Because the earth goddesses mediated the passage from void to substance, it seems natural that they presided over the return, as well, from light (life) into darkness (death). And so it is that goddesses such as the Sumerian Erishkigal and the Greek Persephone ruled the lightless underworlds of the dead.

The dark earth mother is no longer worshipped, but her tradition lives on in some unexpected places. We find her in the powerful lady we refer to as "Mother Nature." Some feel the spirit of the goddess in the Madonna, especially when she presides in crypts beneath the light-filled sanctuaries of Christian churches. A vestige of goddess worship may even be seen in the custom of burying the dead. Ancients considered burial a symbolic return to the womb of Mother Earth. The belief that burial is a return is suggested in our ritual phrase, "Earth unto earth; dust unto dust."

Black is associated with that which cannot be seen, that which is beyond awareness, like the dark side of the moon. It is an apt symbol for the unconscious. Black also speaks of the loss of consciousness, as in "blacking out." In psychological terms, loss of consciousness usually refers to the loss of the ego as a locus of awareness. This is an occurrence that human beings, with the exception of dedicated mystics, instinctively guard against.

The ego must be separated out from the unconscious in order to establish a sense of self. It remains somewhat vulnerable to a reverse flow of libido into the unconscious. This robs the ego of the psychic energy necessary to maintain itself, something like a well gone empty when underground waters flow elsewhere. The color black symbolizes the ever-present challenge to ego consciousness.

The dark forces which threatened to overrun the ego were personified by our ancestors and projected as frightening, evil creatures of darkness. The goddess Hecate was such a one. On moonless nights she roamed the land, confronting terrified travelers poised at a crossroads. With the creation of frightful deities such as Hecate, our ancestors sought to contain their fear of darkness by focusing it on an image and encircling the image with beliefs, customs, and rituals. We moderns, not so very different from our ancestors, continue to make a much-needed place for the darkness with our observance of Halloween.

Black is associated with the final mystery, the darkness of death. Lüscher describes black as "the negation of color itself" and adds that it "represents the absolute boundary beyond which life ceases, and so expresses the idea of nothingness, of extinction" (1969:69). Black is used in ritual practices associated with death. Those mourning the death of a loved one customarily wear black. The liturgical color for Good Friday, the day of deepest mourning in the Christian year, is black. Black is also the color of the voodoo god Ghede, a symbol of death. Ghede, by the way, expects black, peppery foods as his ritual offering.

Black is the color of the god Saturn, who stood for the relentless unfolding of time. He was honored in the Roman festival of Saturnalia. This end-of-the-year celebration, coinciding with the "death" of the sun, focused on the sacrifice of the one chosen to reign as king of the festivities. The ritual acted out nature's imperative that the old order must die to make way for the new: the unending cycle of death and rebirth. On a deeper level, this festival suggests that the color black is associated with the understanding of death/rebirth as transitory phases of a deeper continuity.

Native American tradition associates black with the medicine wheel direction of the West (Storm, 1972). In the life of the person walking the circular path of the medicine wheel way, the West coincides with middle age. The burning away of ignorance, attachment, and self-absorption at this time of life makes possible true dedication to serve the creator, Mother Earth, and all her creatures. Some are born understanding the lessons of the West. Others must be brought to an understanding through their life experience.

It is interesting to note the similarity between the Native American teaching of the West and that of medieval Christianity. In both black represents renunciation. Christianity also attached the meaning of penance to the color black. The relinquishment of self-centeredness through practicing austerities is a time-honored way of shedding the false self in Christianity and in the Native American wisdom ways.

In European cultures black signals sad, mournful, or nihilistic feelings. To be in a "black mood" is to suffer a sad and angry state of mind. Turned inward on oneself such negativity can produce suicidal thoughts. When lived through with awareness, the darkening of consciousness can be embraced as having a positive quality. Saint John of the Cross's "dark night of the soul" is an example of this possibility (John of the Cross, 1959). Black in this context suggests the psychological death that precedes the grace of new understanding.

From what I have observed, black in mandalas may reflect feelings of depression, loss, or mourning. That which is lost may be a person, one's social standing, or even an idea, such as a too-tidy picture of ourselves. It is not unusual to find our conscious ego identity threatened when one of our unsavory personality traits comes to light. Black in mandalas may reveal the process of integrating our dark, shadowy aspects into our sense of who we are.

All of us must grapple with the shadow, death, and evil at some point in our lives. Thinking about death challenges our understanding. The existence of evil and dark deeds, our own and others', is something we must come to terms with. Thoughts about such profound questions go beyond the limits of rationality. Still we seek a solution, a way to place these realities within the structure of who we are and what we know.

The color and form in mandalas give us an opportunity to work through our feelings and shape our understanding. For example, if black is our symbol for death or evil, we have a vocabulary with which to work. The mandala serves as a container for a nonrational dialogue between the darkness and the light within us. Allowing the patterns within the mandalas to unfold as they will, we may see strident or ugly designs at first. As time passes, the colors may change, the forms achieve a new harmony, or our judgments about them may change.

As the forms and colors change, you may discover that a shift in your conflicting attitudes has taken place. Where once you experienced unyielding opposites, you may now find a new completeness. Where once you saw ugliness, you may now see a rugged beauty. For in some way the patterns of light and dark that manifest themselves in your mandalas can help create a place within your psyche for the resolution of such matters. The use of imagery allows you to go deeper than words.

Black in mandalas may also suggest a dark, velvety matrix for new life, the boundless creativity of the unconscious, or the allure of the unknown. It can represent the darkness that enriches and gives depth to personality the way black in works of art makes colors appear more vibrant. While black sometimes symbolizes a frightening loss of the familiar, depression, or negativity, the power of black might best be summed up by this observation: All life begins and ends in darkness.

WHITE

White suggests purity, virginity, and spirituality. White is moonlight, milk, and pearls. And white is nothingness, ashes, and bone. Perhaps more basic than any of these meanings, however, is this: white signifies light itself, an element in the creation stories of many peoples.

And God said, Let there be light: and there was light.

And God saw the light, that it was good: and God divided the light from the darkness.

And God called the light Day, and the darkness he called Night. (Gen. 1:4–5).

Light symbolism in creation stories is a metaphor for human consciousness (Neumann, 1973). Eastern adepts have used the imagery of light to convey their intuitive understanding of the seed of the infinite consciousness planted in each person: "Thine own consciousness, shining, void, and inseparable from the Great Body of Radiance, hath no birth, nor death, and is the Immutable Light—Buddha Amitabha" (cited in Neumann, 1973:23). Christianity has similar light imagery associated with spiritual reality. In the words of Jesus: "I am the light of the world: he that followeth me shall not walk in darkness, but shall have the light of life" (John 8:12).

The sacred quality of light imbues the color white with numinosity. White serves as a symbol for the spiritual, nonmaterial, and otherworldly. It suggests purity, timelessness, and ecstasy (Cirlot, 1962). A few hundred years ago science discovered that white light expands into the full spectrum of colors when it passes through a prism. In a very real sense, then, white can be said to represent unity from which multiplicity (colors) flows.

In fairy tales white stands for "daylight, clarity and order" (von Franz, 1986:254). White often appears in fairy tales as the color of special creatures, especially those that cross the boundary between the real and the imaginary. The mythic unicorn, white horses, birds, rabbits, and fair-skinned maidens are important in folk stories. They point to a noncorporeal reality and often bring the hero or heroine into contact with that reality, changing forever the way things were. The white rabbit in *Alice in Wonderland* drew the young heroine into a dreamlike world beyond the looking glass. In Wales the story is told of a young man who rode his white horse to the edge of the sea at low tide. The tide turned suddenly, and his mount could not outrun it. The two were swept away, lost in the cold, dark sea.

A happier example is found in the Japanese tale of Kagua-hime (Fisher, 1981), the pale, beautiful maiden of the moon. Banished to earth from her kingdom in the sky, she lived happily with an old bamboo cutter and his wife until her great beauty attracted attention. Finally, when the Emperor himself asked for her hand, she revealed that she could not marry because she was not mortal. She transformed herself into a shining ball of light before the heartbroken Emperor. This story illustrates the importance of finding the proper way to relate to creatures from the other side. They represent archetypal energies that cannot be wedded directly to ordinary human existence.

As suggested by the name of the light-complexioned heroine in this story, the color white is also a symbol for the moon. The cool, luminous qualities of the moon are usually personified by a woman, a goddess whose colors are white and silver: the Greek Artemis, the Chinese Kuan Yin, the Polynesian Hina. Susanne Langer (1976) suggests that the moon (and by association the color white) is an apt symbol for womankind as well.

The ideal of the pale, pure maiden is seen also in the fairy tale of Snow White. Her mother's wish for a child as white as snow, as red as blood, and as black as ebony was fulfilled when Snow White was born. Unfortunately, Snow White's mother died soon after her birth, and the maiden's life became a dark, dangerous passage finally secured when a prince became her consort. The feminine ideal of virginity typified by Snow White is often associated with the color white.

Lest we think of white only in terms of virginity, it must be remembered that it is also the color of semen, the essence of creativity, and of milk, the sustainer of new life. The color white suggests generativity, as in the Egyptian creation myth which attributes the beginning of time to an ejaculation of the god Atum. Vast lakes of milk are described in the myths of some Central Asian traditions. This image of plenty connects white to the mother and the happy child's sense of the abundance of life. The memory of such feelings may be the basis of the ecstatic celebratory mysticism practiced by the shamans of the steppes.

Ideas about the spirituality of white may have begun when the moon was sacred and white was adopted as the color of the moon. The numinosity of white is reinforced by its liturgical use for observances of Christmas and Easter. White at Christmas signifies the purity of the Holy Child. The baby Jesus is also a reminder of the child that dwells in each of us, that part of us that remembers the simple bliss of life before the separation of self and other. Jesus reminds us of the child within when he says that we must become as little children in order to enter the kingdom of heaven. White symbolizes the innocence of the newborn and those reborn to new awareness of spiritual matters.

At Eastertime, white commemorates the triumph of the spirit over death. The resurrection of Jesus is seen as the fulfillment of his promise of eternal life. In this instance white symbolizes the spirit which imbues the body with life, and endures to dwell with God even after the body ceases to exist. The idea of the invincibility of the spirit brings the imagery of white full circle to connect it with the everlasting innocence of new life.

Turning to the traditions of Native Americans, we find that white has special significance as well. In the wisdom ways of Native Americans, white is the color for the medicine wheel direction of the North (Storm, 1972). The lessons to be mastered in the North have to do with the quieting of the mind, a growing ability to see things clearly, and less vulnerability to the upsets caused by passing emotions. In the words of Dhyani Ywahoo, a Cherokee wisdom teacher:

> The wise person recognizes that from the North we see the seeds of our actions. We recognize the causes that were established in the past without blame or shame; we simply see that these causes bring forth these actions. . . . Then the mind becomes less and less reactive; one understands that these feelings that arise and fall are just feelings. There is an essential nature, there is a stillness. (1987:243–244)

From the stories and traditions related to white, one may notice that the spiritual realm often symbolized by white can bring great good or great loss. For the human being, encounters with the otherworldly can be enlightening or dangerous. In her work with mandalas, Joan Kellogg finds that white often reflects ambivalence about powerful spiritual experiences. White can symbolize "a breakthrough into unknown transpersonal dimensions of the psyche . . . and attendant feelings of awe and wonder of a power outside oneself, against which the ego may struggle" (Kellogg, 1978:61–62).

Sometimes those who are dying describe encounters with the transpersonal. They give accounts of persons and places filled with light (Moody, 1975). As life passes out of the body, the pink glow of life ceases. One is confronted with the paleness of the corpse. It becomes possible to understand the connection between the color white and death. Funeral customs that make use of white seem justified (Birren, 1988).

Alchemical symbolism is another source that can help us understand the significance of white. The process of *calcinatio,* transformation through fire, is reputed to produce a white ash. As Edward Edinger explains, this signifies the *albedo* or whitening phase and has paradoxical associations: "On the one hand ashes signify despair, mourning or repentence. On the other hand they contain the supreme value, the goal of the work" (1990:40). White can represent surviving a psychological baptism of fire which forges a connection between the ego and the archetypal psyche. By this experience the ego becomes aware of its "transpersonal, eternal or immortal aspect" (ibid.).

White sometimes represents silver in mandalas. This may be a conscious choice, or the substitution may not be discovered until one is listing verbal associations for colors in the mandala. The use of white for silver was a convention of heraldry. It occurs today in the drawing of mandalas most often because the media used do not include metallic colors.

Silver is related to the moon, as gold is related to the sun. It recalls the image of armor-clad knights, gleaming jewelry, and the mirror's capacity to reflect. Because the lunar connection of silver places it within the feminine realm, the use of silver in mandalas suggests a heroic undertaking that is decidedly feminine in nature. Initiatives in the areas of healing, relatedness, or creativity might be indicated.

White appears in mandalas in several different ways. It may be white pigment applied to paper. It may be the absence of color which allows the white background of the paper itself to shine through. Or white may appear when white crayon is applied over other colors giving a lustrous pearly look to the work. Each instance has significance when unlocking the meaning of mandalas.

When white is applied directly to the paper, Kellogg finds that "repression can be inferred, something is hidden and left out" (1978:59). This may also suggest a respite from powerful feelings, a flow of libido into the unconscious, or, possibly, an unwillingness to accept the sensations of one's body. Paper left blank, especially at the center of the mandala, shows readiness for an imminent change. (Kellogg, 1978)

The pearly effect in mandalas is related to the symbolism of the pearl. Cirlot (1962) suggests the pearl represents the idea that something of great value may be hidden in obscurity, as the pearl is hidden inside the oyster. A pearl also signifies the process of transforming irritating foreign matter into an object of beauty. The pearl, then, can serve as a metaphor for the inner work of resolving conflicts within the psyche. Kellogg finds that mandalas displaying a pearly effect indicate that one "is approaching and ready for a peak experience, or has indeed already experienced such an event . . ." (1978:83–84). This special use of white in mandalas can signal a heightened sensitivity to the spiritual dimension which allows the realignment of one's experience in a new pattern of memory and meaning. Kellogg states that pearly white in mandalas "is a sign of synthesis" (ibid., 84).

White in mandalas may suggest heightened spirituality, clarity, and readiness for change. It may symbolize an opening to transpersonal dimensions of the psyche that can be a source of inspiration, healing, and enlightenment. It may also announce a loss of energy, a challenge to your sense of who you are, or hidden areas of intense emotion. For some of us white may reveal a reluctance to embrace life in the body, with its compelling drives, rhythms, and frailties. White in mandalas is a reminder of the Light.

RED

The color red has an ancient history, having been a part of rituals of burial, sacrifice, and healing for at least 30,000 years. Neolithic burial cairns show that red ochre was used in funeral preparations. Cave paintings in Europe show the use of red in lively depictions of animals and human beings created, most agree, for purposes of education, ritual celebration, and initiation (Elsen, 1962). Red is still the primary color used in aboriginal Australian and Melanesian art being created by living artists in the neolithic tradition.

Red was important to our ancestors as a sign of life. Intuitive understanding of the stimulating properties of the color red made it a powerful choice for the treatment of illness. On the theory that like heals like, physicians dressed and covered patients with red (Birren, 1988). The physician to Edward II, hoping to prevent smallpox, directed that everything in his patient's room be red. Some physicians even prescribed red medicines, foods, or wrappings of red wool to cure sprains, sore throats, or fevers.

These practices seem quaint by modern standards. Yet, scientific research has demonstrated that red has a measurable effect on the human body. Barbara Brown reports that the "brain electrical response to red is one of alerting or arousal" (cited in Birren, 1988:152). When you see red in your mandala, you might want to consider the possibility that the red signifies the arousal of healing, life-giving potentials deep in the psyche.

Many people, ancient and modern, associate the color red with blood. When it becomes no longer acceptable to sacrifice animals for religious purposes, the color red serves as a substitute for blood. Thus it has come to symbolize the ritual acts of acknowledging sin, sacrifice, and atonement. We see this use of red in the Old Testament in Isaiah, where it is written: "Come now, let us reason together, saith the Lord: though your sins be as scarlet, they shall be white as snow; though they be red like crimson, they shall be as wool" (Isaiah 1:18).

In the early days of Christianity red was chosen to symbolize the Holy Spirit. The early church used blue to symbolize God the Father and yellow was the color of the Son of God. Modern-day Christianity no longer uses this triune color symbolism. It does survive in a few practices, such as the liturgical custom which prescribes the use of red in vestments and altar furnishings for Pentecost, a time set aside to honor the passionate fire of the Holy Spirit.

For Saint Hildegard, red also symbolized God the Holy Spirit. In one of her drawings a fiery red head reveals the spirit of God aroused to become "the rod of freedom from unbending injustice" (Fox, 1985:104). For her, red expressed the zealous, justice-seeking impulse born from God within.

Red as a symbol for sacrifice is more commonly associated with Jesus in the rituals, art, and legends of Christianity. In religious art Jesus is often shown wearing a red robe over a flowing white garment. In a familiar legend, the white rose presented to the Christ child by a shepherd's daughter turned red when he touched it, foretelling his future suffering. The symbolism of red as blood shed in sacrifice continues in the communion sacrament. This ritual feast consists of bread with red wine which symbolizes the body of Christ and the blood he shed.

One last image is offered here as an example of red associated with Jesus, God incarnate. This striking image was revealed to the Christian visionary Saint John the Divine.

> His eyes were as flame of fire, and on his head were many crowns;
> and he had a name written, that no man knew, but he himself.
> And he was clothed with a vesture dipped in blood; and his name is
> called The Word of God. (Cited in Birren, 1988:49–50)

Much of the power of red derives from the fact that it is the color of blood. Many responding to a color questionnaire make this connection. It is interesting to note that an equal number of respondents associate the color red with fire. Fire suggests warmth as well as the power to destroy, refine, and transform.

The use of fire in the crafting of clay and metal provides an apt metaphor for the changes human beings must endure in order to achieve wisdom. For just as firing makes clay pots strong and resonant, the emotional fire of human suffering can bring transformation and a deeper wisdom. Tibetan mandalas, which serve as psychic maps of the pathway to enlightenment, are encircled by a ring of fire (Tucci, 1961:39). It marks the point of beginning and symbolizes the burning away of ignorance, wrong thinking, and self-importance. In the same way, Siegfried is compelled to plunge into a ring of fire to release the imprisoned Brunhilde with whom he is destined to create a new world (Wagner, [1876] 1960).

To medieval alchemists red was a vital sign of progress toward achieving the *magnum opus* (great work), transmuting base matter into gold. Seeing red in their arcane chemical procedures heralded the appearance of gold. To alchemists the attainment of their goal was a gem of worth beyond measure, of knowledge beyond knowing. Their writings suggest that the alchemists were motivated by something other than simple greed.

Carl Jung has pointed out that the alchemical process was really a metaphor for the psychological transformation required to become a whole person. Jung felt that wholeness, like the goal of the alchemists, is really an unattainable ideal. There is, nonetheless, an urge to grow toward wholeness that causes aspects of the psyche to become differentiated and organized in a pattern approaching wholeness. These aspects include the functions of feeling, thinking, sensing, and intuiting. Jung (1973b, 1974) often saw the color red symbolize the feeling function in the artwork of his patients. Harmony of the inner person was reflected in artwork which successfully balanced the colors red, blue, green, and yellow, representing differentiated aspects of the psyche.

Cherokee Indian teachings present a similar challenge to those who choose to walk the path of wisdom. For the Cherokees, red represents a sacred inner fire that symbolizes the choice "to articulate and live in a sacred manner" (Ywahoo, 1987:41). It is one of three sacred fires which must be honored by right thoughts and actions in order for the person to fulfill the birthright of human beings to become wise and serve others. It is through achieving balance of the triune energy system that the task is accomplished.

The ancient science of astrology provides another way of thinking about color as an aspect of human life. The color red is associated with Mars, the god of war. Mars rules over those born under the signs of Scorpio and Aries. It is thought that Mars influences those under his sign toward passion, vigor, and reckless courage. From this point of view red might be thought of as the natural expression of the active temperament some associate with masculinity.

As most often seen in mandalas, red has positive meanings that suggest the energy we need to survive, be healthy, and transform ourselves to greater inner wisdom. The negative meanings of red have to do with wounds, destructive rage, and suffering. The appropriate meaning for us can be determined by referring to patterns and meanings suggested by the mandala as a whole. Women studying their mandalas will notice that they tend to use more red during menses. This is a natural response to the fluctuating hormonal balance in their bodies, and should be remembered when arriving at interpretations.

Kellogg finds that red in mandalas can be an indicator of "the will to thrive" (1986:17). A series of mandalas with little or no red may indicate passivity, or lack of self-assertion. A touch of red in your mandalas is desirable. Red may not appear in every one, but, perhaps, in every third or fourth mandala in a series.

It is important to realize that red is present in colors such as purple, orange, and pink. When red is mixed with another color, it suggests that energy is present but strongly bound up with whatever is symbolized by the color with which the red is blended. For example, purple might show us that energy (red) is aligned with the archetype of the mother (blue).

Please remember that red means something a little different to each of us. To Lüscher (1969) red is a warm, energetic color that is physically stimulating to behold. Expressing a different point of view, Kellogg finds red suggests "the physical life of man—lust, blood, and atavistic emotions associated with killing and assertiveness" (1977:124). Jacobi, too, finds that red symbolizes "burning, surging emotions" (1979:98). That which one person experiences as warmth may, for another, be intensely emotional. Neither is "right." Both are correct.

In my work with the mandala red often seems to express the raw energy called libido. It is associated with blood, anger, and suffering. Red can show a commitment to life, the will to survive, and an acceptance of the body. Red can also mean fire: the fire of emotion, spirituality, or transformation. What red means for you may be one of these traditional meanings, or it may be something entirely different.

BLUE

Blue is reminiscent of a clear sky, vast stretches of water, and cool shadows. Blue suggests calmness, serenity, and peace. In fact, research has shown that the brain electrical response to blue is one of relaxation (Birren, 1988). Could this be the reason most people like blue? Or could it be the fascination for something beyond our reach, as suggested by Goethe?

> As the upper sky and distant mountains appear blue, so a blue surface seems to retire from us. But as we readily follow an agreeable object that flies from us, so we love to contemplate blue, not because it advances to us, but because it draws us after it. (Goethe, [1840] 1970:311)

The vast pleasantness of blue skies, the awesome stature of faraway mountains, and the terrifying depths of the ocean, each amaze and delight us in shades of blue. Early peoples believed these blue, distant mysteries were the dwelling places of gods, spirits, or ancestors. From such thoughts the color blue itself has become associated with religious feeling. We find blue in religious imagery from all over the world.

Blue is the attribute of Jupiter and Juno, the Roman god and goddess of heaven. In Tibetan mandalas blue symbolizes a spiritual condition in which the whirlwind movement of passion has been transcended and only the clear motionless brilliance of consciousness remains (Tucci, 1961). In Cherokee Indian wisdom, blue is the color of the sacred fire of pure intention which each person must bring to fullness within (Ywahoo, 1987). Early Christians chose blue to symbolize God the Father. Today's Christian church most often uses blue as the color of the Virgin.

According to Jung, blue "means height and depth" (1974:287). We can see how this might be so because the spacious sky is always overhead, and as far up and away as the eye can see. The ocean, too, challenges our mind beyond its limits trying to imagine the breadth and depth of its expanse. Our experience of blue in nature teaches us of realities beyond the human scale, and stirs our intuition toward understanding the vast scheme of things of which we are all a part. The use of blue in holy images is a way of bringing this vastness down to a scale which can be comprehended by the human mind.

In Christianity we see blue appearing as the special expression of the feminine, and feminine attributes such as compassion, devotion, loyalty, and unfailing love. Saint Hildegard wrote of receiving a vision of a sapphire blue man within the glow of a golden disk. He represented an aspect of the trinitarian God for Hildegard. Yet, interestingly enough, she described him as the essence of "motherly compassion" (Fox, 1985:24).

Motherly qualities are most often associated with the Virgin Mary in Christianity. As the mother of Jesus, she typifies the feminine ideal of the good mother. Mary is the embodiment of the virtues of love, patience, and compassion. In liturgical art it is customary to show the Virgin wearing shades of blue. This Christian tradition has linked the color blue with the feminine, especially the positive aspects of the archetype of the mother.

The connection between blue and the mother is suggested in another thread of human experience as well. Kellogg tells us that blue connotes "that fantastic place where one is completely and utterly supported and cared for, where no demands are made at all" (1977:124). This is the experience of the nurturing uterine environment. It is the seed for our idea of the good mother.

Before birth we exist as underwater creatures gently rocked by the movements of our mother. The amniotic fluid in which we swim is a saline solution very like sea water. Could it be that our prenatal experience predisposes us to connect the ocean, with its gently rocking rhythm, to the mother of our earliest memory? If so, then it follows that blue, the color of water, would also be linked with mother.

Blue as a symbol for water suggests other meanings as well. Water cleanses, nourishes, and cools. Water transforms substances by dissolving them. Alchemists relied on water to reduce incompatible substances to the same liquid state so they could be mixed together. They called this procedure *solutio.*

Water is the element with which the ritual of baptism is performed. Baptism, it will be remembered, is the symbolic death and rebirth by which Christians enter the life of the church. The water serves to sanctify and dedicate the life of the person baptized.

The biblical story of Jonah and the whale illustrates another type of underwater passage. Like the storm-tossed sea of Jonah's trials, blue can suggest qualities that are dangerous, unpredictable, and terrifying. Blue then becomes an apt symbol for the unconscious itself. The plunge underwater then becomes a metaphor for the eclipse of the ego by the unconscious, and suggests the personal transformation that may occur with such an event.

Others have discovered quite different meanings for blue. Jungian psychologists find it is often associated with the function of thinking. While cautioning that "the correspondence of the colours to the respective functions varies with different cultures and groups and even among individuals," Jolanda Jacobi notes that blue, "the colour of the empty air, of the clear sky, is the colour of thought . . ." (1979:97). In his explication of the mandalas of "Miss X," Jung (1959c) also reports that light blue represents thinking.

Lüscher feels that blue represents complete calm. Contemplating blue "has a pacifying effect on the central nervous system. Blood pressure, pulse and respiration rate are all reduced, while self-protective mechanisms work to recharge the organism"

(1969:54–55). According to Lüscher, blue represents tradition, devotion, and lasting values. One might recall the saying that a loyal friend is "true blue." In his work Lüscher finds that blue suggests a desire to perpetuate the past.

In astrology, the color blue is associated with Jupiter (Birren, 1988). He is the ruler of those born under Sagittarius and Pisces. The influence of Jupiter is thought to make a person honest and blessed with a deep moral sense. Jupiter endows one with prudence and suspicion. He grants the strength of will to accomplish one's ambitions.

In mandalas the meaning of blue often relates to mothering. Lighter shades of blue seem to suggest unconditional love, nurturing, and compassion. Darker shades of blue may relate to mothering that is engulfing, devouring, or impersonal. In a woman's mandala, the appearance of blue points to positive feelings about mothering. A great deal of blue in a man's mandala, on the other hand, can suggest passivity (Kellogg, 1977).

Dark shades of blue, especially indigo, convey the feeling of the night sky, darkness, or a stormy sea. These may be metaphors for inner darkness: the unconscious, sleep, and death. Indigo speaks of that aspect of the mother archetype that is the beginning and the end of consciousness. Mother Nature, the goddess Kali, the primal chaos of Tiamat: at one and the same time, womb, and tomb. Kellogg explains that "dark blue represents the terrorizing aspects of 'Mother' which is not only mother but the enormity of nature: the fact that everything gets eaten up, dies and is destroyed" (cited in DiLeo, Graf, and Kellogg, 1977:81–82).

In Christian art one sometimes sees a sad or mourning Mary dressed in this color. Mary, then, stands as witness to the life embraced by her son, to live and to die a suffering death. Through her recognition of the entire cycle of life and death, she becomes the special intercessor for humankind. She mitigates the stark power of the dark feminine through her consciousness and compassion.

Kellogg (1978) notes indigo in the mandalas of those who have experienced a life-threatening event. She also finds it to be an indicator of difficult experiences in infancy, producing a lack of trust in the mother. Based on her clinical experience Kellogg contends that a great deal of indigo in a mandala can point to deep-rooted conflicts with the mother. For such persons mother may be seen as a frightening person. This negative connection to mother, while depriving the person of feeling nurtured, does seem to develop the ability to empathize with others.

Indigo in your mandalas may reveal the awakening of intuition, the attainment of wisdom, and the development of a deeper and more meaningful philosophy of life. It may also relate to the trying experience of a dark night of the soul: feelings of depression, loss, or confusion. Like the dark night that must be endured before the dawning of enlightenment, the appearance of indigo in mandalas can presage a psychological rebirth. Indigo, then, speaks of the opening of an ability to see beyond the cycle of death/rebirth to the timeless reality beyond visible forms.

YELLOW

Yellow is the color of the sun. The light, warmth, and life-giving power of the sun are symbolized by yellow. Goethe saw yellow as the color nearest the light, writing that "in its highest purity it always carries with it the nature of brightness, and has a serene, gay, softly exciting character" ([1840] 1970:306–307).

Perhaps because of its association with the sun, our greatest source of light, yellow has become a symbol of the ability to "see," or understand. It suggests the god-like quality of consciousness which enables the person to rise above instinct to think, plan, and imagine things unseen. In her work with mandalas, Kellogg finds yellow an important indicator of the development of consciousness, awareness of self, and individuality.

> [Yellow] appears to reflect the point in human evolution when identification with the tribe ceases and the individual will becomes apparent. The child will become highly aware of being a distinct and individual person, much as our common ancestors upon standing up must have felt different from the rest of the tribe. I believe this internalization of the sun within themselves made for a leap in consciousness which, in turn, made them alien from those others who remained earthbound. Yellow can be interpreted as correlated to aspects of the hero, individual missions. . . . (1978:73)

Worship of the sun was one of the earliest and most widely practiced forms of devotion in the world. The color yellow became the attribute of solar deities such as Apollo, the Egyptian god Ra, and the sun gods of the Incas and Aztecs. The sun gods of these cults symbolize a heroic, courageous force that creates and guides the orderly existence of earth's creatures. Countless stories and myths celebrate the active, life-giving powers of such deities.

In Egyptian mythology the sun's warm, penetrating rays are thought of as the golden sperm of Ra. Greek mythology gives us the story of the beautiful young woman Danaë whose father, fearing his fated death at the hands of his grandson, locked his daughter in a small chamber. The only opening was in the roof. She was courted by the amorous Zeus who transformed himself into golden drops of sunlight. The fruit of their union was the hero Perseus. He fulfilled the prophecy when he killed his grandfather.

The imagery of light as a source of life has even found its way into Christianity, as shown in this version of the Annunciation:

> Now on a certain day, while Mary stood near the fountain to fill her pitcher, the angel of the Lord appeared unto her, saying, Blessed art thou, Mary, for in thy womb thou has prepared a habitation for the Lord. Behold, light from heaven shall come and dwell in thee, and through thee shall shine in all the world. (Pseudo Matthew cited in Campbell, 1949:309)

Light imagery in Christianity is also expressed by the choice of yellow by early Christians to symbolize Jesus. Biblical allusions to Christ as the "Light of the World," and even the homophonic words "son" and "sun" offer intriguing clues that ancient beliefs regarding the sun have enriched Christianity. Certainly, Jesus as the bringer of the Word, the carrier of the Logos, can be seen as the ultimate fulfillment of the heroic consciousness first embodied in pre-Christian solar deities.

Beliefs regarding the influence of the sun are also a part of astrology. It is thought that the sign of Leo is ruled by the sun. The color associated with this sign is yellow (Birren, 1988). Those born under this sign are said to be magnanimous, wise, and free in thought and action. Leos are thought to be especially favored to be the great men of the day. They are destined, according to this ancient science, to be ruled by passion and high aspirations.

Cherokee Indian teachings associate yellow with the sacred wisdom fire of actualization, the capacity to actualize the creator's intention through the individual's right efforts (Ywahoo, 1987). Yellow is also the color for the medicine wheel direction of the East. (Storm, 1972) The teaching of the East is said to be illumination. With the wisdom of the East one can see things clearly far and wide, like the eagle that flies high above. The yellow of the East is like the brightness of the morning star.

Jungian psychologists have found that yellow symbolizes the ability to grasp a pattern of meaning in a scatter of facts and impressions. They identify this ability as intuition, one of the four psychological functions. Jung (1973b) comments that "Miss X," the creator of a beautiful series of mandalas, used yellow as a symbol of intuition. In her work Jolande Jacobi discovered that

> yellow, the colour of the sun which brings the light out of the unfathomable darkness and vanishes again into the darkness, is that of intuition, the function which, as though by sudden illumination, apprehends the origins and tendencies of things. . . . (1979:97–98)

Yellow suggests the active, fructifying principle in nature associated with the masculine. It is often seen in mandalas as a symbol of the father. For women, the color yellow may be an attribute of the animus. For both sexes yellow is associated with the development of autonomy. A new chapter in your life may be announced by the appearance of yellow in your mandalas.

Lüscher emphasizes the "hopeful volatility" of yellow. He finds that a preference for yellow expresses "the hope or expectation of greater happiness" (1969:63). He also finds that yellow implies the need for release from conflict. A preference for yellow suggests one is a person who presses forward into the future seeking the new, the modern, the developing, and the unformed.

When yellow in a mandala predominates or appears overly bright or fluorescent, Kellogg finds this to be an indicator of inflation. In her experience, "this expansion of the psyche can also hide the shadow, or dark, black opposite" (1978:73). As she suggests, a lot of yellow in a mandala can speak of a polarization of light and dark aspects of the psyche. For example, one might experience an alternation of moods of elation and despair, with little in between.

In her work with the mandalas of art therapy clients, Kellogg found that:

> A good clean yellow in either a man's or a woman's mandala reflects in most cases a good mind, curious, and alert. It very often speaks of a good relationship with an admired father. (1977:124)

A darkened yellow may symbolize a negative attachment to the father. This might be lived out as difficulties with authority, a hard time meeting deadlines, or problems in relationships with men.

When yellow appears in your mandalas, you may be feeling robust, energetic, with a well-defined sense of self. The ability to see things clearly, set realistic goals, and accomplish the goals you set will seem to be functioning when yellow appears in your mandalas. Yellow can show you that you are ready to learn something new, to venture out into the world with energy and drive to pursue some new project. On the other hand, yellow in your mandalas may be a clue that you are seeking change for the sake of change, and that you may be in need of the balance that cool, calm deliberation can bring. Perhaps you need the refreshment that time with a few close friends can give you.

You may discover that yellow in a mandala represents the precious metal gold for you. What does this mean? Gold suggests riches. As is more often the case in mandalas, the wealth is of the spirit, like the gold sought by the alchemists. Sometimes your unconscious uses the imagery of gold to remind you that you carry the imprinted potential for wholeness within you: the archetype of the Self.

GREEN

Green is the color of nature, teeming with growing things and redolent of fresh scents. Green reminds us of the cyclical renewal of the natural world which dies and is reborn each spring, fresh and full of potential. Green symbolizes the principle of natural, healthy growth, and the ability to nurture growing things.

The Native American medicine wheel tradition uses green as a symbol for the South (Storm, 1972). The South exemplifies the innocence of being close to nature, trusting, and knowing one's own heart. The animal associated with the South is the mouse, a creature with keen discrimination regarding things close by. The wisdom of the South is the capacity to cherish loved ones in a natural, accepting way.

The association of green with nature, with concrete reality, explains its frequent choice as a symbol for the function of sensing. According to Jacobi, "green, the colour of earthly, tangible, directly perceptible vegetation, represents the function of sensation" (1979:98). Jung (1973b) also saw green used to represent sensation in the art work of analysands.

Saint Hildegard placed great importance on the color green. To her it was the symbol of an energy source which kept the affairs of men "moist" with life. Green was expressive of the presence of God in earthly matters. Hildegard's conception of the deity encompassed both masculine and feminine attributes. Her choice of green as a symbol of God is similar to Kellogg's view of green as representing the archetypal parents in harmony. Kellogg writes:

> Mythologically, [green] is the mother (blue) and the father (yellow) united. . . . It can show a capacity for nurturing, both the internalized nurturing of oneself and the nurturing of others. Green can signify reaching a point in maturity when one introjects both mother's and father's conscience and begins to serve as one's own parent. (1977:124)

Cirlot suggests that the colored knights of European mythology are symbols of particular stages of human growth. For example, the Green Knight encountered by Sir Gawain in the English tale "Sir Gawain and the Green Knight" stands for an early stage of development. According to Cirlot, "the Green Knight is the pre-Knight, the squire, the apprentice sworn to Knighthood" (1962:162). In other words, the student who has embraced the path toward enlightenment.

Green is the water from which Venus, the goddess of beauty, emerges. Green remains associated with her and all things beautiful. Venus is the namesake of the planet which rules the astrological signs of Taurus and Libra. Venus influences a person "to love beauty, to be amiable, . . . to have confidence and faith. For all these virtues, however, he may be vain, irresolute, easily tempted, and not very strong to overcome adversity" (Birren, 1988:75).

Green is the color of water sprites, wood nymphs, and fairies (deVries, 1976). These creatures are survivors of older, earth-centered religions. They represent a capricious, playful force that is often at cross-purposes with authority. Free spirits who are guided by this principle are sometimes considered outlaws, like Robin Hood and his merry band dressed all in green. At odds with the lawmakers of the day, the creatures of green serve a higher authority in harmony with the laws of nature.

Green is a pleasant color to most people. Goethe explained the feeling of harmony conveyed by the color green with the theory that green occurs at the juncture of the opposites black and white. According to Goethe, blue results from lightening black, and yellow is created by the darkening of white. Seen from this point of view green results from mixing blue, a derivative of black, with yellow, a darkened white (Goethe [1840], 1970).

Green is sometimes encountered as a symbol of negativity. One may recall that the poisonous venom of snakes is green. The dark green woods of fairy tales is a place of danger. Vegetation, as it rots, becomes a darker and darker green. The human body, too, allowed to pass through a natural process of death and decay, assumes a greenish tint. Folk wisdom tells us of the unpleasant state of being "green with envy."

Green is often seen in the mandalas of those in the helping professions. Kellogg finds that green in mandalas reflects "the ability to nurture, to parent and protect" (1977:124). It connotes an ability to take care of oneself and offer support to others as well. However, a great deal of green in mandalas "can speak of being overly controlled by the internalized values of the parents, at the expense of true autonomy. . . . rigidity or a tendency to overcare for, overpossess, or overprotect other people" (ibid.).

Dark and light shades of green have special significance when considering mandalas. Kellogg finds that dark green

> points to threatening aspects of the nurturer and speaks to the memories of "the dark forest where the witch lives." In analytic terms, this refers to the frightening aspects of the pubic area out of which we were all thrust. . . . Medium green and some lighter shades speak in a positive way of the harmonious blending of active and receptive forces in the psyche, of growth and fertility. There are instances also where the use of a bright chartreuse green, heavy with a yellow hue will reflect a harsh superego of an authoritarian kind and may reflect a conflict in the previous developmental stage. (1978:76–77)

Green might best be thought of as the symbol of Mother Nature herself. This mythic figure survives in today's thinking as a vestige of times when the miracle of life itself was revered. When you see green in your mandalas, it may be a reminder of the power of life to create, heal, and renew itself. And in knowing this power, perhaps you too can discover the presence of the divine.

ORANGE

Orange is the color of the harvest moon, pumpkins, and autumn leaves. Goethe writes that orange "gives an impression of warmth and gladness, since it represents the hue of the intenser glow of fire, and of the milder radiance of the setting sun" ([1840] 1970:309). Orange suggests energy one step removed from its primal source. If we think of red as raw energy, then orange might be thought of as energy tempered by the yellow of insight, understanding, or thought. Orange is something like fire within rightful boundaries, such as the fire around which a group gathers for stories on a winter evening.

Orange is not a traditional liturgical color in the West. Nevertheless, the color has important spiritual symbolism. Orange has been associated with the Job-like experience of deepening one's spiritual understanding through misfortune, rejection, or alienation from one's fellows. Orange is sometimes a symbol for the outcast. In an alchemical text, Cirlot discovered this reference to orange:

> A man and a woman coloured orange and seen against the background of a field coloured sky-blue, signifies that they must not place their hopes in this world, for orange denotes desperation and the blue background is a sign of hope in heaven. (1962:54)

In India orange was once the color of clothing worn by condemned criminals on their way to execution. Ascetic beggars adopted clothing of this color to show their status as persons outside ordinary society. The Buddha donned orange robes to signify his renunciation of a life of princely pleasures. To this day many embarking on a life of austerities in pursuit of enlightenment follow his example and wear orange.

Looked at another way, we might think of orange as energy (red) invested in relationship to the father (yellow). It is traditionally the father's task to teach the skills needed to go forth and function in the world. What began as "his" ideas become "yours" when you hear a familiar voice in your head saying such things as, "do it right," "use your head," or "teamwork gets the job done." Orange, then, has to do with self-assertion, pride, and ambition. Concerns about one's power, or lack of it, seem implied by the use of orange in mandalas.

Orange in your mandalas may suggest energetic striving, a strong sense of identity, and healthy assertiveness. On the other hand, orange may also symbolize a willful use of power, a hostile attitude toward authority, or no self-discipline. In her observations of color in mandalas Kellogg found that

> A great deal of orange in a mandala reflects an ambivalent feeling about maleness and about ego strivings. In a female's mandala, orange has a great deal to say about her attitude to men. It usually implies an attachment to father and can also be a reflection of great self-esteem, ambition, and the like. (1977:124)

In my art therapy workshops orange is often identified by participants as their least favorite color. Orange is not used very often in the mandalas I see. The consistency with which orange is rejected intrigues me. I have some thoughts, by no means conclusive, as to why this might be so. It seems to me that many of us dislike orange because we are uncomfortable with that which the orange sometimes symbolizes: power.

Another reason orange is an unpleasant color to many may relate to its suggestion of entropy. Respondents to the color questionnaire chose orange most often as the color associated with autumn. Orange, as Goethe tells us, is identified with sunsets as well. Because of our culture's emphasis on newness and youth, it is hard for us to see the beauty in cycles coming to an end. Perhaps this is the reason why it is difficult for us to see the beauty of orange as well.

PURPLE/VIOLET

Purple is the color of royalty, the wine-dark sea, and violets in the snow. Since the color purple was once a rare and expensive dye, it naturally became the perquisite of the rich and royal. Yet, paradoxically, purple appears gratis in nature's display of spring flowers:

violets, crocus, iris, all there to be enjoyed. In these lovely flowers purple is a sign of life, alive for its own sake, blooming wherever it happens to be.

Purple is a mixture of blue and red. It is a separate color and yet it retains something of both red and blue. It is an amalgamation of the energy of red and the serenity of blue. For Lüscher purple represents identification.

> This identification is a sort of mystic union, a high degree of sensitive intimacy leading to complete fusion between subject and object. . . . In a way, this is enchantment, a dream made fact, a magical state in which wishes are fulfilled—so the person who prefers violet [purple] wants to achieve a "magical" relationship. He not only wants to be beglamored himself, but at the same time he wants to charm and delight others, to exert a degree of fascination over them. . . . Violet [purple] can mean identification as an intimate, erotic blending, or it can lead to an intuitive and sensitive understanding. (1969:65–66)

Purple is associated, above all, with royalty. "To the purple born" is an expression used to describe those of royal lineage. The use of purple as a designation of authority has been carried into the Christian church. Purple is the color worn by bishops.

The use of purple for spiritual symbolism seems more clearly understood when we recall that blue can also be a symbol for spirituality. Then purple becomes energy (red) invested in spirituality (blue). This carries the suggestion of sacrifice and the sublimation of personal drives in the service of spirituality. From this line of thinking we can understand the choice of purple as a liturgical color for the Lenten season, a time for observing austerities.

Purple dress for those of high rank within the Christian church brings together both sacred and profane meanings of the color. It suggests personal dedication to spirituality. At the same time purple conveys the authority of those who rule by "divine right." In this connection Goethe has wryly observed that the bishop's purple "unceasingly aspires to the cardinal's red" ([1840] 1970:313). Goethe concluded that purple has a restless, striving quality.

In pre-Christian times the cultivation of grapes and the making of wine were the province of the Greek god Dionysus. He appears dressed in royal purple robes, always holding a cup full of wine.

Dionysus was a god of generosity, conviviality, and ecstatic abandon. As the patron of fruit-growing, he was associated with the yearly death and regeneration of plants. The Greeks considered him a symbol of the death and resurrection of human life as well.

Worshippers of Dionysus engaged in orgiastic springtime celebrations that made liberal use of sacred wine. These rituals were eventually banned by the authorities because of excesses. Robert Johnson (1987) has written of the banishment of Dionysian worship as a metaphor for the suppression of the feeling function in the Western psyche. When the color purple appears in your mandala, you might consider the possibility that it expresses the emergence of the feeling function.

The sacramental use of wine is an important part of the Christian tradition as well. The power of wine to intoxicate in some way suggests the experience of the Holy Spirit. The process of winemaking itself serves as a powerful metaphor of change. The crushing of the grapes to be transformed into the substance of wine (spirit) commemorates the blood sacrifice, death, and resurrection of Jesus.

The color purple may also signify the process of personal growth. It can suggest the restless motive energy of something seeking to become free at a new level of being. Kellogg suggests that purple speaks of the psychological unity with the mother experienced by everyone prior to the ego's emergence from the maternal matrix. The psychological separation from the mother is revealed by the appearance of red where once there was purple. "The purple precedes the clarification of red, which may be seen to symbolize the freeing of energy in the service of individual goals" (1977:123).

Purple may reappear in mandalas after the initial separation when, for example, one seeks a temporary respite from independence, or reaches into deep layers of the psyche as a source of inspiration. The reappearance of purple in mandalas may usher in the development of a more genuine, personal spirituality. On the other hand, it may also reveal an increased need for emotional support.

Purple in mandalas suggests a vivid imagination, which can be useful for creative endeavors. Those who like purple seem to have an ability to generate excitement, to attract attention. This can earn one a special place within the family or community. Kellogg has identified some negative connotations to a preference for purple.

These include "a self absorption and a vision of oneself as beyond or above the human condition" (ibid.). She finds that, for some people, feelings of persecution and paranoia are symbolized by purple.

Idiomatic sayings highlight the specialness of purple. We say that we experience a purple passion or read purple prose. In small amounts purple enlivens, delights, and may even enhance your concentration on your mandalas. Its dazzle in large amounts in mandalas might reveal that you are self-centered, authoritarian, or unrealistic. Of one thing you can be certain: purple is not ordinary.

LAVENDER

Lavender is pale, yet intense. The color takes its name from the flowers of the lavender plant, valued for its aromatic fragrance since Roman times or even earlier. Lavender has come to be associated with virtue, industry, and acknowledgment (DeVries, 1976). Para-doxically, it has also been linked to distrust and precautions. In astrology lavender is related to the planet Mercury whose influence endowed a person with excellent memory, and scientific and artistic aptitude. The god Mercury, messenger of the Olympian gods, was thought to rule the nervous system, for "the nerves are messengers on the biological plane" (Cirlot, 1962:198). Its association with Mercury suggests that the color lavender may in some way be related to the functioning of the nervous system.

Lavender can be produced by adding white (spirituality) to purple (royalty). It can be looked upon as symbolizing energy in a highly refined state of spirituality. Lavender can also be produced by mixing light blue (positive mother) with pink (flesh). The meanings of these component colors suggest that lavender can connote a melting bliss such as the experiences described by Saint Teresa of Ávila (1961).

The use of lavender in mandalas may reveal a proclivity for mystical experiences. It may also herald a spiritual awakening that can produce a psychological rebirth. There are pitfalls associated with the experiences symbolized by lavender. Having so little red, lavender conveys a sense of dissociation from the physical body. This seems especially worth considering in situations where a great deal of lavender appears in the mandala. Kellogg finds that "much use of this color [lavender] indicates a dependency on fantasy and an escape from reality, fleeing as it were from embodiment" (1977:125).

The selection of lavender for mandalas may suggest physical conditions that cause oxygen deprivation. Kellogg sees this happening in the mandalas of those who suffer from respiratory illness. According to her, it is sometimes seen in the mandalas of those with life-threatening illnesses and it may also represent the memory of a birth experience that was oxygen deprived. However, she emphasizes the spiritual nature of lavender:

> When we find it [lavender] in a mandala we can say with some assurance that we are dealing with a very mystical person and that his use of this color represents a positive spiritual development for him. (Ibid.)

PINK

Pink is the color of flesh. It is a mixture of white and red. White (spirit) imbued with red (energy) suggests a robust innocence, like that of a healthy infant. DeVries (1974) finds that pink has traditionally connoted sensuality, emotions, and youth. Viewing pink as the color of flesh, the Gnostics used it as a symbol of resurrection (Cirlot, 1962).

Pink is associated with the physical body. In mandalas pink often reveals the pleasures and pains of life in a physical organism. Kellogg writes that "human beings identify . . . pink and flesh tones with those tender, sensitive organs, muscles, and connective tissues most responsive to emotional stress" (1977:124). She finds that the use of a great deal of pink in mandalas "can be an admission of vulnerability, fear of exposure, and a need for caring" (ibid.). Pink may be chosen by people who are experiencing physical symptoms due to illness or stress, even though the symptoms are unrecognized by the person. For example, Kellogg finds that women in menses frequently use pink.

> Women seem to be closely influenced by their biological state and are aware, at a subliminal level, of what goes on in their bodies; they may use pink at times of menstruation, even though they may not speak of any preoccupation with the body. (Ibid.)

If pink appears in your mandalas, it may be an indicator that your health needs attention.

Pink is a feminine color. Girl babies are dressed in it. Pink has long been considered an appropriate color only for young females. However, this custom has been challenged recently by growing numbers of American men choosing to wear pink shirts, sweaters, and ties. Perhaps this speaks of the integration of the feminine by modern men. Pink in the mandalas of men and women may refer to the young feminine: the inner child for women, the anima for men.

Pink can also be considered the solution to the opposition symbolized by red and white. Red and white represent dualities in many cultures. Take as an example the traditions of alchemy. In alchemical symbolism red stands for the active, masculine principle. White signifies the passive, feminine principle. The transcendence of these opposites is symbolized by a marriage between the two. The consummation of this marriage is signified by the mixture of red and white which produces pink.

While working with the mandalas of "Miss X," Jung (1973b) learned that for her pink stood for the feeling function. When seen in your mandalas, the positive pole of pink might relate to your emotional life, an acceptance of the human condition, or enjoyment of the sensuous possibilities of the flesh. The negative pole of pink points to a preoccupation with the body, pressing needs of your inner child, or, possibly, the presence of a physical illness. Pink in your mandalas can direct you to look for what is new and in need of protection in yourself.

PEACH

Peach is the color of mangoes and canteloupes as well as peaches. It recalls the sensuous pleasure of biting into a ripe fruit, being flooded with the taste sensation of sweetness, and reaching quickly for a napkin as juice drips from the corners of your mouth. The color is produced by mixing a bit of yellow (consciousness) with pink (body). Peach, like pink, suggests sensuality. It is not, however, the sensuality of the infant. It is, rather, the responsiveness of the mature adult: sexuality.

The peach originated in China where it is a symbol associated with Taoist sexual mysticism (Walker, 1988). The peach symbolizes the feminine vitality that creates life, and, on a concretistic level, it represents the female genitalia. Peaches from a sacred garden were said to be the vital ingredient for producing the god's elixir of immortality. To the Chinese it provided a clue to long life for mortals as well. "The symbol of human longevity was the old man, Shou Lu, always slyly shown with his finger stuck into the cleft of a fuzzy peach, to reveal the Way to his secret of long life" (Walker, 1988:493).

In Europe the peach has also served as a symbol of the vulva, the feminine principle, and of marriage (DeVries, 1976). The peach is an attribute of the Virgin. In astrology it is associated with Venus. It was thought to counteract the negativity of Mars. Clearly, peach is the color of woman, seen as the embodiment of a garden of delight.

When peach appears in your mandalas, you may find you are ready for a rich and meaningful sexual relationship. The positive pole of peach connotes a feminine coming of age, sexual maturity, or the release of generative potentials within the psyche. The negative meanings may have to do with a compulsive indulgence in sexuality, or possibly an overly romantic notion of sexuality and its place in your life. In my experience the use of peach in mandalas usually proclaims the presence of feminine energy generated from the hidden depths of one's being which, when freely given to others, is received as the bouquet of the goddess.

MAGENTA

Magenta is a bright purplish red. It is also known as fuchsia, after the flower of that name. Magenta was so named because the dye that creates it was discovered during the same year that a battle was fought in northern Italy near the town of Magenta. The year of this discovery was 1859.

Magenta is a relatively new color. It seems to express vitality, excitement, and restlessness. Magenta is frequently chosen by to-day's women for clothing that makes a bold, dramatic, and individualistic statement. It is an interesting synchronicity that the women's movement began about the same time as the battle that gave magenta its name.

One could look at magenta as red (energy) with a touch of blue (feminine). Magenta can be read, then, as a statement of the freeing of energy from the traditional feminine, the matriarchy, or as a feminine form of energy. I see it in the mandalas of women who are establishing autonomy, identifying their vocation, and enlarging their world view. These women are taking action while staying grounded in their true feminine nature.

It seems significant that magenta was the color selected for the goddess Kali plate of Judy Chicago's *Dinner Party* installation (Chicago, 1979). Chicago's remarkable assemblage expresses in the feminine symbolism of a dinner party the heritage of women. Beautiful place settings of china, hand-worked linens, and gleaming flatwear honor outstanding women, many unrecognized or overlooked by historians. Most of the place settings honor specific individuals. The Kali plate, however, is there to honor the primal energy source of womanliness. She is the vortex of nature's power to create and destroy with ceaseless abandon.

Magenta in your mandalas may well reveal your readiness to undertake a course of study, to initiate a creative project, or to voice your own opinions. The positive meanings of magenta include motivation, focus, and liveliness. The pitfalls of living out the energies indicated by the presence of magenta in your mandalas revolve around a loss of relatedness that can lead to inflation. Negative possibilities to consider are impatience, egotism, or a loss of focus in excess emotionality. Most often I see magenta in mandalas announcing the arrival of a time of productivity when one moves out into the world as an individual.

BROWN

Brown is reminiscent of fertile soil, of fields harvested and ready for planting. Perhaps because empty fields suggest something once there and now gone away, for some people brown bespeaks renunciation, sorrow, and penitence. DeVries (1976) mentions that a certain "nutbrown maiden" appears often in ballads. She is tested and found steadfast by her banished lover. Like this maiden, the color brown also suggests a down-to-earth trustworthiness.

Brown can be created by several color combinations. It can be a mixture of red and green: the red of libido and the green of control.

When this is the case brown may express a feeling of being stuck between the impulse to go and the inhibition not to go. Brown can also be made with orange (striving for autonomy) and blue (feminine). This combination may suggest a conflicted relationship with the mother.

Lüscher (1969) considers brown a darkened red. The muting of the active vitality of red to him suggests passive receptivity, such as that of the bodily senses. Jung (1973b) also mentions that brown symbolized the sensation function in the mandalas of his client "Miss X." Lüscher, however, had a more specific meaning associated with brown, although it does not contradict Jung's interpretation.

Lüscher came to see brown as an indicator of the need for emotional security, experienced in the physical body as symptoms of discomfort. He found that people displaced by World War II often put brown in a prominent place in his color preference test. From this he concluded that "brown . . . indicates the importance placed on 'roots:' on hearth, home and the company of one's own kind, on gregarious and familial security" (1969:68). According to Lüscher a preference for brown suggests the need for

> release from some situation which is bringing about a feeling of discomfort. [The situation might be one of] insecurity, of actual physical illness; it may be an atmosphere of conflict, or the existence of problems with which the individual feels unable to cope. (Ibid.)

We cannot overlook the fact that brown is also the color of excrement. Feces is a waste product and this influences, to some extent, meanings associated with the color brown as well. For example, Kellogg discovered that use of brown, especially when placed in the center of a mandala, often means that "the person has very low self-esteem, feels worthless and dirty" (1977:124). It should be remembered, though, that manure is a rich fertilizer, and that the dungheap was often the source of the prima materia with which alchemists sought to create gold. That which is rejected within us may yield some of our most sterling qualities.

Brown mixed with red produces a deep maroon, not unlike the color of dried blood. Kellogg has discovered some special meanings associated with this color in mandalas. She finds that brown-tinged red reveals feelings associated with sexual identity. In the mandalas of a man this color calls to one's attention:

areas of taboo, such as incestuous wishes. In the work of a female, questions arise as to feelings of unworthiness by virtue of being female, preoccupation with the body, and in severe cases gynecological disorders. (1978:63)

When maroon appears in your mandalas, perhaps it is a message from your unconscious to reexamine old wounds that may yet need some attention in order to heal.

Because brown is the color of fallow fields, it is appropriate in art work with an autumn theme. Mandalas produced in the fall of the year, at the end of an important life cycle, or near the end of a healing process may tend to have brown in them. When brown appears in your mandalas you might want to consider the positive meanings of brown such as earthiness, fertility, and opportunities for new beginnings. Since brown is a mixture of other colors it "can point to energy buried or tied up" (Kellogg, 1978:63). You may also want to look at whether brown reveals an unjustifiably low opinion of yourself, blocked energy, or a need for more security.

TURQUOISE

The color turquoise takes its name from the gemstone. It is a greenish sky blue. Turquoise has been useful in healing for centuries. It was associated with the goddess Isis who bore the title Lady of the Turquoise (DeVries, 1976). Iranians believe that it wards off the Evil Eye and brings good health. Europeans thought turquoise made an excellent horse amulet, and that wearing it protected a rider from falling, or at least softened a fall (Walker, 1988).

Native Americans of the Southwest use turquoise for personal adornment, as an offering to important deities, and sometimes crush it for sand paintings (Bahti, 1966). Window and door frames of Mexican-American homes are often painted turquoise. The same custom is observed in the Eastern United States in areas with African influence. It is felt that turquoise halts the unwelcome flow of ghosts through these openings.

To illustrate the significance of turquoise in mandalas, Joan Kellogg (1983) tells the story of Turquoise Lady, based on Native American traditions. Turquoise Lady is an honorary position assigned to a woman who has suffered a terrible loss. Her family may have been wiped out, a beloved son, daughter, or husband lost. She needs some activity to help her bridge from her former existence as a caretaker to her new status as a matron in the tribe.

The bereaved woman is designated Turquoise Lady for the period of two years. It is her job to see that protocol is observed when visitors call. At tribal gatherings she sees to it that dignitaries are seated in the right place so that proper respect is shown to all. Performing this activity diverts the woman's attention from her personal tragedy.

The role of Turquoise Lady gives the woman a place in the tribe. Because she is busy, time passes. Her grief is eased. At the end of the two years, she relinquishes her position as Turquoise Lady and embarks on a new life.

In my work with the mandala, it seems that using turquoise is a bit like becoming Turquoise Lady. Turquoise often appears when healing is necessary in order that you may get on with your life. As a temporary measure, you may need to distance yourself from painful events, to suppress the pain of loss that might threaten the ego's ability to cope, and to begin closure with the past so that you do not suffer the constant visitations of the spectre of how things might have been. The appearance of turquoise in your mandalas may indicate that the psyche is controlling the flow of memories which might be too painful.

Turquoise is light blue (positive mothering) and green (nurturing, control). We can look at turquoise as a statement of traditional mothering (caring for others) being redirected toward an increased ability to care for oneself. When you select turquoise for your mandalas it may be a reminder of the capacity of the psyche to heal itself in ways you cannot know or understand. The difficulty turquoise may bring to your attention could be a tendency to resist emotion, fearing the deeper unconscious imagery it might arouse.

GRAY

Gray is a neutral color. In nature gray is associated with stone, ashes, and mist. Gray is a Lenten color. It is traditionally associated with atonement, as in the Biblical practice of donning sackcloth and ashes to expiate guilt. Cirlot (1962) finds that the connection with ashes results in gray also symbolizing depression, inertia, and indifference. The gray hair of old age gives the color gray connotations of wisdom, retrospection, and relativism (DeVries, 1976).

Gray suggests the balance of opposites since it is a mixture of black and white. The balance achieved by gray does not include the colors of the spectrum. Since color has to do with emotion, gray, as a noncolor, suggests a lack of feeling. In psychological terms, a lack of emotion is considered a symptom of depression. From the viewpoint of age and experience, however, the neutrality of gray may reflect an equanimity such that one is no longer tossed about by transitory emotions.

Kellogg saw the use of gray in mandalas created by heroin addicts whose drug abuse caused all sensations, both positive and negative, to fade away. She deduced that their addiction was in some way used to numb guilt feelings "related to hopelessness and depression connected to the right of one's organism to life" (1978:70). Non-addicts may also experience such existential guilt. Kellogg suggests that the roots of such feelings may even reach back to a struggle for survival within the uterine environment. They may also occur in persons who are "programmed to accept the responsibility for imposing great pain on the mother . . ." (ibid.).

In my work with mandalas, I have observed that gray sometimes stands for stone. Stones have been revered as sacred objects for thousands of years. They have received the numinous projections of Celtic, Native American, and Japanese peoples, to name a few. Stones are related to the symbolism of the mandala itself. They have been used in many traditions to define sacred space. Perhaps gray in your mandalas is a call to honor your own sacred space.

When gray appears in your mandalas you might ask yourself whether you are discovering some insight into the paradox of human existence, glimpsing the possibility of wholeness, or finding a restful middle ground on some troublesome moral issue. You may also want to consider whether you are in some way cutting off your feelings, experiencing a misguided guilt for being your own person, or passing through a depression that may be a natural station in the pilgrimage of life.

These color meanings are offered as an aid to understanding colors in your mandalas. They are the compilation of one person, myself, and they reflect the limitations of an individual viewpoint. There are many possibilities not included. Please use this chapter as a tool for your own personal exploration of color. It is by no means the final word on the subject of color in mandalas.

The interplay between colors is another dimension of meaning that should be considered when looking at mandalas. The colors dance together in harmony or dissonance. Tradition brings meaning to some color combinations. Psychology offers another way of understanding the significance of colors that appear together. In the chapter that follows we will take a look at relationships between colors and what they may be telling us in our mandalas.

4 COLOR SYSTEMS

COLORS HAVE RELATIONSHIPS, just as people do. Some colors create an impression of harmony together. They convey through mandalas a message of balance, peace, or healing. Other color combinations appear to clash. They suggest conflict, vitality, or disharmony. Knowing how colors interact with one another can help you understand their messages in your mandalas.

Some color relationships are established by what is seen in nature. For example, the rainbow always displays the same ascending pattern of colors: red, orange, yellow, green, blue, indigo, and purple. The rainbow, honored in many traditions as a sign of blessing from the gods, creates a feeling of excitement, anticipation, and joy. The rainbow colors are bright, and yet they remind us that a storm is nearby.

The changing of the seasons creates another family of colors in many parts of the world. The pastel pinks, lavenders, and yellows of spring ripen into the rich greens and golds of summer. Autumn brings a dark, earthy palette of colors followed by winter's extremes of dark grays, black, and white. The colors of all the seasons together can signify a complete yearly cycle of growth. These colors can also serve as a metaphor for the seasons of a human life.

Ancient human activities such as pottery-making, metallurgy, and wine-making established certain ideas about color as well. As clay hardens, metal heats, and wine matures, their colors vary. The colors seen during the processing became significant markers of the transformations taking place. For example, the potter knew that her pots should be heated until they were a bright cherry red to assure that they would have the desired strength and resonance once they cooled. The alchemists, craftsmen of the inner world, used color as an important indicator for their work as well.

The artist's experience with mixing paint determined the kinship of some colors. For example, artists discovered that the color orange can be made by an equal mixture of red and yellow. Orange is a color in its own right, but it also suggests to the eye the qualities of both red and yellow. All three colors—orange, red, and yellow—suggest warmth, energy, and vitality.

The practical experience of artists and craftsmen is handed down to us in traditional systems of color such as the color wheel (Plate 2). Peoples who lived close to nature incorporated the natural colors they saw around them into systems of philosophy, morality, and conduct. We are not so different from these ancient artists, craftsmen, and philosophers. We respond to the same natural patterns of color that moved people of other places and times. When trying to understand the role of color in mandalas, these traditional color systems can be helpful. Therefore, in this chapter we will look at some ways of approaching color relationships I have found useful in my work with mandalas.

First we will examine the artist's color wheel, which establishes primary and secondary color relationships, and the ways that seasonal colors relate to work with the mandala. Then follows a brief description of the Native American medicine wheel. Next I will suggest ways in which colors associated with kundalini yoga may help you understand your mandalas. I will describe Goethe's hierarchy of colors, which grew out of European traditions, as well as alchemical color symbolism. Finally, we will look at some of Joan Kellogg's observations of significant color combinations in mandalas.

Perhaps some of these color systems will prove useful for you, as they have for me, in working with mandalas. There are no doubt other ways of looking at color not included simply because I do not know about them. You may prefer others that will be more appropriate for your work. The systems outlined here are offered as suggestions of some ways in which color relationships in mandalas can be approached. They are by no means *the* way to decode color.

The color wheel was devised by European artists as an aid to achieving color harmony in their work. It is an arrangement of the colors red, blue, yellow, green, orange, and purple in a circle. The circle is subdivided by two triangles. At the points of one triangle, placed along the circumference of the circle, the colors red, blue, and yellow are positioned. Pigments in these colors can be mixed in varying amounts to produce virtually all other colors. Because they are basic building blocks of the colors used by artists, they are called primary colors.

Secondary colors are produced by mixing equal parts of two primary colors. For example, purple is the product of red and blue. Orange is created by combining red and yellow. Green is the result of mixing blue and yellow. On the color wheel secondary colors are placed between the primary colors of which they are comprised. Secondary colors on the circumference of the color wheel are connected with lines to create a second color wheel triangle.

In mandalas the primary colors seem to reflect the basic drives of a human being. Red appears to express the libido or life force necessary to sustain existence as an organism. Blue seems related to the ability to form bonds and to give nurturing. Yellow reveals the capacity for consciousness. The appearance of these colors in a series of mandalas often points toward the functioning of these primary human impulses.

When considering secondary colors in mandalas, one looks to the primaries that comprise them and their symbolic meaning as well as the meanings of the secondary colors themselves. That is to say that purple is considered as being red and blue as well as being purple. In deciphering the meanings of secondary colors in mandalas, one collects associations for all three colors: the color itself, and each of the primaries that create it. For example, the final meaning for the secondary color purple will be an amalgamation of the associations compiled for red, blue, and purple.

Let us consider the color purple in this way of unlocking meanings in your mandalas. My associations to purple might be "royalty, authority, and lofty mountain tops." Red, for me, speaks of "raw energy, drive, and anger." Blue means "tranquility, justice, and nurturing." When purple appears in my mandala the message to me might be something like this: "Behind my distant, authoritative exterior burns a raw energy seeking expression in relatedness."

Another possibility might be, "My sense of specialness is the result of burying my anger and assuming the role of a nurturer." Yet another formulation might be, "I am achieving nobility through my struggle to maintain a difficult relationship with a woman in my life." The correct statement would be determined by my sense of whether it brings me information that seems relevant to my present situation.

Colors that are opposite one another on the color wheel are called complementary. When these colors are placed side by side in art work they create a vivid impression. To some observors they even appear to vibrate. The Impressionists made use of this optical effect to enliven their paintings. Complementary colors are red/ green, yellow/purple, and blue/orange.

When complementary colors are used next to each other in mandalas, they may suggest the tension of opposites. For example, red (energy) might compete with green (control). Yellow (autonomy) with purple (connection with the mother) could suggest the clash between the desire for independence and the habit of relying on the parents. Blue (nurturing) next to orange (striving) may symbolize the conflict between a desire for relatedness and the ambition to accomplish.

The relationships established by the color wheel are useful guidelines for understanding colors in our mandalas. I find looking at the meanings of the primary colors that comprise secondary colors is especially helpful. The clash of colors opposite one another on the color wheel can give us clues to understand conflicts we are experiencing. We should remember that some conflict is part of being alive, just as strident colors may give our mandalas a vitality that can be pleasing.

We do not lead lives so intimately intertwined with natural rhythms as did our ancestors. Even so, we are aware of our natural surroundings. They influence our thoughts about colors, even though we may often be unconscious of nature's effects on us. Evidence of our sensitivity to the natural world is demonstrated by the Seasonal Affective Disorder associated with a deprivation of natural light during winter.

The four seasons each have colors that distinguish them one from the other.* The orderly passage of seasonal colors may sometimes

* Associations of seasons and colors are based on the results of questionnaires

be a symbol for our own psychological growth process. Projects, concerns, and relationships come and go with a natural rhythm that mirrors that of the seasons. Looking at the colors in your mandalas in terms of the seasons they represent can be another way to understand your choices of colors.

Spring is associated with bright, cool pastels: yellow, pink, lavender. Green is a spring color, especially pale shades. Violet (purple) is often identified with spring as well. These colors in your mandalas could point to something new, tender, and full of potential in your life.

Summer shades include green, golden yellow, orange, red, peach, and sky blue. The colors of summer have a rich, warm, vibrant quality. It is as if they each contain a tiny drop of golden yellow, the color of the sun which dominates this season. When the colors of summer appear in your mandalas, you might consider whether they indicate the fulfillment, abundance, or maturity of something.

Fall colors, most agree, are brown, orange, gold, and maroon. These colors evoke the feelings of harvest time: happiness that the crops are ripened and brought in, but sadness about the passing of the excitement of the growing season. When fall colors find a place in your mandalas, they may suggest that you are reaping the rewards of a season of personal growth. These colors may also be a reminder to attend to the grieving process that is a natural part of the passing of familiar ways of being, the completion of projects, or the fulfillment of obligations.

Winter colors are black, white, and gray. These colors suggest cool winter days with gray skies, long dark nights, and the brightness of snow. Winter colors in your mandalas could be telling you that it is a fallow rest time in your inner growth cycle. Even though mandalas in winter colors look cool and detached, they carry the message that the quickening of spring begins hidden beneath the snows of winter.

Colors have been useful teaching devices in times and places where the written word was rare. Natural patterns of color in nature provided a framework for organizing the insights of folk psychology. The colors yellow, green, black, and white are frequently used

---

completed by 294 participants at conferences on religion and psychology sponsored by the Journey into Wholeness during 1988–89.

as aspects of the Native American medicine wheel (Storm, 1973). Perhaps ancient Native American elders linked the four directions with the four seasons, and let the color of the season determine the color of the directions.

The medicine wheel is a device used for teaching lessons about life, morality, and one's place in the community. It is a circle marked by the four directions arranged like the cardinal points on a compass. Each direction is assigned a color. North is white, East is yellow, South is green, and West is black. Each direction has its own distinct qualities, lessons to learn, insights to gain, or skills to master.

Native American tradition attributes a different world view to each direction. The East (yellow) is the direction of illumination. It is like the springtime, the dawning of the day, and the youthful discovery of knowledge. The South (green) is the place of trust and innocence. It seems like summertime, the fullness of noontime, and the generative time of life. The West (black) is the place of intro- spection. Like autumn, afternoon, and middle age, it conveys the natural necessity of reviewing and letting go. The North (white) is the place of wisdom. It suggests the white snows of winter, the long hours of nighttime darkness illumined by a bright moon, and the rich treasure of wisdom.

According to the medicine wheel way each person comes into the world with the understanding of at least one of the directions. The challenge of living is to learn the lessons of the other directions, mastering each in order to grow in wisdom. Hyemeyohsts Storm explains that

> any person who perceives from only one of these Four Great Directions will remain just a partial man. For example, a man who possesses only the Gift of the North will be wise. But he will be a cold man, a man without feeling. And the man who lives only in the East will have the clear, far sighted vision of the Eagle, but he will never be close to things. This man will feel separated, high above life, and will never understand or believe that he can be touched by anything.
>
> A man or woman who perceives only from the West will go over the same thought again and again in their mind, and will always be undecided. And if a person has only the Gift of the South, he will see everything with the eyes of a Mouse. He will be too close to the

ground and too near sighted to see anything except whatever is right in front of him, touching his whiskers. (1973:6)

Bringing the four directions into balance within is a way to make oneself a whole person, in harmony with nature. In the words of Storm:

> After each of us has learned of our Beginning Gift, our First Place on the Medicine Wheel, we then must Grow by Seeking Understanding in each of the Four Great Ways. Only in this way can we become Full, capable of Balance and Decision in what we do. (Ibid., 6–7)

When white, green, yellow, or black appear in your mandalas, you may want to remember the lessons of each, as taught by the medicine wheel. The colors might be the gateway to go deeper into the Native American teachings of the four directions.

Now let us turn to a different system of color relationships. It is based on the folk psychology of India, where spiritual and psychological thought are intertwined in a way to which we are not accustomed in the West. So ancient that their inception precedes the dawn of recorded history, these ideas are probably based on careful introspection. Interestingly enough, contemporary psychologists have formulated theories of a hierarchy of human needs not unlike those of traditional Indian thought. To understand the role of color in this theory, we must first briefly describe the system itself, which is known as kundalini yoga.

Kundalini yoga holds that unseen energy flows through certain pathways in the body. Especially important is the flow of energy

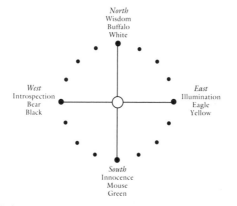

The Native American medicine wheel. (After Storm, 1972: 6)

upward from the base of the spine to the crown of the head. It is felt that along this channel of energy flow there are certain nodal points that function to concentrate and transform the energy. These are called chakras.

Each chakra has a developmental task associated with it. As mastery of the task is achieved, it is felt that the kundalini energy flows more freely upward to meet the challenges of the next chakra. There are seven chakras spaced several inches apart along the spine and at points on the head. The lower chakras have to do with survival and basic needs. The upper chakras relate to spiritual awakening. One cannot fully open the upper chakras until the lower chakras are cleared.

Each chakra has a color associated with it, assigned in the order of the spectrum: red, orange, yellow, green, blue, indigo, and purple. The first chakra at the base of the spine is associated with red, "the colour of blood, of dark passion" (Jung, 1976b:11). The next chakra, a few inches below the navel, is given orange, "the colour of the dawn or the last rays of the sun" (p. 11). Moving up the spine we find the next chakra in the areas of the solar plexus. Jung describes this as "the place where the sun rises" (p. 23). It is given the color yellow.

The color of the next chakra, located near the heart, is green. Moving a few inches higher, we find the fifth chakra located in the throat area. Its color is blue. The sixth chakra is located in the head, at a point between and above the eyes. Its color is indigo. On top of the head is located the crown chakra. Its color is purple (often shown as lavender).

The concerns of the person working with energies of the first chakra relate to basic survival needs and to the health of the body. It resonates with experiences during infancy. When red occurs in your mandala it is worth considering whether it might be telling you something about your health. Perhaps there is an illness you need to treat with more care. Another possibility could be that the stress you are experiencing is beginning to affect your physical well-being. I have observed that women who are menstruating tend to use more red than when they are not. Red may also symbolize memories of times when your basic needs for security were not fulfilled.

The second chakra relates to the development of autonomy. Its color is orange. Kellogg (1978) suggests that our experiences as toddlers seem related to this chakra. Our sense of self-worth, judgments about the effects of our actions on our surroundings, and gender identification are some of the concerns during this phase of development. The appearance of orange in your mandalas may reveal a continuing concern in these areas, or may herald the reworking of some of the choices made much earlier in life.

The third chakra is located behind the navel. It is associated with self-consciousness or the emergence of the ego as a point of reference. The color for this chakra is yellow. The concerns of this chakra are reminiscent of the experiences of the child leaving home to go to school. The issues here relate to independence, and the ability to learn, think, and plan. Effective interaction with the environment is important to the person working with the energies of the third chakra. Yellow in your mandalas may reveal a readiness to learn, the dawning of awareness about something, or a willingness to own your unique point of view. Yellow may also relate to memories of earlier events when independent action was taken.

The fourth chakra, near the heart, is associated with caring for others. The color is green. The challenges of adolescence and young adulthood seem related to this chakra. Relevant issues include the relinquishment of unconscious claims on one's parents, the ability to nurture oneself and others, and the readiness to relate to another in the intimacy of sexual relationship. Green in your mandalas may announce coming into your own as an adult, or a revision of earlier experiences related to this period of personality development (DiLeo, Graf, and Kellogg, 1977).

The fifth chakra is in the neck. Light blue is assigned to this chakra. The ability to love without receiving anything in return is the developmental challenge associated with this chakra. This chakra also has to do with sharing your gifts, talents, and abilities without the expectation of rewards. The fifth chakra relates to growing spiritual awareness since, in the yoga tradition, it is thought that this chakra is the gateway to the return through which the individual becomes reunited with the larger self, the Atman. Blue in your mandalas may suggest the awakening of your spiritual nature.

Spiritual awareness is felt to deepen at the sixth chakra, placed just above and between the eyes. Energies of this chakra seem related to the development of intuition, sometimes called the third eye. The color is dark blue. The challenge of this chakra is to integrate a sense of the timeless order behind events with our personal finite ego consciousness. When dark blue appears in your mandalas, you may be experiencing an awareness of the deeper reality behind events in your life.

The seventh chakra crowns the top of the head. The color is purple or lavender. In yoga tradition it is associated with an ability to transcend one's separate existence and to experience a mystical connection with the cosmos. When lavender appears in your mandalas it might symbolize a peak experience from the recent past or near future. Lavender might also recall the bliss state of infancy, revisited as a place of rest, healing, or inspiration.

The chakra system colors are those of the rainbow. Some of us may create mandalas that incorporate all these colors together. There is a special dazzle to these mandalas. Kellogg finds that such mandalas reveal an intense arousal that can be healing. She calls it the "rainbow experience" (1977:125). Kellogg has written that "in developing an understanding of rainbow symbolism, one becomes very aware of rain in its fertilizing aspects and the bow as the cosmic vagina. . . . The rainbow signifies a new birth under magical circumstances" (1978:81). When you create a rainbow mandala, it is as if all seven chakras are activated. You may sense a profound reordering of your point of view about yourself and past experiences. A rainbow mandala may accompany a feeling that you are being reborn.

The color wheel and the spectrum give us useful systems for understanding colors. There are two important colors, however, that do not have a place in either of them. These are the colors black and white. Some artists will tell you that black is the absence of all color. Others will say that black has within it all colors. The same can be said for white. What is the significance of black and white in your mandalas?

In one sense black and white are complementary colors. The presence of one implies the other, in the same way that darkness suggests light, its opposite. Black and white have traditionally symbolized the opposites of darkness and light. They are apt metaphors for other opposites as well.

Black and white placed together in your mandalas may show that you are experiencing the tension of the opposites. Mandalas composed of black and white without other colors suggest that you are viewing the world in cool, intellectual terms. Generally speaking, colors represent emotions. An absence of color suggests that emotions have gone underground temporarily. This may happen when conflicts have generated powerful feelings and the body decrees a temporary respite to recover.

Just as many creation myths begin with the separation of darkness and light out of chaos, black and white mandalas can signify a new beginning for you as well. These mandalas suggest bare-bones simplicity, a condition in which everything superfluous has been burned away. While painful to achieve, this simplicity is necessary to make a place for something new. Your black and white mandalas may be a sign that chaos has been purged and your psyche is ripe for the planting of a seed that will blossom into a renewed involvement in life.

Black and white are central to Goethe's theory of color. His philosophical romanticism was based on classical traditions. Goethe's profound love of nature made him a careful observer of color in the natural world. He also created laboratory situations to demonstrate his ideas about color under controlled conditions.

Goethe's color theory is based on the properties of light and dark. According to Goethe, all colors are included between the opposites of absolute darkness (black) and pure light (white). He writes that "light and darkness, brightness and obscurity, or if a more general expression is preferred, light and its absence, are necessary to the production of colour" ([1840] 1970:lvi). Colors flow organically from one to the other as proportions of light and dark vary. Goethe thought of black as a symbol for matter. White represented spirit for him. According to Goethe, as matter becomes filled with spirit it changes. The coming of light into darkness suggested to Goethe the process by which spirit enters matter.

When light is added to darkness, as with the coming of the sun in early dawn, black changes to blue. Goethe saw the lightening of black into blue as a metaphor for the spiritualization of matter. Conversely, as spirit descends into matter, it is transformed in a way that is illustrated by the shift of white to yellow as white darkens. To Goethe the colors blue and yellow represent the body and soul of human beings.

Green is produced by mixing equal amounts of blue and yellow. The fact that mixing equal amounts of blue and yellow produces green was an affirmation for Goethe of the state of harmony that can be achieved by human beings who balance within themselves both body and soul. Since blue and yellow are derived from black and white, green also represents the resolution of the opposites symbolized by darkness and light. Goethe felt that the position of green at the center of the color hierarchy accounted for the sense of harmony conveyed by the color green.

The color red appears as yellow darkens and blue lightens. This deepening of yellow to red can be observed in a colored liquid to which more and more yellow dye is added. Goethe writes that "the intensest and purest red . . . is produced when the two extremes of the yellow-red and blue-red are united ([1840] 1970:lvi–lvii).

Goethe's hierarchy of colors helps us understand the close connection of blue (the maternal) and black (the ground of being). It also suggests the relatedness of yellow (the father) and white (the formless, colorless void). When you see black and white followed by blue and yellow in a series of mandalas, a special resolution of the opposites is suggested. This movement, using Goethe's theory, is a step towards the center, toward harmony. Blue and yellow can express the understanding of opposites on the human scale, in terms of masculine and feminine. The conceptualization of the opposites as masculine/feminine opens us to the possibility of resolving the opposition through a sacred inner marriage which produces a new unity symbolized by the color green.

Goethe's color theory relates color to the dynamic rhythms of nature. The whole system is predicated on a conceptualization of the dualities of nature as symbolized by darkness and light. For Goethe everything was either dividing itself out of a state of unity, or moving toward such a state of unity.

> To divide the united, to unite the divided, is the life of nature; this is the eternal systole and diastole, the eternal collapsion and expansion, the inspiration and expiration of the world in which we live and move. (Ibid., 293–294)

Goethe's theory of color can help you see the movement of your own psychic life, mirrored in your mandalas, as you move from the differentiation of black and white, through blue and yellow, to the unity of green, and back once again to black and white.

The next family of colors existed before Goethe's time. The system of which the colors are a part was rejected during the age of rationalism as being unscientific. Its significance for modern persons was revealed by Jung. This is the color symbolism of alchemy.

Alchemy is a body of formulas and procedures purported to create invaluable substances from base matter. Activities such as burning, dissolving, and drying were performed in a tightly-sealed vessel. Jung believed that these activities were really a projection of the psychological experience of personal growth, which he called individuation. Consequently, the alchemical opus can be read as a metaphor of the psyche's unfolding toward wholeness. In M. Esther Harding's words,

> The hermetic vessel is oneself. In it the many pieces of psychic stuff scattered throughout one's world must be collected and fused into one, so making a new creation. In it must occur the union of the opposites called by the alchemists *coniunctio* or marriage. (1973:431)

Many processes are mentioned in alchemical references. Edward Edinger (1990) has singled out four as being especially informative when looking at alchemy as a metaphor of psychological growth. These are *calcinatio* (burning), *solutio* (dissolving), *coagulatio* (drying) and *sublimatio* (evaporating). Each stage moves the prima materia from its point of beginning through an operation governed by each of the four elements: fire, water, earth, and air. Each operation symbolizes an inner, psychological transformation. Certain colors are associated with each procedure. By matching the colors in your mandalas with those of the alchemical processes you may get clues about the energies that are shaping your inner experience at the moment.

The prima materia with which the process begins was said to be a nondescript, dark color. The first step of the alchemical procedure requires that the prima materia be sealed tightly in a vessel. Harding notes that some alchemical texts show the seal being placed by a man and woman together. Psychologically, this points to the importance of engaging masculine and feminine aspects of the person in the work of transformation. The colors red (man) and white (woman) are associated with this couple.

Red and white together in a mandala may announce the constellation of the alchemical vessel which, in psychological terms, may be an experience of an obstacle or the frustration of desires. Sealing the prima materia in the alchemical vessel is the first step towards transformation. This means staying with the frustration. It causes the material to darken into black. This stage is the *nigredo*. In terms of personal growth, this activity compares to facing one's dark side, a necessary but unpleasant step for coming to terms with one's shadow. When looking at a mandala that is very dark, you might consider whether the darkness mirrors this necessary stage of individuation: a time when the ego feels wounded, self-esteem is low, and depression is not uncommon.

Calcinatio is the next step in the alchemical work. It requires the burning of the material at red-hot temperatures. On its way to a bright red, the blackened prima materia lightens to purple. Some sources describe iridescent colors like the peacock's tail as the heat intensifies. The appearance of these colors in your mandalas suggest the transformation of the psyche through a kind of psychological cooking powered by intense, contained emotion. When the red in your mandala has a fiery quality, you might consider the possibility that it is the psyche's fire of transformation that guides your choice of this color.

When the fire burns out, all that is left behind is white ashes, called "white foliated earth" by the alchemists. These ashes contain the essence of what has been burned. They hold everything needed to continue the process of refinement outlined by alchemy. White in mandalas may signify the ego's having survived an ordeal of the archetypal energies of the unconscious. It can suggest the emergence from a dark night of the soul into a new, untried, and unknown way of being in the world.

The alchemists prescribe mixing the ashes with water. This is the process of *solutio*. What was once solid and irreducible is thereby made the same, and can freely interpenetrate in the liquid medium. This image corresponds to the return to an earlier level of functioning. A temporary regression can be helpful for the reordering of the contents of consciousness. When blue, the color of water, is prominent in our mandalas, perhaps the process of *solutio* is at work in the psyche.

To create a new, refined substance out of the solution, the alchemists employed the process called *coagulatio*. For this work they sometimes used sulphur. Sulphur is yellow and flammable, attributes it shares with the sun. In psychological symbolism, it will be recalled, the sun represents consciousness. Linking these two images together, Jung wrote that "sulphur represents the active substance of the sun or, in psychological language, the *motive factor in consciousness* . . ." (1976a:151).

When yellow appears in your mandalas, it might indicate that the dynamism of consciousness, the will, is actively engaged. That which was vague and unresolved in the psyche may become clear, meaningful, and substantial. The ego, wounded and eclipsed in *nigredo,* shines forth once again as the carrier of an expanded consciousness.

Sublimatio is the operation through which solid matter passes directly into a gaseous form. Edinger suggests that this operation is a metaphor for a dynamic movement between the opposites. When one experiences awareness of one's contradictory aspects over and over again, some sense of the center may result. Edinger explains that

> the repeated circuit of all aspects of one's being gradually generates awareness of a transpersonal center uniting the conflicting factors. There is a transit through the opposites which are experienced alternately again and again, leading finally to their reconciliation. (1990:143)

The paired opposites of complementary colors (red/green, orange/purple, blue/yellow, black/white) can express this oscillation between the opposites. The appearance of these pairs of colors in your mandalas may indicate that you are experiencing the rise to consciousness of opposing aspects of your psyche. With the constellation of your contradictory nature comes the possibility for a different, more complete resolution of these facets of your personality. The colors in your mandalas will reflect the changing pattern, sometimes preceding your ability to understand.

The completion of the alchemical opus is the mystical marriage of the opposites, the *coniunctio.* The unity of this wedding brings into being the alchemists' longed-for treasure. This marriage comes as the result of having successfully differentiated the opposites (spirit/matter, conscious/unconscious, good/evil). The opposites can then be rejoined in a union within which each continues its unique existence, yet, paradoxically, becomes part of a larger, more inclusive whole. Whereas the work is begun when an ordinary man and woman together seal the vessel, the alchemists envisioned this final coming together as the marriage of a royal pair.

Harding describes the couple so vital to the successful completion of the alchemical work:

> . . . the king, that is, gold or spirit, must be thrice purified; . . . She herself [the queen, or body] must also undergo a purification, usually represented as a washing or bathing, by which she is changed from the black earth, the nigredo, into the white earth or the silver. Thus another text referring to marriage or insemination reads: "Sow your Gold in White Earth." (1973:451–452)

And she clarifies the meaning of the mystical marriage from the viewpoint of personal growth:

> Psychologically this surely refers to the fact that the union of body and spirit or of conscious and unconscious can be safely attempted only when both have undergone a purification brought about by the earlier stages of analysis, in which the conscious character and the personal unconscious are reviewed and set in order. (1973:452)

In other words, we must carefully attend to our inner work in order to experience the reward of the mystical inner marriage.

The colors associated with the sacred marriage of opposites are mentioned in the alchemical writings referred to by Jung (1976a, 1974), Harding (1973), and Edinger (1990). Shades of red, reddish yellow, or the creamy resolution of red and white into rosy pink bespeak the *coniunctio*. When these colors appear in your mandalas, you may be reaping the reward of a moment poised near wholeness, hard-earned through earlier stages of personal growth and holding the tension of the opposites to expand consciousness. This is a state of grace. It never seems to last long, but we take the memory as a seed into the prima materia with which we will work as we begin the cycle once more.

Before moving to the next chapter, which will introduce ways of looking at shapes in mandalas, there is a bit more information about color I wish to share. This is based on significant color combinations identified by Joan Kellogg in her clinical work with mandalas. While our interest in the mandala is for personal growth rather than for clinical information, Kellogg's observations can provide additional information for studying our own mandalas. When you find these color combinations appearing in your mandalas, you may want to look at the meanings Kellogg associates with them, and ponder whether her insights are relevant for you.

According to Kellogg (1978) black and pink together reveal negative feelings about oneself. When these colors appear in your mandalas, it may be a signal to initiate interventions that enhance your health and well-being, both physical and emotional. For example, it may be appropriate to guard against accidents, to renew the supportive connections between yourself and loved ones, and to sort out and challenge self-derogatory thoughts. This color combination may appear before you are aware of your negativity, and so alert you to take preventive action that can eliminate unnecessary pain.

Black and red in mandalas are identified by Kellogg as indicators of depression and rage experienced simultaneously. These two colors together in a mandala suggest that the feelings may be acted out in explosive behavior. In using the mandala for your own personal growth, you may find the drawings you do a satisfactory substitute for foul moods, angry words, or punishing behavior which might otherwise be inflicted on others.

The combination of blue and red in mandalas signals a certain kind of conflict. Kellogg links these colors with the mythological dragon fight, a struggle during which the young hero challenges the dragon and achieves mastery. The hero's battle seems to express the universal struggle to free oneself—one's consciousness and identity—from the parental matrix of childhood. Kellogg sees this conflict revealed through the colors in mandalas when, during a series of drawings, purple is replaced by dark blue and red, which, in turn, make way for yellow.

> Red and dark blue separate out from the original dark purple, only to become antagonists. The conflict is finally resolved when the ego and self-consciousness are born in the sun of self, yellow. (1978:58)

The use of yellow with black or dark blue in mandalas reveals a vulnerability to inflation alternating with low self-esteem. "The expansive pose of the ego is constantly at hazard from the opposite polarity. One must be All . . . or Nothing at all" (ibid., 75). Yellow with black or dark blue may also symbolize mood swings between the extremes of elation and dejection. When these colors appear in your mandalas you might consider the need to do serious inner work to discover your true self and your own rightful power.

Kellogg finds that red and green together in mandalas can point to conflict. This could be the case when red symbolizes need and green stands for parental control, which inhibits the expression of the need. Red and green are associated with Christmas for many people. The intense, often contradictory emotions we experience during this holiday season seem attached to this color combination. These colors in your mandalas might be a signal that you need to nurture your own inner child.

This chapter has given brief descriptions of different systems of color relationships. It has been an attempt to show that colors in mandalas have another layer of meaning determined by their relationships to one another. As with the color meanings suggested in the previous chapter, these color systems are not intended for use as hard and fast rules. They merely provide guidelines that may prove useful in understanding the meanings in your mandalas. The true test for whether a meaning is the right one is whether or not it nourishes your growth process. As the mandalas unfold, you have the opportunity to confirm insights as the same colors appear again and your understanding of your color vocabulary deepens.

5 NUMBERS AND FORMS

WHEN THE BIOLOGIST adjusts a microscope to focus on the world of one-celled life, he pays attention to the shapes beneath his lens. Their distinctive forms help the biologist identify miniscule plants and animals. When we look at our mandalas, we are a bit like the biologist: we, too, seek understanding by studying shapes. With patience and experience, we can begin to discern the meaning of the forms we see in our mandalas.

Forms are comprised of line and color. (Refer to chapters 3 and 4 for information about color.) The quality of a line you draw is a reflection of the muscular tension in your body. When your emotions are aroused, tension in your body tends to be greater, and this causes you to bear down and make heavier lines. You make pale lines when you are tired or feeling weak from illness or depression. The thickness of your lines is also affected by the media you use. The softer your drawing material, the more likely it is that you will produce heavy lines.

Mandalas may include curved lines, straight lines, or both curved and straight lines. Curved lines are most often drawn by women. Straight lines appear somewhat more commonly in the mandalas of men. Kellogg finds that

> curved lines usually reflect a nonrational approach to life and an emotional way of handling situations. A curving line is very significant in regard to femininity. On the other hand, the straight line usually represents a rational way of handling problems. It is more representative of a masculine orientation. . . . (1977:125)

The distinction between straight and curved lines carries into shapes. For example, the shape of a triangle is comprised of straight lines and therefore suggests "masculine" rationality. A flower drawn with curved lines suggests "feminine" emotionality.

The line around the outside of the mandala seems to reflect the psychological boundary which separates oneself from the environment and other persons. Jung notes that a thick line here "denotes hardening or sealing off against the outside" (1973b:44). Kellogg agrees with Jung that a heavily defined boundary may reflect a defensive posture, but she also finds that such boundaries can indicate "deep introspection" (1977:126). A pale or nonexistent boundary suggests an openness to others, sensitivity to elements in one's environment, or possibly a diffuse sense of personal identity. A visible, but not overly thick, outer line usually indicates a well-defined sense of identity, with clearly established psychological boundaries between oneself and others.

Most mandalas will contain several shapes, perhaps even many. The forms may overlap, or suggest layers that create the impression of depth. Shapes can appear in random arrangements, or they may create orderly patterns. Take note of the shape that appears in the center of your mandala. It will probably be especially important for you at this time. Forms appearing in the bottom half, generally speaking, relate to material in the unconscious. Shapes appearing in the top half usually symbolize material closer to consciousness and therefore easier to decipher. (See page 35 for more information about placement in mandalas.) The variety of forms in mandalas is limitless. There is no right or wrong design. Your mandala is simply what happens when you fill a circle with color and form.

When analyzing the shapes in your mandala, you should always consider numbers too. Sometimes you may unconsciously include the graphic form of a number in your mandala design. For example, you might discover a squiggle that looks like the number nine. More often than not, however, a number will be an aspect of other forms. A flower may have six petals, so the number six can be important in your symbolism as well as the flower symbol itself.

Counting the number of shapes in your mandala can be helpful when unlocking its meaning. You might take note of the number of points on a star, the number of "pink drops," or even the number of colors you intuitively chose to use. When analyzing the significance of a number, you might also want to ask yourself what life was like for you at the age indicated by the number.

All the lines, numbers, and shapes that appear in your mandalas are significant. They are right, relevant, and informative for you at that point in time. The act of creating your mandala and seeing these forms can be deeply meaningful. You may be satisfied with your experience at that point, and want to go no further. However, you may find delving into the meanings of your symbols can make the mandala experience even more rewarding.

The symbolic meanings of forms in your mandalas can often be discovered with some of the simple techniques for keeping a journal described in chapter 2. To stimulate further insight into your symbols, the rest of this chapter is devoted to descriptions of some of the numbers and shapes often seen in mandalas. I have woven together traditional symbolism from religious liturgy, psychology, and mythology. Reading this information can help you amplify the meaning of your own symbols.

ONE

The number one stands for the individual, unity, and beginnings. One symbolizes the initiation of a process. Like the single acorn with which a tree begins, one suggests the potential to become much more. Singular shapes or designs in mandalas can suggest a nascent potential expanding with the psyche.

One, being the first number, in some way stands for all numbers. Since it has the capacity to suggest both itself and an infinite number of numbers, one is a symbol of unity. Jung saw the number one as *"the* unity, the One, All-oneness, individuality and non-duality—not a numeral but a philosophical concept, an archetype and attribute of God, the monad" (1965:287).

The number one stands for a state of mind as well. It is a way of thinking which does not contain opposites. All is experienced as a seamless unity uninterrupted by categories of things. This unitive consciousness is described by mystics. As strange as this may sound, each of us has experienced such a point of view.

In psychological terms, the experience of unity is one we all had as infants (Jung, 1976b). Prior to the separation of our identity from the world of experience, all was one. As persons mature, the functions of thinking, feeling, sensing, and intuition become differentiated and available to consciousness. The mind-set experienced by a person for whom only one of the four functions is conscious is still very close to the beginner's mind. As described by Jung, this is a time when "man still naively participates in his surroundings in a state of uncritical unconsciousness, submitting to things as they are" (cited in von Franz, 1986:124).

When you create a mandala containing one symbol, or perhaps even devoid of shapes and filled only with color, you may be experiencing a state of consciousness similar to the one described by Jung. It will recall the feelings that you knew when quite young. You might feel passive, blissful, and loving. As an adult you may identify this as a transpersonal state.

The number one may also suggest a quite different attitude. It can convey the essence of individuality. A statement such as "I'm number one" expresses a high degree of self-awareness, even egotism, which seems very different from the mystic's impression of reality. Yet it expresses a truth that we all know: each of us is a distinct individual, one of a kind. The number one can be a symbol for the singularity of the individual, with her/his unique potentials for being and becoming. It can symbolize the whole person.

It is well to remember that all mandalas, being a single circular design, carry the meaning of "one." Because the number one expresses the idea of unity, wholeness, and individuality, when you create a mandala, you place before yourself an image of your beingness. This is one reason that creating a mandala can be so comforting. It mirrors back to you the facts and possibilities of your own singular existence, your integrity, and your wholeness.

TWO

The number two "divides, repeats, and engenders symmetries" (von Franz, 1986:74). Gerhard Dorn, the alchemist, believed that the number two came into being on the second day of Creation, when the waters were separated from the earth. Even before the time of Dorn, during the time of Pythagoras, the number two was used to symbolize matter. (Von Franz, 1986)

The division into water and earth is a step away from the primordial unity that marked the beginning. Two has come to be a symbol for this first step of differentiation, out of unity and into the opposites. This was considered by many to be a movement away from harmony into strife. Therefore, the number two, according to Dorn, was associated with "the beginning of all confusion, dissension, and strife" (cited in von Franz, 1986:90).

Two also became associated with Eve, she being the second human creature created, according to the biblical story. Through time, two came to connote the "bisexuality of all things, or dualism" (Cirlot, 1962:222). Two also symbolizes the coming together of the sexes and marriage. By extension, two can suggest the harmonious resolution of the clash of opposites, or a state of equilibrium in opposing forces.

Some sources equate two with the shadow, and use it to suggest a second, lesser aspect of the person which, nonetheless, has a powerful connection with the person. The notion of a reflected image is also associated with two. Many folk stories revolve on a theme of twins, separated at birth to live in very different circumstances, happily reunited later in life. Other stories, such as the tale of Lucifer, the angel who falls to become the devil, speak of a rejected sibling split off and relegated into the darkness.

In your mandalas you might find the number two associated with imagery of the archetype of the shadow. However, when two identical shapes appear, they suggest something different. Jung observed that a paired motif "indicates conscious realization, since a content rising out of the unconscious splits at a certain moment into two halves, a conscious and an unconscious one" (1973b:86). For example, two identical flowers, twin human figures, or double geometric forms may symbolize contents emerging from unconsciousness. Learning what the designs mean through personal associations can help us understand the information coming to us.

The number two is built into the human body. Many of our organs and appendages are paired. We look at the world through two eyes. We grasp the world with two hands, although we sometimes find that the right hand does not know what the left hand is doing. Our bicameral nature even extends to the form and function of our brain.

The number two is built into our relationships as well. Lovers form a pair. The ritual of marriage transforms lovers into husband

and wife. With parenthood, a new being is introduced through a connection between mother and child. Twoness suggests intimacy.

In his work with the four functions, Jung noticed a particular state of mind experienced by the person who has raised two functions to consciousness while the other two remain unconscious. It is characterized by "a dualistic world- and God-image [that] gives rise to tension, doubt, and criticism of God, life, nature, and oneself" (cited in von Franz, 1986:125).

Viewed as a fall from unity, two conveys strain, separation, and conflict. Considered as the sacred marriage of opposites, two is a healing connection which announces the return of harmony. Your mandalas may suggest either message. Use your associations to help determine which reflects your experience in the present.

THREE

Three is a number suggesting vitality, energy, and motion. Von Franz comments that three is "connected with the principles of intellectual and physical movement" (1986:101). According to Chinese tradition, three and all odd numbers greater than three partake of the energetic quality of yang, the masculine principle. Fairy tales are often built upon three adventurous encounters which intensify the flow of events.

In a general sense, the number three can be said to symbolize any dynamic process. The vitality of three comes as the result of the resolution to the impasse of duality suggested by two, through the creation of something new. To Pythagorus, the number three represented completion. He took three to represent a beginning, a middle, and an end.

Three is significant as a marker of the stages of life of the family and its members. Three can symbolize the family unit created with the birth of a child. Three may also represent the individual's striving to establish his identity separate from that of his parents. We most often think of the push for independence as typical of the toddler and adolescent phases of development. However, threeness may become prominent in your mandalas whenever the energy powering independent thinking or doing is on the rise.

When three of the four functions are separated from the unconscious and available to consciousness, the individual experiences a

PLATE 1 *Sea Flower*, a mandala created by a middle-aged woman.

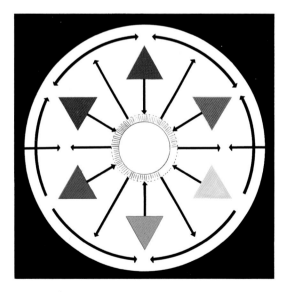

PLATE 2 The color wheel.

PLATE 3 Debbie's mandala accompanied the making of an important decision.

PLATE 4 Nita Sue's first mandala predicts an intensification of conflict.

PLATE 5 In Nita Sue's second mandala, the flower sealed inside the black box suggests a process of inner transformation.

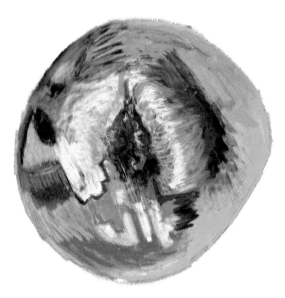

PLATE 6 Heavy pressure caused a tear in the center of this mandala by Nita Sue. This destructive act accompanied a breakthrough to new ways of being.

PLATE 7 Nita Sue's next mandala shows the re–formation of ego boundaries in a new configuration symbolized by an "eye" that stands
for "I."

PLATE 8 This drawing by Nita Sue is a rainbow mandala indicating a
profound reordering of psychic energy.

PLATE 9 Nita Sue's last mandala of the series shows the consolidation of her inner work.

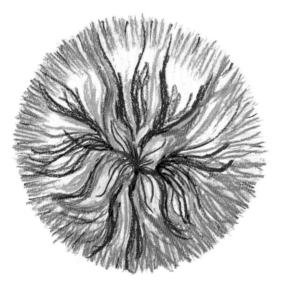

PLATE 10 Marilyn's first mandala reflects a great deal of energy.

PLATE 11 Marilyn created her second mandala to help contain her energy.

PLATE 12 Laurie's first tree mandalas were leafless figures silhouetted by
the moon.

PLATE 13 The tree in this mandala by Laurie pushes out to fill the space inside the circle.

PLATE 14 The huge wave poised to inundate the tiny boat symbolizes Laurie's encounter with death.

PLATE 15 Laurie used mandalas as positive visualizations during radiation treatments for cancer.

PLATE 16 Laurie's last tree mandala reflects her resurrection from a state of near-death.

particular mind-set. Jung writes that the state of mind characterized by three "denotes insight, the rise of consciousness, and the rediscovery of unity on a higher level" (cited in von Franz, 1986:128). Elsewhere Jung states that "three suggests the predominance of ideation and will" (Jung, 1974:267). Von Franz explains that the consciousness typified by threeness tends to be ego consciousness. That is, what can be known tends to be intellectual and based on a "purely imaginary standpoint on the world" (von Franz, 1986:128). This is determined by the fact that while three of the four functions are available to ego consciousness, the fourth remains shrouded in the mystery of the unconscious. The wisdom of a well-rounded point of view comes from contact with the unconscious through the fourth function.

The number three has been imbued with sacred meaning since the dawn of history. For example, the Christian God is a trinity of three beings in one. Other religions have incorporated trinitarian concepts of the deity as well. Pagan goddesses worshipped long before Christianity often manifested three distinct forms: the virgin, the mother, and the crone. The three-sided triangle appeared as a symbol for the goddess. Three was considered a feminine number in paganism.

The notion of three dark days, or three nights in the underworld, is a theme that appears in sacred literature, myths, and folk stories. Christ was entombed for three days. Jonah remained in the belly of the whale for a similar duration. In another version of this story theme, the moon goddess retires for three nights during the dark phase of her cycle. The legends of many cultures from the South Pacific to the British Isles contain similar story lines.

Jung described the motif of three days or nights as a stereotyped expression in hero tales for the "night sea imprisonment" (1976b:331). This is a period of incubation during which the hero is transformed. It is a metaphor for an encounter with the unconscious which is both frightening and transformative. These stories provide a framework helping the individual understand his or her experience of contacting the unconscious through the fourth, undifferentiated function which remains hidden there.

When your mandala is characterized by threeness, you may be experiencing vitality, excitement, and an urge for independence. You may be expressing some aspect of your spirituality or personal belief system. Three may announce the commencement of a heroic journey into the darkness, there to encounter teachings of wisdom through dreams, stories, or surprising discoveries about yourself.

FOUR

Four suggests balance, wholeness, and completion. Four sets boundaries, defines limits, and organizes spaces. Our year is divided into four seasons. We orient ourselves in relation to the four directions. We measure land and lay out cities with reference to the four-sided square.

Fourness occurs in nature in flowers, crystals, and four-legged creatures. The Greeks, through their study of nature, identified four elements (earth, air, fire, and water) of which they felt all things are composed. Paracelsus, a Christian alchemist, identified a fourfold quality of mind corresponding to the natural order described by earlier thinkers (Jung, 1983). Jung affirmed Paracelsus' intuitive insight with his own clinical research when Jung distinguished the four functions by which the brain processes information.

The straight-side logic of the square typifies the rationality some associate with masculinity. Nevertheless, four has traditionally represented the feminine as the matrix of all things. The Chinese associate four with yin, the dark, damp, receptive feminine. European alchemists considered four a feminine number as well. The complete alchemical process was expressed in their axiom of Maria, the mathematical statement $3 + 1$, or four (Jung, 1983:151).

The rhythms by which the universe comes into being are thought to have a fourfold quality by some cultures. The sacred syllable OM, the "mother of mantras," is considered by Indians the seed sound of all creation. It is chanted by voicing the three sounds "ah," "oh," "oo," and breathing in silently. Thus, the complete chant consists of four elements. In a similar way we can see how the qualities of time are four: past, present, and future are completed by static space, in which changes of state occur (Jung, 1979).

It seems that fourness has often been used in symbols which attempt to define a relationship with a reality which exceeds the limits of human knowing (von Franz, 1986). It is used in sacred art, architecture, and mythology to suggest the interrelated workings of the universe. Buddhist temples are enclosed by a walled square entered through four gates. This arrangement, it is thought, mirrors the divine order of the cosmos. The Native American medicine wheel, also a microcosm of the universe, is laid out in four quadrants. In Egyptian mythology the four sons of Horus stand like pillars to support the heavens. The four evangelists of Christianity echo earlier Biblical themes, such as the four cherubim in the vision of Ezekiel, who lift up a firmament of crystal.

Four is common in the symbolism of individual mandalas. If we agree with Jung that the mind has a fourfold quality, then the number four can represent activity in all four functions. The process by which this is achieved brings that which is dark and hidden in the unconscious (the least developed function) into relationship with consciousness (the three more differentiated functions). One of the functions is and always will remain in the province of the unconscious, while the other three are available to consciousness.

When the connection between conscious and unconscious is opened, a new state of mind is experienced. According to von Franz, "our mental processes no longer revolve about intellectual theorizations, but partake of the creative adventure of 'realizations in the act of becoming' " (1986:131). There is an increased depth of awareness as "the observer experiences himself as a participant on the level of a thinking and *experiencing* being" (ibid., 128).

Fourness emerges in our mandalas when our identity is closely aligned with the patterns of the archetype of the Self. This may occur when we feel strong, heroic, and bursting with energy. Oddly enough, the influence of the Self may be most apparent during times of transition when we feel deflated because our customary ego functioning is disturbed or challenged. At times like this, the fourfold patterning of the Self shines through our mandalas, revealing its function as matrix and guarantor for the ego. The Self acts as a bridge to new ways of being, sometimes rewarding us with lovely mandalas when we badly need encouragement to go on.

Beyond psychological wholeness, however, the number four can suggest an intuitive attempt to know one's place in the cosmos. Jung (1973b) viewed mandalas characterized by fourness as a natural attempt on the part of the psyche to establish a symbolic structure through which an understanding of ultimate reality could be achieved. The creation of a mandala establishes for the individual a psychic equivalent of the cosmos, of which the person is an essential element. According to von Franz (1986) the rhythmical configurations of the number four play an especially outstanding role in this process.

When you construct mandalas with a pattern of fourness, your hand is guided by the need to experience balance, harmony, and order. Through arrangements of four, diametrically opposed opposites can be brought together in a pattern of wholeness. This mirrors the inner process through which your psyche unfolds, heals, and creates itself anew striving toward the pattern of wholeness established in you by the archetype of the Self. With fourfold mandalas you are intuitively reaching for understanding of yourself, the universe, and your place within it through an ancient symbol.

In relation to the number four, you may want to also see the sections on the cross (page 120) and the square (page 134).

FIVE

Five is a number of natural wholeness. It often occurs in nature, as the number of petals in a blossom, the lobes of a star fish, or the segments of an apple core. Five refers to the physical reality of the body as well. Each of our hands has five digits, as does each foot. When we stand firmly on the ground with feet apart, and stretch out our arms, the points of our body number five: hands, feet, and head.

This firm-footed stance, grounded and reaching to maximum extension, is one of the traditional meanings associated with the number five. It suggests the person, reaching outward to engage reality. As Jung says, "Five is the number assigned to the 'natural' man, in so far as he consists of a trunk with five appendages" (1973b:89). In the context of Christianity the fiveness of natural man is transposed to the conscious vulnerability of God become man: the wounds of Christ number five.

Because it is often seen in plant forms, five also suggests the budding of spring. According to Cirlot five "signifies the organic fullness of life as opposed to the rigidity of death" (1962:225). By extension, five may also symbolize health, love, and sexuality as well.

In China the number five is a symbol of wholeness that corre-

Man, the microcosm. (After Cirlot, 1962: 188)

sponds to the European concept of the number four. As von Franz explains, five represents a "centered four ⁙ " (1986:120). To the Chinese the number five stands for the element of earth, that which carries and focuses all number of things "at the center of the foundations of existence" (ibid., 123). A similar idea regarding the number five is found in the medieval natural philosophy of the West. It is the concept of the *quinta essentia*, the purified essence, which is related to the philosopher's stone. According to von Franz, "the *quinta essentia* is additively joined onto the first four as a fifth element, but represents the most refined, spiritually imaginable unity of the four elements" (ibid., 120–121).

Mandalas characterized by five may reveal your active engagement with the real world in making your own personal vision a reality. A feeling of mission may inspire in you an active, energetic approach to your goals. Your drive will be tempered by a clear sense of your ability, what can be accomplished, and how to work within existing social structures to accomplish it. When you see five objects, or a design of fiveness in your mandalas, you might consider whether the meaning has to do with the organic fullness of your body, with your ability to take hold, or with your heartfelt desire to give the world something of yourself.

SIX

Six is the number of creativity, perfection, and equilibrium. The Biblical story of creation describes the sixth day as the one on which God made man and woman and said to them: "Be fruitful, and multiply" (Gen. 1:28). The Greeks, too, considered the number six "most fit for generation" (Jung, 1983:266). In their philosophy of numbers they considered it meaningful that six is comprised of two and three because they attributed gender to numbers. Two was feminine and three masculine, thus six represented the sexual union of masculine and feminine. As Jung explains, ". . . the number 6 means creation and evolution, since it is a *coniunctio* of 2 and 3 (even and odd = female and male)" (1973b:88).

Six, by virtue of its symbolism as the union of sexual opposites, may represent wholeness. This concept is beautifully illustrated in the Sri Yantra, a mandala which is part of the sacred art of Hinduism. It consists of interpenetrating triangles. The downward-pointing triangles represent the receptive female principle while the upward-pointing triangles stand for the active masculine principle. Six-pointed stars are created by the intersecting pairs of triangles. To the Hindu the Sri Yantra suggests the interrelatedness of all life forms.

Six also has an ancient tradition of feminine symbolism. The

The Sri Yantra mandala.

Pythagoreans referred to six as "the Mother." To the Chinese six was also a feminine number endowed with the passive receptive qualities of yin. Six was used in sacred imagery alluding to the sexuality of the goddess Aphrodite. Walker suggests that it was this connection with the sexual aspects of feminine divinity that prompted Christian authorities to call six "the number of sin" (1988:68).

Six may also represent the completion of a cycle of creativity, as did the Biblical sixth day. Like a flower that has opened as fully as it possibly can, or a fruit at the peak of its ripeness, six may connote the cessation of growth, activity, or the creative impulse. It suggests the pause that follows the completion of a creative act. This moment is rich in beauty, harmony, and fulfillment, yet it holds within it the portent of dissolution.

When six appears in your mandalas you may be completing a project that has commanded a great deal of your time and energy. Perhaps you will be experiencing a pause during which you can enjoy a feeling of satisfaction, fulfillment, even pride. Your accomplishments might be on the emotional level as well. You may sense within yourself the crystallization of many elements into a harmonious pattern such that you resonate on physical, mental, and spiritual levels. Six in your mandalas can signify the achievement of goals, a slowing of creative activity, or a deepening sense of spirituality.

SEVEN

Seven is rooted in the number mysticism of the ancients. The seven planets were revered as gods, and the number seven seen elsewhere inspired a sense of awe. Seven colors were identified in the rainbow, which was thought to be a bridge for the gods to earth. Each god was given his own day, and the seven-day week was established to mark time. Even our seven-tone musical scale derives from the celestial harmonies once thought to be produced by the seven planet-gods.

Seven is associated with methods of orientation, and the designation of sacred space. In the Native American tradition, there are seven directions. In addition to the usual four directions of north, south, east, and west, they include up, down, and the center, or oneself. Native Americans address each of the directions when establishing a place for rituals. This is the necessary beginning for any ritual observance.

In ancient literature the number seven denotes the completion of a cycle of time. The Biblical story of creation tells us that God ended his work and rested from his labors on the seventh day, and that he blessed the seventh day because it marked the conclusion of his work. In another story the friends of Job came to comfort him and they "sat down with him upon the ground for seven days and seven nights" (Job 2:13).

The number seven appears in many other contexts in Judeo-Christian tradition. Jacob bowed seven times before his brother to convey his humbleness. Elsewhere there are references to the sevenfold gifts of the Holy Spirit, the seven deadly sins, and to the seven joys and seven sorrows of the Virgin. The frequent appearance of the number seven attests to its numinosity in European cultures. This tradition continues in the conviction that seven is a lucky number.

Ancient pagans venerated the number seven because it is comprised of the integers three and four. In goddess tradition the number three is feminine because it is related to the three-sided triangle, symbol of the primordial divine mother. The number four was thought to be masculine. Hence, seven represented the union of masculine and feminine, a sacred wholeness.

Alchemical tradition also assigns the number seven an important place. The work of transforming base matter into something of timeless value took place in seven phases. (Jung, 1983) The arcane chemical procedures described by the alchemists paralleled their own inner work, through which the alchemists aspired to pass from ignorance to enlightenment. Seven, then, could represent the last stage of this difficult transformation process. According to Jung, " 'seven' stands for the highest stage of illumination and would therefore be the coveted goal of all desire" (1974:137).

When seven appears in our mandalas, we may be resonating with ancient sacred traditions that make the number seven special. Perhaps we will want to give attention to the natural rhythms of time, and honor them with the reverent consideration of our ancestors for whom each day of the week was holy. Seven may also suggest the completion of a phase in our lives, a project brought to resolution, or an ambition fulfilled. The balancing of masculine and feminine aspects of ourselves may be highlighted by the number seven as well. The number seven trails its numinous past into our mandalas where it brings us the good fortune to find ourselves.

EIGHT

Eight is a number of stability, harmony, and rebirth. In Christian tradition, eight is associated with the resurrection, because Christ rose from the grave eight days after his entry into Jerusalem. Baptism is thought of as a rebirth that commemorates Christ's resurrection. In the Middle Ages, eight was a symbol of the waters of baptism. Ferguson (1961) notes that many baptismal fonts incorporate the symbolism of resurrection with their octagonal shape.

The graphic form of the number eight suggests meanings that have little to do with enumeration. For example, the number eight resembles the sign for infinity, and can indicate the limitless spiraling movement of the cosmos. By virtue of its shape, eight resembles the interlacing serpents of the caduceus, or physician's symbol (Cirlot, 1962). It can, like the caduceus, signify the balancing out of opposing forces. Because of its double-looped shape, eight also suggests a closely connected pair, such as lovers, mother and child, or husband and wife.

Eight also appears in the eight-spoked wheel, a venerable symbol of the sun as the divine instigator of endless change (Cirlot, 1962). As the wheel turns, half of it goes up and half of it goes down. A point on the edge of the wheel is sometimes up, sometimes down, and always moving from one transitory state to the next. The wheel, then, aptly symbolizes the opposites dancing together to create transformation in the lives of individuals. The number eight can signify the inexorable turning of the wheel of life.

Jung considered eight a symbol of wholeness because it is a multiple of the number four, a preeminent symbol of the Self. In the mandalas of his analysands Jung observed that a pattern of fourness often expanded into a pattern of eight or more design elements: "the quaternity found at the centre of a mandala often becomes 8, 16, 32, or more when extended to the periphery" (1974:279).

Eight in your mandalas reveals the strong influence of the

archetype of the Self. The Self provides a central point of focus for your inner life, but its patterns lie beyond your abilities to understand. The surprise of sudden change is as much the gift of the Self as is transcendent harmony. You may find that eight in your mandalas represents an exquisitely balanced organization of paired opposites, ideas, or persons, that presages significant changes in your life.

NINE

Nine represents a band of angels, careful synthesis, and the enigma of human existence. Jung writes that by ancient tradition nine represents "a company of gods" (1974:139). The Bible mentions that there are nine choirs of angels. The most mysterious element of the Trinity, the Holy Ghost, was symbolized by the number nine in medieval Christianity. Nine has been a traditional symbol for benevolent spiritual beings.

In European esoteric philosophy nine symbolized a cosmology based on three planes of existence. Believers of these obscure mystical ideas accepted that the universe and all its creatures exist in a physical, intellectual, or spiritual reality. Nine was considered a complete image of these three worlds. While each plane was unique and separate, under certain conditions elements could be mixed from different levels with efficacious results. This was especially true in the preparation of healing potions. Repeated distillations and mixtures potentized the medicine even more. Mixing the elements of three levels together three times was the best possible procedure. According to Cirlot, "in medicinal rites, [nine] is the symbolic number *par excellence,* for it represents triple synthesis, that is, the disposition on each plane of the corporal, the intellectual and the spiritual" (1962:223).

In our numbering system nine is the last number in the numerical series before its return to the unitive number one in the number ten. It suggests the differentiation that seems to precede a new and simpler unity. The progressive cycle of differentiation and simplification associated with nine is captured in an old folk tale mentioned by Jung. It is a story of hidden treasure. According to Jung, "the treasure . . . is said to take nine years, nine months, and nine nights to come to the surface and, if not found on the last night, sinks back to start all over again from the beginning" (1974:158).

Symbolism associated with the number nine expresses mysterious realities of human existence. We are creatures of different levels. We are physical beings who think and have souls. Nine in our mandalas may suggest the fact that we live a more complete existence when we integrate all three: the physical, the mental, and the spiritual. The number nine symbolized truth in mystic Hebrew tradition. Perhaps it appears in our mandalas to remind us of our own true nature.

Nine in your mandalas may signal an opportunity for synthesis in your life. It may announce the presence of benevolent spiritual energies which can enhance your efforts toward personal growth. Nine may be a reminder of your need to balance physical, mental, and spiritual aspects of your being. Nine is a trinity times three, and you might also consider it a powerful reiteration of the message contained in threeness. While nine can be an awkward design in mandalas, it appears to reflect a state of energy, arousal, and potency generated by spirituality.

TEN

Ten is the traditional number of perfection, morality, and realism. In European mysticism ten is symbolic of the return to unity. Judaism uses the number ten to symbolize God, who is thought to incorporate ten intertwining divine attributes. It is customary that ten elders be present in order for Jewish religious services to be convened.

Judeo-Christian tradition contains the well-known moral code called the Ten Commandments. These statements continue to serve many people as an ideal by which to guide one's conduct. They are so familiar that the number ten itself may symbolize a moral code. This is even more so given the tradition that ten represents perfection.

The number ten is rooted in nonspiritual traditions as well. It is the number of our fingers with which we touch, hold, and caress. Ten is the basis of a numbering system that allows us to count and calculate. Mathematics is very abstract, and yet it seems reasonable to suppose that it all began long ago with the counting of fingers.

Ten may symbolize our remarkable fingers and the robust, two-handed grasp of reality they can give us.

In its graphic form ten sometimes symbolizes marriage (Cirlot, 1962). The zero suggests feminine sexuality while the one resembles maleness. The pairing of these two forms in the number ten is a visual representation of male and female intimately related. The number ten can show a balance between the sexual opposites.

Ten in your mandalas may suggest your adherence to, or rebellion against, a traditional moral code. It may reflect an active approach to the realities of life or suggest to you a group of elders who stand in support of what you do. Ten might highlight your relationship with the opposite sex. The number ten in your mandalas may reveal spiritual inspiration, a sense of balance, or a hands-on approach to life.

ELEVEN

Eleven is a symbol of transition, conflict, and the challenge to find balance. Since eleven is more than ten, and ten has traditionally stood for perfection, eleven is thought by some to represent excess (Cirlot, 1962). Its departure from the perfect ten has also caused eleven to be associated with change, peril, and even martyrdom. It might be thought of as a symbol for the breakdown of static perfection.

In the Jewish mystical tradition of the Kabbalah, existence is thought to come into being through ten emanations from the One, or God. The ten emanations constitute a world, and four progressively denser worlds evolve from each other to finally manifest the world we know. At the point of transition from one world to the next is an eleventh invisible emanation called Daat, or Knowledge. The spirit of God passes through Daat as it leaves the old world and begins to generate a new one. So it is that the eleventh governs death and rebirth.

The Chinese have a different way of looking at eleven. According to von Franz, among the Chinese, eleven "is not taken in the quantitative sense of ten plus one. Rather it signifies the unity of the decade in its wholeness" (1986:65). As a symbol of wholeness, the Chinese use the number eleven to represent the Tao, a sacred way of life. The Chinese concept of Tao is difficult to put into

English. Jung suggests that a suitable translation may be "to go consciously, or the conscious way" (1983:20). He further explains:

> If we take the Tao to be the method or conscious way by which to unite what is separated, we have probably come close to the psychological meaning of the concept. . . . There can be no doubt, either, that the realization of the opposite hidden in the unconscious . . . signifies reunion with the unconscious laws of our being, and the purpose of this reunion is the attainment of conscious life or, expressed in Chinese terms, the realization of the Tao. (Ibid., 21)

European tradition sees eleven as the mark of discord, death, and rebirth. The Chinese view it as symbolic of a model way of life. These points of view regarding eleven seem mutually exclusive, yet they may not be. Bringing the opposing aspects of ourself into consciousness creates disruption. Jung described it as a "violent and agonizing process of transformation" (ibid., 107). Perhaps the number eleven in your mandalas reflects conflict which is an important transition in the process which moves you toward a more complete realization of who you really are.

TWELVE

Twelve is symbolic of cosmic order, Herculean tasks, and salvation. It corresponds to the signs in the zodiac, and the number of months in a year. Twelve sometimes represents the completion of a cycle of time. It appears in myths, dreams, and fairy tales. Twelve is also part of the symbolism of diverse religious groups. Jung identifies twelve with the growth process he calls individuation.

Twelve is prominent in Greek mythology. The gods and goddesses of Mount Olympus number twelve, not including their leader, Zeus. The story of the Greek hero Heracles is notable for the occurrence of twelve. As atonement for the murder of his loved ones while temporarily insane, Heracles is directed to spend twelve years serving the despised king Eurystheus. Eurystheus demands that Heracles perform twelve impossibly difficult labors to earn his freedom. Heracles at last succeeds, with the timely aid of divine intervention.

The twelve tasks of Heracles were eventually equated with the twelve signs of the zodiac (Graves, 1981). The completion of the twelfth labor released Heracles from bondage and closed a chapter in his life. In the same way, the twelve-month year marks a phase in our lives. The close of the year provides an occasion to look back, review, and assess our experiences.

Twelve is an integral part of the religious traditions of Judaism, Christianity, and Buddhism. The Jews trace their ancestry to the twelve sons of the patriarch Jacob. The descendents of Jacob's sons formed the twelve tribes of Israel. Twelve gems adorned the ceremonial breastplate of the high priest, and within the life of Moses twelve celebrated episodes occurred.

Christians use twelve as a symbol for those who have accepted the faith. It represents the apostles, those persons chosen by Jesus to be the first Christians. Sometimes the meaning of twelve is expanded to symbolize all those baptized, the entire Christian church (Ferguson, 1961). Twelve recalls the season of Christmas which is traditionally celebrated during the twelve days from December 25 through January 6, the Feast of the Epiphany.

Buddhism incorporates the concept of the horoscope of twelve months into its belief symbol. The horoscopic circle is conceived of as a lotus with twelve petals. Each petal, representing a month, is named after an animal. The attributes of the animal correspond to the qualities of the season in which that month occurs. Buddhists also believe that years are grouped in cycles of twelve according to the order of the zodiac. Each year has the traits associated with the symbolic animal with which it coincides.

Twelve appears in many fairy tales, often as the number of individuals in a significant group. For example, twelve good fairies come to offer their blessings in the tale of Sleeping Beauty. Other stories include "The Twelve Brothers" (Grimm, 1944), in which a family of princes is released from bondage as crows by the steadfast faithfulness of their sister. In "The Twelve Huntsmen" (Grimm, 1944), a princess and her servants disguise themselves to be near the princess's beloved who is betrothed to another. Eventually the lovers are united. In each of these tales the group of twelve seems to be a metaphor for the passage of time which must be endured while something new comes into being.

Jung encountered the number twelve in the dreams and drawings of the people with whom he worked. In the analysis of "Miss X," the number twelve appeared as radiating bands encircling a globe early on in a series of mandalas. In her words it denoted a "climax or turning point of the process of development" (cited in Jung, 1973b:22). For her, twelve seemed to introduce an intensification of the individuation process. Elsewhere Jung has written that "the number twelve is a time symbol, with the subsidiary meaning of the twelve labors, that have to be performed for the unconscious before one can get free" (1973a:119).

The "twelve labors" suggest the hard work of individuation. In another source Jung (1979) equated the number twelve with wholeness, the goal toward which individuation moves us.

Twelve in your mandalas is related to the turning wheel of the zodiac, and calls attention to the passing of time and the completion of a cycle. For example, you may see patterns of twelve in your mandalas when you finish a project, end a relationship, or bring closure to unfinished business from the past. Twelve might also represent the challenges ahead of you dictated by the mysterious pattern of the Self. Twelve in your mandalas suggests completion, wholeness, and the never-ending movement of the spiral of growth.

THIRTEEN

Thirteen is associated with faithlessness, betrayal, and unfortunate endings because it was the number of people seated at the Last Supper. The thirteenth fairy in the tale of Sleeping Beauty is the one who casts a spiteful curse on the young princess. A witches' coven is traditionally comprised of thirteen.

The number thirteen may also have a positive value. In fact, some suggest that its connotation as unlucky comes from the distortion of its numinous qualities. For example, the powerful Olympian gods and goddesses of Greek mythology number thirteen. The first group of Christians numbered thirteen: Jesus and the twelve apostles. The lives of the twelve were transformed by Jesus, the thirteenth member of the group.

Thirteen can mark a new beginning as well as an ending. Since twelve connotes the completion of a cycle, thirteen, being one more than twelve, points to the beginning of another one. At times it is difficult to distinguish a beginning from an ending. Sometimes we experience an ending and a beginning at the same time. Our feelings are bound to become confused. The ambivalence surrounding endings and beginnings may be the source of the traditional idea that thirteen is unlucky (Cirlot, 1962).

When you see thirteen in your mandalas, perhaps the message conveyed is that you have moved into a new phase in your life. Thirteen might also be telling you that the weight of the past may hamper the new direction in your life, especially when you do not bring closure to what has gone before. Thirteen in your mandalas may be a clue that a powerful process is in force within you, and that you might do well to prepare for a freeing of your energy after what seems like a time of tribulation, hard work, and confusion.

ANIMALS

Animals often symbolize instinctive, nonrational, or unconscious aspects of being. According to Cirlot, the appearance of animals in dreams "expresses an energy still undifferentiated and not yet rationalized, nor yet mastered by the will (in the sense of that which controls the instincts)" (1962:13).

Jung considered animal symbolism "a visualization of the unconscious self" (1979:145). The more primitive the animal, the deeper the stratum of the unconscious it represents. Contents from deeper layers of the psyche are more difficult to assimilate because they are further removed from ordinary consciousness. In other words, a dog could symbolize unconscious energies easier to integrate into consciousness than would a snake which represents " 'cold blooded,' inhuman contents and tendencies of an abstractly intellectual as well as a concretely animal nature: in a word, the extrahuman quality of man." (Jung, 1979:187).

Developing the proper attitude toward the unconscious is crucial in the fostering of consciousness. A separation must be made so that the ego is no longer simply controlled by instinct. As Jung writes, "Man becomes human through conquering his animal instinctuality" (1976b:262). Ideally a respectful attitude toward the unconscious can be cultivated so that creativity, meaning, and collective wisdom are available to the ego. According to Jung, the way in which animals appear to us in dreams and drawings is an indicator of our attitude toward the unconscious:

> If [our attitude] is negative towards the unconscious, the animals will be frightening; if positive, they appear as "helpful animals" of fairy-tale and legend. (1976b:181)

Some cultures use identification with an animal as a way to integrate the unconscious. Native American traditions encourage young persons to discover through dreams the animal that will be a spirit guide and companion in their contacts with the spirit world, which we would call the unconscious. Young persons receive a name that honors their special connection with the animal. This also helps them integrate the qualities of the animal into their identity.

Symbolism associated with an animal is traditionally based on its natural attributes. Lions are known for their beauty and fighting spirit. The king of beasts is the "possessor of strength and the masculine principle" (Cirlot, 1962:181). The wolf, a fierce defender of its kin, symbolizes valor and loyalty. In Native American traditions, the wolf is considered a pathfinder, for other animals follow its trails.

The bull is a symbol of the feminine because its horns resemble the crescent moon. It was associated with the lunar goddess worship of Crete. Paradoxically, the bull has also been a symbol of masculine sky deities such as Thor: its bellow is associated with thunder. The bear is considered a lunar animal because its periodic withdrawal for hibernation is reminiscent of the disappearance of the moon during its dark phase. The bear also symbolizes the alchemical phase of *nigredo,* the point of beginning in a process. The bear stands for instinct and for dangerous aspects of the unconscious.

Elephants are long-lived, intelligent beasts, and this probably explains their use as symbols of moderation, wisdom, and eternity. Cirlot states that elephants also stand for strength and the power of the libido (1962:92).

In contrast to the elephant's laudable qualities, the ass is found to be a symbol of wrongful behavior in Egyptian mythology. In the *Golden Ass* of Apuleius (cited in Jung, 1983:183) the hero is punished for his dissolute life by being given the form of an ass. He is eventually saved from his unfortunate state when he seizes an opportunity for redemption by the goddess Isis.

The lamb is significant in Christianity as a symbol for Christ. Its attributes are meekness, purity, and innocence. Another level of meaning is that of an unjustified sacrifice. Cirlot has found an interesting juxtaposition of meaning between the lamb and the lion in medieval symbolism for Christ. Over the entrance to a Romanesque church he found the epigraph, "I am the death of death. I am called a lamb, and I am a strong lion" (1962:168).

The fish is also a symbol for Christ, but not due to its qualities. The connection comes by virtue of the fact that the five Greek letters spelling the Greek word for "fish" *(ichthys)* are the first letters of the words "Jesus Christ God's Son Savior." The fish, the duck, and the frog, though quite different from each other, are all water animals. Their affinity for water connects them with the idea of "primal water." Because of this, all three animals can symbolize "the origin of things and the powers of rebirth" (p. 10).

The horse works in concert with its human rider and is a symbol of the instincts properly channeled. A wild, untamed horse has the opposite meaning of unbridled instinct. Horses in legends are often clairvoyant and give their masters timely warnings (Cirlot, 1962:145). Of all animals, the dog is most closely associated with human beings. Its intimate involvement in our lives determines its symbolism as a faithful helpmate and companion. However, a dog can occasionally carry the contrary meaning of bestiality: for example, Mephistopheles first appeared to Faust as a dog.

Imaginary animals combine parts of several different animals or extraordinary additions to familiar animals. The sphinx, unicorn, phoenix, dragon, and winged horse are examples. In legends these creatures are supernatural consorts of divinities. According to Cirlot, such animals "stand for flux and transformation, and also for purposeful evolution towards new forms" (p. 10).

Gods are often shown as part animal. Three of the four sons of Horus are seen with human bodies and animal heads: an ape, a jackal, and a hawk. The Hindu god Ganesha has an elephant's head and a man's body. Fauns, half man and half goat, are woodland spirits allied with the goddess Diana. These entities personify the challenge of human beings to integrate within themselves animal instincts and godlike consciousness.

Animal symbolism in your mandalas can be a way for you, too, to come into contact with that part of your psyche that recalls a deeper than human reality. Through honoring and acknowledging the animal aspects of your own nature, you may develop a relationship with the deeply etched patterns of instinct that guide the behavior of animals and reside in human beings as an ageless source of wisdom.

BIRDS

Birds are ancient symbols of the human soul, of the element of air, and of the process of transformation. In Egyptian hieroglyphics, a bird with a human head stands for the soul or the idea that the soul departs from the body after death (Cirlot, 1962). In early Christian art, the bird was used as a symbol of the "winged soul" (Ferguson, 1961:12). In contrast to these meanings, birds have also been known as bringers of lightning, war, and death.

Birds have come to stand for the spiritual, as opposed to the material. Jung (1976b) said that birds could represent spirits, angels, or supernatural aid. Birds were sometimes viewed as messengers in the ancient world. The Romans regarded birds as the givers of omens and enlightenment. In a secular sense, birds might represent thoughts or the flight of thoughts, especially fantasies and intuitive ideas (Jung, 1974).

Certain kinds of birds carry special meanings. The eagle shares with the lion qualities of courage, strength, and nobility. It is honored by Native Americans as the source of wisdom through the gift of clear-sightedness. The eagle is believed to fly higher than any other bird, and its closeness to the sun imbues it with the essence of light. Since light is a metaphor for spirit, the eagle has become a symbol of spirituality.

Cirlot points out that the eagle is not a symbol of peace. "From the Far East to Northern Europe, the eagle is the bird associated with the gods of power and war" (1962: 87). It is also thought to express the masculine principle because it is identified with the sun. The "male" activity of the sun, which fertilizes "feminine" nature, makes the eagle a symbol of the father as well.

The owl is the opposite of the eagle. It is a night bird that has come to symbolize darkness, death, and knowledge. It is associated with goddesses of wisdom such as Athena, Minerva, and Lilith. This connection with goddesses survives in the place owls have with witches at Halloween. According to Barbara Walker, witches are a vestige of the tradition of the wise Crone Goddess. She points out that the Latin and Italian names for wise woman or witch also mean owl (1988:404).

The dove is significant in Judeo-Christian tradition. It is a symbol of purity and peace. A dove sent out by Noah returned with an olive branch. This was a sign that flood waters had receded and that God had made peace with humankind. During the time of Jesus, doves were used as offerings in Jewish Temple rites of purification following the birth of a baby.

In Christian art the dove is often seen as a symbol for the Holy Spirit, one aspect of the trinitarian Christian God. This symbolic meaning of the dove can be traced to a passage in the Bible describing the baptism of Christ: "And John bare record, saying, I saw the Spirit descending from heaven like a dove, and it abode upon him" (John 1:32). As suggested by this passage, the dove descending can symbolize a spiritual initiation.

Birds are sacred in the beliefs of some peoples. The Hindus of Vedic times depicted the sun in the form of a huge bird: an eagle or a swan. Native Americans personify lightning and thunder as the great Thunderbird, source of creation and healing. The peacock was the sacred attribute of Juno, queen of heaven, and symbolized the deification of Roman princesses.

The mythologies and folkways of Europe are filled with birdlike creatures. Among the Celts women are thought to have once been winged creatures. Norse Valkyries dressed themselves in feather garments belonging to the goddess Freya. The feathered clothing and ritual objects used by Siberian shamans recall birdlike flight as a symbol of spirituality. The expression "to learn the language of the birds" was a common metaphor for mystic enlightenment (Walker, 1988:396).

While single birds might be divine messengers or even deities, a flock of birds can take on negative implications. This is according to the esoteric law that multiplicity is a step away from unity, which is considered divine. Greek mythology gives us the example of the flock of birds in the Stymphalian Marsh. These pesky birds harassed their victims, poisoned crops, and then retreated to a swamp too wet for walking, and too dry for boating. The sixth labor of Heracles was to rid the swamp of these birds.

A flock of birds can suggest negativity, wicked desires, or even danger. One might remember the menacing presence of birds in the Alfred Hitchcock movie thriller *The Birds*. On the other hand, numerous birds can also represent a positive force. Pioneers in Salt Lake City, Utah, erected a statue to honor the memory of a flock of birds which saved their crops from a plague of locusts. They believed the birds were heaven sent.

Birds are important alchemical symbols for "forces in process of activation" (Cirlot, 1962:26–27). Their precise location gives more specific information. In the imagery of alchemy the bird

> soaring skyward expresses volatilization or sublimation, and swooping earthwards it expresses precipitation and condensation; these two symbolic movements joined to form a single figure are expressive of distillation. (Ibid., 26)

Birds in your mandalas suggest the activation of your intellectual capacities. They also reflect volatile spiritual processes. Birds flying upwards may connote ideas being released or brought to light. Birds gliding downwards could suggest something about yourself becoming more solid or acceptable. Birds moving up and down or around may suggest the refinement of insights, knowledge, or bringing self-awareness to a higher level.

BUTTERFLY

 The butterfly is a symbol of transformation because of its dramatic life cycle. It begins as a homely caterpillar, then enters the dormant phase of the chrysalis, and finally emerges as one of nature's most beautiful creatures. In Christian tradition the three stages of its life are equated with life, death, and resurrection. The butterfly stands for the risen Christ and, in a more general sense, the resurrection of all people (Ferguson, 1961).

Spiritual associations for the butterfly are not limited to Christianity, however. The Greeks used the word "psyche" to connote both "soul" and "butterfly." They believed that human souls became butterflies while searching for a new reincarnation. European poets have used the butterfly's plain cousin the moth as a metaphor for the soul. In the way that the moth is attracted to the light, they see the image of the soul's longing for God.

When you see a butterfly in your mandala, you might find that it is an affirmation of the power of the psyche to continually create itself anew (Jung, 1976b). It may also reveal your departure from a dark night of the soul. A butterfly could be the announcement of a dramatic shift to a new way of being. Butterflies in your mandalas reflect your beauty, spirituality, and self-renewal.

CIRCLE

The circle encloses a space. That which is inside the circle is protected, strengthened, and delimited. The circle recalls the form of a matrifocal village, of ancient sacred spaces, and of countless forms in nature. The circle suggests movement: the spinning of the planets, the stirring of the waters, and the spiraling steps of ceremony, worship, and play.

The sun is often represented by a circle. The full moon also is suggested by a circular form. Time itself may be symbolized by a circle, especially a circle that conveys movement, such as the Gnostic uroboros, a snake circling to bite its own tail. The circle is a widely accepted symbol of eternity: a line with no beginning and no end represents time with no beginning and no end. This makes the circle an appropriate symbol for God. According to Ferguson, "[The circle] represents not only the perfection of God but the everlasting God, 'Who was in the beginning, is now, and ever shall be, world without end' " (1961:153).

The Chinese symbol for heaven is a disk with an empty circle in

The uroboros, the snake biting its own tail.

the center. The hole signifies the path of transcendence. An empty circle in the center of a mandala is like the motionless center point at the hub of a wheel. This motif suggests the idea known in Western alchemy as the "window of eternity" (von Franz, 1986:260). According to von Franz this symbol represents an experience of the Self. It frees the individual from a point of view limited by time and space. She writes that "through this 'window' man touches the eternal in himself, and at the same time the eternal can reach into his timebound world in the form of synchronistic events" (ibid., 261).

The mandalas we draw are circles. Jung relates the mandala circle to the "protective circle" or "charmed circle" of countless folk customs. "It has the obvious purpose of drawing a magical furrow around the centre, the temple or *temenos* (sacred precinct), of the innermost personality, in order to prevent an 'outflowing' or to guard by apotropaic means against distracting influences from outside" (1983:24). Because the circular form contains and organizes whatever is placed within it, mandalas lead us to understand and experience unity in our inner diversity.

> Through the ritual action [of drawing the circle], attention and interest are led back to the inner, sacred precinct, which is the source and goal of the psyche and contains the unity of life and consciousness. (Ibid., 25)

The Chinese symbol of heaven. (After Cirlot, 1962: plate XVI)

Smaller circles within your mandalas may protect, enshrine, or liberate some aspect of yourself. Circles sometimes overlap, creating an almond shape called a mandorla. In religious art this form surrounds Christ and the Virgin Mary when they stand at the juncture between earth and the heavenly realm. You may draw a mandorla when experiencing a state of grace. A mandala with an empty center suggests that you are open to change, receptive to the transpersonal, or apt to have experiences that defy the rules of logic. Circles in your mandalas can remind you of the flow of life whose currents spiral in and out of things bound solid in time and space.

CROSS

The cross is the conjunction of a vertical line with a horizontal one. It is reminiscent of the form of the human body, standing in perfect balance, with feet together and arms outstretched. The cross is used to mark a special place. It also symbolizes a state of mind.

The upright position of the cross connects it with other symbols of the vertical, such as the tree, mountain, and ladder. These symbols suggest a connection between the earth and the sky, which is traditionally associated with the gods. The vertical connection is thought of as a pathway linking the spiritual world with the ordinary reality of earth. It is also a focal point, marking the place on earth where the superordinary exists side by side with the mundane. This vertical/horizontal connection is sometimes called a "world axis." Cirlot writes that ". . . the cross stands for the 'world axis.' Placed at the mystic Centre of the Cosmos, it becomes the bridge or ladder by means of which the soul may reach God" (1962:65).

The cross is closely related to the symbol of the tree. Medieval Christian art depicts the cross as a living tree, sometimes with flowers, fruit, or thorns. Legend has it that the cross on which Jesus died was hewn from the Tree of Paradise grown in the Garden of Eden. The Christian cross takes on the meaning of the Tree of Life because it is through the sacrifice symbolized by the cross that one is granted eternal life.

The cross is found in other religious traditions as well. The Druids tied large tree branches high up on a sacred tree, giving it the appearance of a living cross. The crossing of roads were considered sacred sites by adherents to goddess-centered religions in Europe. They were places for ritual sacrifices to Hecate, goddess of the underworld. While condemned by Christian authorities as the Queen of Witches, she was honored as the deity of safe passage, and remained important as a link to the earlier earth religion. In fact Hecate was so important to common folk that in the tenth century A.D. legal measures were taken in order to eliminate her rituals. A woman was threatened with a legally imposed three-year fast if found guilty of dedicating her child at the crossroads to the Earth Mother (Walker, 1988).

Perhaps the most important meaning of the cross is that of the conjunction of opposites. The precise joining of vertical and horizontal in the cross makes it an apt symbol for the wedding of the spiritual (vertical) with the material world of phenomena (horizontal). The cross may symbolize many other pairs of opposites as well: dark/light, conscious/unconscious, life/death. Jung saw in the cross a symbol for the balance of the opposites within the whole person.

> The cross, or whatever other heavy burden the hero carries, is *himself,* or rather *the* self, his wholeness, which is both God and animal— not merely the empirical man, but the totality of his being, which is rooted in his animal nature and reaches out beyond the merely human towards the divine. His wholeness implies tremendous tension of opposites paradoxically at one with themselves, as in the cross, their most perfect symbol. (1976b:303)

The cross expresses life's difficulties, with its "cross-roads of possibilities and impossibilities, of construction and destruction" (Cirlot, 1962:68). The cross is associated with the human challenge to attain consciousness through the attempt to know one's dark, hidden side. The task of separating oneself from the world of unquestioning instinct is symbolized by the heroic act of slaying the dragon. It should not surprise us that the hero's sword is another version of the cross.

A shift of the cross a few degrees off the vertical and horizontal produces the X. As suggested by the phrase "X marks the spot," this figure also designates a point in space, a singular position or point of view. Supplicants visiting the New Orleans tomb of voodoo priestess Marie Laveau inscribe an X where they are standing when they make their petition. The ancient custom of indicating poison with a skull and crossbones gives to this form of cross the meaning of entropy, decay, or loss. St. Andrew was crucified upon such a cross. One may, however, take another view of the X. Cirlot indicates that in esoteric tradition, the X may also represent the "union of the Upper and Lower worlds" (1962:66).

If you imagine a cross fixed and allowed to whirl about its center, you will understand the derivation of the swastika. This ancient symbol was widely known centuries before it was adopted by Nazi Germany. The swastika is a symbol of the sun and its movement across the sky (Cirlot, 1962). Its four equal legs created a balanced pattern that Jung (1973b) has identified as a symbol of wholeness. The swastika is a dynamic symbol related to bringing the ideal into manifestation through increased consciousness.

In your mandalas crosses with something attached to them, or objects resting near the base, may indicate a time of sacrifice. Crosses rotated to form an X may also suggest the ending of a cycle. These figures carry the message that you may be called upon to surrender familiar ways of being. They herald a time when the ego may be called upon to endure a period of testing, the dark night of the soul.

When you see a cross in your mandala it can be a clue that you are waging a hero's battle and carving chunks of consciousness out of that which has hitherto been dark and unknown. You may find yourself struggling to make a decision or embarking on some new venture. Perhaps a cross is telling you that you are integrating a new ego center (Kellogg, 1977). When a cross appears in your mandala you might want to consider the possibility that you are balancing, more or less successfully, the contradictions that are part of human nature.

In relation to the cross, you may also want to see the sections on the number four (page 98), the square (page 134), and the tree (page 138).

DROPS

Raindrops bring moisture to the earth nourishing vegetation, filling lakes and streams, and helping crops to grow. It is not surprising that rain is associated with fertility in mythology (Jung, 1976b). The Chinese used rain as a symbol for maleness in their art. In Greek mythology, the maiden Danaë became pregnant when the god Zeus showered her with his golden droplets.

Rain falls from the heavens. Its celestial source and its lack of minerals give it a purity ordinary water does not have. Therefore, in some traditions, rainwater is used for cleansing rituals. Raindrops may symbolize the act of purification. The daunting realities of the twenteith century have given rain new meanings. The deadly rain that falls following a nuclear explosion, and the acid rain that results from pollution, are both examples of rain that is antithetical to growth and life.

Raindrops are related to human tears, which are said to "fall like rain." Tears may come from sadness, disappointment, anger, joy, or relief. Tears may be a release from emotion too intense to contain. Like the rain of purification, tears can wash away grief or anger, and make a place for forgiveness.

Blood may also fall in drops. Serious injury creates a bleeding wound. The notion of a blood sacrifice for the purpose of atonement is very ancient. Rituals of sacrifice, such as the Eucharist, incorporate the symbolism of blood. Sometimes we ignore the fact that the bodies of ordinary women are created to sacrifice blood each month. In Native American tradition, the woman's "moon time" is honored and acknowledged as a worthy spiritual gift which benefits the whole community.

When you see drops in your mandalas you might want to ask yourself, "What do I need to cry about?" You may also consider the possibility that you are being fertilized and that new seeds are being planted which, now unknown to you, will materialize in the future as an inspiration, a new project, or perhaps even a child. Black drops might suggest there is something in your environment that you find detrimental to the full use of your potential. When the drops are red, purple, or brown, you may find that you are making some sort of sacrifice. When your mandala contains forms like drops of rain or blood, perhaps you are witnessing the signs of a natural, inner process of purification.

EYE

 The eye is the organ of sight, and so it is associated with the ability to see both literally and metaphorically, in the sense of "understanding." The eye may also symbolize the superordinary ability to see, as in clairvoyance. It is used to represent the omnipotent, all-seeing, ever-present sight of God. The Bible contains many scriptural references to the eye of God, such as this one: "The eyes of the Lord are over the righteous, and his ears are open to their prayers" (1 Peter 3:12).

In Egyptian tradition the eye is a sacred attribute of the gods Horus, Thoth, and Ra. The goddess Maat, however, was the original All-Seeing Eye and Mother of Truth. Her name is based on the verb "to see." According to Walker, "The universal mother-word Maa was both the name of the goddess and a hieroglyphic eye" (1988:308).

The association of the eye with the feminine is found in Indian culture also. Here the eye stands for the female genitals. This connection is pointed out by Jung in reference to the myth of Indra: "Indra, who, as punishment for his wantoness, was smitten with yonis [vulva] all over his body, but was so far pardoned by the gods that the shameful yonis were changed into eyes" (1976b:268).

The presence of eyes in unusual places on the body is also a traditional way of showing clairvoyance. The "third eye" positioned above and between the ordinary two, is symbolic of "the super human or the divine" (Cirlot, 1962:95). One sees fantastic beings, such as the Greek demigod Argus, depicted with eyes on hands, wings, torso, or elsewhere. Cirlot maintains that the eye takes on meaning in association with the part of the body where it is placed. For example, an eye located in the hand would denote "clairvoyant action" (ibid.).

Jung writes that the eye "is the prototype of the mandala."

> Our mandala is indeed an "eye," the structure of which symbolizes the centre of order in the unconscious. The eye is a hollow sphere, black inside, and filled with a semi-liquid substance, the vitreous humour. Looking at it from outside, one sees a round, colored surface, the iris, with a dark centre, from which a golden light shines. (1973b:52–53)

Thus, the eye, like a mandala, contains these elements: a circular form with a central focus which suggests the light hidden in the darkness within.

The presence of many eyes in your mandala has both positive and negative connotations. Numerous eyes may be a symbol for the unconscious, with its uncanny way of picking up information from everywhere. The eyes might be a message to pay attention to what it is that your unconscious "sees." On the other hand, eyes in your mandala may express feelings of being watched by others. You might want to reflect upon what it is these eyes see in you, and test this information against reality.

A single eye in your mandala may serve as a symbol for "I," or the ego. Looking at the design of the eye can reveal information about your ego in relationship to the archetype of the self. An eye may signal a heightened ability to receive information by extraordinary means or suggest you are concerned with issues related to women or your own feminine identity. It may even be a symbol for the Self, the archetypal basis of the mandala itself.

FLOWERS

 The blooming of flowers announces the return of spring. So it is that the flower has become a symbol of spring itself, of the transitory nature of life and beauty, and of the eternal renewal of life. From ancient times flowers have been given as tributes of love, awarded in ceremonies to honor achievement, and carried in nuptial celebrations. Flowers have been a final parting gift in rituals for the dead.

Flowers are circular with petals emanating from a center marked by contrasting color. Because of their shape and focus at the center, flowers are natural mandalas. They are used by some mystics as an object of contemplation. This is most appropriate because, according to Cirlot, the flower is "an image of the 'Centre,' and hence an archetypal image of the soul" (1962:104).

Alchemists considered flowers symbolic of the work of the sun whose activating force produced their much sought after gold. According to the alchemists flowers take on different meanings depending on their colors. For example, red flowers bespeak the vitality of animal life, with its blood and passion. Orange and yellow flowers reiterate the sun symbolism of the flower itself. The blue flower is a symbol of the impossible, and alludes to the soul's connection to God or the "mystic Centre" (ibid., 105). Alchemical symbolism apparently helped Jung interpret the meaning of the blue "soul-flower" in the mandalas of "Miss X" (1973b:54).

Flowers symbolize the womb that nurtures divine infants in the religious traditions of India, China, and Europe. Jung (1973b) points out that Buddha and other Indian deities are frequently pictured in lotus-flowers. The golden flower of Chinese mysticism is described as the "altar upon which consciousness and life are made" (Jung, 1983:23). In European tradition the Son of God is sometimes said to dwell in a flower. The Virgin Mary is compared to a rose in this Christian prayer cited by Jung (1973b:79):

O Rose-wreath, thy blossoming makes men weep for joy.
O rosy sun, thy burning makes men to love.
    O son of the sun,
    Rose-child,
    Sun-beam.
Flower of the Cross, pure Womb that blossoms
    Over all blooming and burning,
    Sacred Rose,
    Mary.

Flowers in your mandala may be a harbinger of spring revealing the quickening of your personal growth cycle. They may signify the womb in which a divine child, your own individual being, is born within you. Flowers may also signal the fulfillment of a goal or task which has taken much dedication on your part. When studying the flowers in your mandalas, take notice of how many flowers appear, their color(s), and the number of petals each holds. Incorporating this information will help you interpret the meaning of your flowers. You may want to consider the possibility that flowers reveal your soul's work, a growth process unfolding through your relationship with the archetype of the Self.

HANDS

With our hands we take hold, create, and reach out toward others. With our hands we accomplish things. Hands set human beings apart and, in partnership with the brain, they make possible the skills with which civilization is built. To the Egyptians, creators of one of the world's most remarkable cultures, the hand stood for manifestation, action, and husbandry (Cirlot, 1962:130).

The hand communicates meanings with its gestures. In esoteric European doctrine, as in the Hindu practice of yoga, the position of the hand, and the arrangement of the fingers, convey precise symbolic meanings. In Christian symbolism, the hand raised with palm outward conveys the blessings of God. The hand outstretched, palm up, is a supplication. A tightly closed fist indicates defiance. Hands clasped suggest a "virile fraternity" (ibid., 131) or the union of marriage. In early Christian art, the hand with a pointing finger was seen as a symbol for God.

Each hand has five fingers. It should not be surprising, then, that the symbolism of the hand(s) is related to the numbers five and ten. Five suggests love, health, and humanity while ten traditionally symbolizes unity or perfection (Cirlot, 1962). The hand may also stand for the whole body by virtue of the fact that the body's extremities number five (hands, feet, and head). In Jung's opinion, the hand may also suggest generativity (1976b).

The right hand traditionally stands for rational, conscious, logical, "masculine" qualities. The left hand connotes emotional, unconscious, intuitive, and "feminine" qualities. Interestingly enough these folkloric traditions are in keeping with the modern split-brain theory. The left brain, the organ of logical thinking, controls the right side of the body. The right brain, seat of wholistic modes of perception, directs the left side of the body.

With the hands one takes hold of things. The appearance of hands in your mandala may signal your readiness to engage with life. Hands may symbolize your ability to influence your surroundings, to take an active part in relationships, or to begin an occupation or project. When hands appear in your mandala, you should consider the meanings of the numbers five and ten. You might want to remember that the health of your body could be symbolized by a hand.

When the hand in your mandala has a pointing finger, pay special attention to the area indicated by that finger. It may contain an important message for you. In a general sense, the appearance of a hand may reveal your readiness to shift from a mode of "being" into a mode of "doing." When hands appear in your mandala you may be experiencing a sense of vitality, a desire for action, and justified confidence in your own abilities.

HEART

The heart is a symbol of love. Most often, the love symbolized is that between persons. However, the heart may also represent spiritual fervor. In mystic doctrine the heart symbolizes love as the source of illumination and happiness. This spiritual love is sometimes represented in Christian art as a flaming heart. In either personal or spiritual love symbology, a heart pierced with an arrow can represent devotion despite trying conditions.

The heart was once considered the center of being and the "true seat of intelligence" (Cirlot, 1962:135). The Egyptians preserved the heart intact after death because it was thought indispensible for the person's afterlife. The heart is also associated with courage, sorrow, and joy. In esoteric thought the heart corresponds to the sun. For the alchemists the heart was an image of the sun within man, in the same way that gold was thought of as the image of the sun in the earth (Jung, 1983).

Heart references abound in language. We encourage people to "take heart," to "get to the heart of the matter," or not to be "hard-hearted." A person is described as having "the heart of a lion," or "wearing his heart on his sleeve." Persons are said to have a "heart-to-heart talk." We say our heart is "bursting with joy," or "broken with sadness." All of these expressions reveal how much a part of our thinking are the old ideas regarding the heart as the center of emotion, understanding, and will.

Hearts appearing in your mandalas can reveal a concern about relationships. They may also be a reminder to focus on that which is really important in a situation. Hearts may speak of wounds and suffering, especially if they are purple, "broken," or pierced with an arrow. If you see a wounded heart in your mandala, you might also want to confirm the physical health of your heart. Hearts suggest that your emotions are aroused. When you see hearts in your mandalas there is a good chance you are experiencing the altered state known as love.

INFINITY

Infinity symbolizes unlimited time, space, and number. It suggests the hypothetical end of a continuum that passes from the known to the unknown. The concept of infinity is a bridge from rational thought to unknown, possibly unknowable, realities. With the infinity symbol, the infinite can be transposed to the finite scale of mathematical calculations.

The mathematical sign for infinity is a double loop. It is formed by the interlacing of a clockwise circle and a counterclockwise circle. Although derived from the Arabic numbering system, India is the true source of the mathematical precepts upon which infinity is based (Walker, 1988). According to Indian tradition, the clockwise movement of the right half of the infinity sign is associated with the male, solar principle. The counterclockwise movement of the left half corresponds to the female, lunar principle.

The infinity sign represents the harmonious union of two principles which are opposites. While the infinity demonstrates a separation into dualities, it does not depict a conflicted pair. The two loops are created and joined by one continuous line. This is a statement of the balanced order which is the background of the multiplicity of ordinary reality. In the words of one mathematician, infinity postulates "a complete orderedness which was not invented but discovered" (cited in von Franz, 1986:83).

The infinity sign in your mandala may reveal a desire to relate to the Infinite, or God. It may also express an attempt to balance the opposites. Sometimes the infinity sign reflects our experience in a relationship within which the opposite can be projected and integrated. Thus, a good connection with another human being, such as a friend, lover, or therapist, may be signified by the infinity sign in your mandala. The repetitive tracing of the infinity within a mandala has proved to be an effective personal ritual for my own relaxation, centering, and concentration.

LIGHTNING

Lightning is a flash of light from above that sometimes burns or even kills. Its frightening, dynamic quality led ancient peoples to attribute lightning to the gods. The Greek god Zeus was armed with thunderbolts which he launched like spears to banish enemies. The Norse god Thor threw a mighty hammer as quick as lightning and just as deadly. With the rolling of his chariot wheels he produced thunder.

Lightning became a symbol for the activating force of the spiritual realm of the gods working upon the earth and its mortals.

According to Persian mythology, the Heavenly Father fertilized the Mother-Stone with lightning bolts and she gave birth to the savior Mithra. Among the Chinese it was thought that the great Yellow Emperor was conceived in the womb of a royal concubine by a flash of lightning (Walker, 1988). In the beliefs of early peoples lightning was equated with "the creative mana, the power of healing and fertility" (Jung, 1974:105).

The flash of illumination produced by lightning has also come to symbolize a bolt of insight, such as that characteristic of intuition (Jung, 1973b). For medieval alchemists lightning was a symbol for "sudden rapture and illumination" (Jung, 1983:317). Some believe that lightning represents the attainment of wisdom. For example, the Navaho's mighty Thunderbird, source of lightning and thunder, is also bringer of the gift of enlightenment.

Lightning may also signify the beginning of a new cycle, just as springtime thundershowers mark the beginning of a new growing season. Jung describes the solid black mandala of a woman in deep depression. Her recovery, resulting in the lifting of her depression, was announced when she drew a black mandala penetrated to the core by lightning. The lightning proclaimed the dawning of a new day for her. Jung characterizes this lightning as a symbol of energies in the psyche that are "illuminating, vivifying, fertilizing, trans-forming, and healing" (1973b:30).

Lightning in your mandala suggests the activation of energies within you which may have been dormant. The claiming of your intuitive powers may be indicated by lightning. It can also symbol-ize a powerful spiritual awakening. When you see lightning in your mandala, consider whether you are experiencing a dramatic change, a startling insight, inspiration, or profound healing.

RAINBOW

The rainbow is a dazzling natural display of color. It shimmers in the cloud-dark sky following a thunder-storm. The silent beauty of the rainbow after the drama of thunder, lightning, and rain is an uplifting sight. It signals the return of the sun.

The rainbow has been a symbol of the special connection be-tween gods and man from the earliest times. In the Biblical story of

Noah and the Ark the rainbow is given as a token of God's promise never again to bring great floods to destroy humankind. The Greeks named the goddess of the rainbow Iris. She was the messenger of the gods and provided a link between gods and mortals. In Wagner's mythic opera *Das Rheingold,* the rainbow serves as a bridge from earth to Valhalla, the heavenly fortress of the gods.

Seven colors comprise the rainbow: red, orange, yellow, green, blue, indigo, and purple. The seven colors of the rainbow are sometimes substituted for other mystical sevens. The seven planets of ancient astronomy, the gods associated with the planets, and the seven days of the week dedicated to those gods all have colors associated with them. Close inspection of hair, skin, and other organic matter in bright sunlight reveals rainbow colors. This fact led some ancients to conclude that the rainbow was the basis of all things.

Folklore tells us that there is a pot of gold at the end of the rainbow. However, as we have no doubt learned from experience, the end of the rainbow cannot be found by ordinary means. The search for rainbow gold is like the quest for the grail, or the alchemist's attempts to refine the philosopher's stone. The rainbow, like the grail and alchemical treasures, is a symbol for that which has great value but cannot be discovered by ordinary means.

The rainbow, perhaps because of its association with life-giving rain, signifies fertility. The shape of the "bow" in the rainbow alludes to a cosmic womb (Kellogg, 1978). Thus, the rainbow represents the sacred conjunction of male and female principles, the archetypal parents. We find this symbolism in a creation myth of the Australian aborigines. It is their belief that the Rainbow Serpent Mother created the world and gave birth to all its people (Walker, 1988). Indian peoples of the American Southwest look to the rainbow god as a benevolent guardian and bringer of good medicine.

Jung (1973b) found that the alchemists considered the colors of the rainbow a symbol for the peacock. The gold alchemists sought was thought to come from peacock's eggs. Rainbow colors marked an important transition in the procedures of the alchemists. They presaged the appearance of the gold. According to Jung the metaphorical language of the alchemists describes the process of becoming one's true self. He suggests that the appearance of rainbow colors in mandalas is related to wholeness, the goal of individuation.

Kellogg describes mandalas that are bright with the seven colors of the rainbow as indicative of the "rainbow experience" (1977:124). This is a rebirth of the person occasioned by a profound reordering of the psyche. She states that rainbow-experience mandalas are characterized by "the use of many colors in a fragmented, shattered pattern" and she proposes that "the rainbow experience may be looked on as the first step in a process whereby, in order to achieve a new integration, disintegration of the old self is necessary" (ibid., 125). Kellogg (1978) finds rainbow-experience mandalas point toward Oedipal conflicts and suggest the means to resolve them. When you create a rainbow-experience mandala, you may want to request extra emotional support from your circle of friends and loved ones to help you keep your feet on the ground.

When rainbows appear in your mandalas you may be celebrating the joy of having come through a dark time. Perhaps some of the wounds of your inner child are being healed. A rainbow may suggest that the number seven has special meaning for you also. Rainbows in your mandalas can be like a gift of encouragement from the gods. The rainbow experience can be your psyche's way of liberating powerful energies for healing.

SPIRAL

 The universe flows in spirals. When we blow smoke the air cascades away from us in vortical movement. The water we stir creates similar patterns. The same forces which shape the air and water join with gravitational contraction to create atoms, solar systems, and galaxies. The spiral depicts this orderly movement of both the large and the small in our universe. It is a symbol suggesting circular motion toward and away from a center point.

The spiraling order of the cosmos "both structures and reflects our consciousness" (Purce, 1974:8). This order is expressed by the spiral motif in ancient stone carvings such as those found in England, Ireland, and France. To early peoples the spiral may have symbolized the pathway of the moon, the growth of plant life, or whirling dances of healing and incantation. It is thought that spiral figures may have been used to induce a state of ecstasy (Cirlot, 1962).

Human beings are drawn to move around and toward the center, which is also the Center, where God dwells. Ritual circumambulation is practiced by the devout of varied religions in their approaches to sacred places. Japanese pilgrims wind upward around the sacred Mount Fuji. Muslims circle the holy of holies in Mecca. In much the same way, Christians intone prayers as they retrace the patterns of spiral labyrinths on floors in Gothic cathedrals.

This impulse to circle around that which is sacred shapes the inner workings of the psyche as well. Jung has observed that the growth cycle of the psyche itself describes a spiral pathway. He writes, "We can hardly escape the feeling that the unconscious process moves spiral-wise round a centre, gradually getting closer, while the characteristics of the centre grow more and more distinct" (1974:29). Jung is referring to the process of individuation through which the ego takes up its proper position as an entity revolving around the Self, the true center of the personality. The transformation that brings about this reorientation is described metaphorically as a chemical cooking process in the imagery of alchemy in which ". . . the spiral emphasizes the centre and hence the uterus, which is a synonym frequently employed for the alchemical vessel . . ." (ibid., 254).

The sinuous design of the spiral alludes to the form of the snake. It sometimes conveys the potent imagery associated with the serpent. In Jung's words, "The serpentine line . . . is analogous to the healing serpent of Aesculapius" (ibid.). Jung also finds the spiral reminiscent of the tantric symbol for life force. Hindus envision this energy as the kundalini serpent coiled three-and-a-half times around a point at the base of the spine. The awakening of this imaginary serpent frees subtle energy in the body to begin the process that culminates in the joining of pure cosmic energy (Sakti) with pure consciousness (Siva). The spiral, then, serves as a symbol of the revitalization of life through contact with the divine, creative, healing energies of the deepest layers of the psyche.

Spirals in your mandala may show your "spiral tendency" which is "the longing for and growth towards wholeness" (Purce, 1974:9). A quickening of energy may be indicated. Spirals may accompany a flow of images from the unconscious in the form of uncanny knowledge, inspirations, and insights about the nature of reality. The spiral in your mandala may bring you the shaman's challenge: to translate your knowledge into a form that can be useful to others.

Spirals in your mandala may appear to turn to the right or to the left. Clockwise-turning spirals often indicate something moving into consciousness or manifestation (Jung, 1974). Counterclockwise spiraling suggests an involution of energy back to the center, or into the unconscious. When you see spirals in our mandalas perhaps you are feeling in tune with cosmic rhythms that help you know your place in the universe. Creating spirals can express the flow of your psychic energy in patterns that mirror the universal.

SQUARE

The square gives the impression of firmness, stability, and balance. With its four equal sides, the square is an expression of the number four. It suggests a balance of four equal but different elements. The square is rarely seen in nature. A square is usually the product of human effort—it must be carefully measured and laid out in order to be accurate. Perhaps for this reason, in the West the square is often a symbol of rational thought, human accomplishment, earthly existence, and goal-directed behaviors. In Egyptian hieroglyphics, for example, the square represents achievement while the square-shaped spiral stands for "constructive, materialized energy" (Cirlot, 1962).

In the East, the square has somewhat different traditional associations. The Chinese use a black square to stand for the earth with its feminine yin quality. In India, the square signifies the *padma* or lotus and alludes to the archetypal feminine *yoni* (Jung, 1974). The liturgy of Tibetan mandalas uses the square to designate a palace or sacred precinct. It defines the sacred place where the symbol of the deity is placed. In these cultures the square represents matter and symbolizes the principles that guide the embodiment of spirit in matter.

The squaring of the circle, which upon completion appears, rather, to be the circling of the square, is an alchemical figure bringing together the symbol of heaven, the circle, with the symbol for earth, the square (Cirlot, 1962). It represents an attempt to

The squaring of the circle.

balance the opposites through synthesis, thus producing something new from that which was diametrically opposed. Jung tells us that the squaring of the circle is a symbol of the alchemical work conceptualized as breaking down ". . . the original chaotic unity into the four elements and then [combining] them again in a higher unity" (1974:198). From Jung's point of view the circle represents unity and the square stands for the four elements.

Jung (1973b) mentions the squared circle as one of the mandala forms he saw most often in the work of his patients. He considers it evidence of the dynamism of the Self, that uncanny archetypal force of nature that regulates the harmony of the individual's psychic life. Jung saw that this mandala, and all mandala forms characterized by fourness, was born of the psyche's attempts to balance the often competing possibilities offered by the four functions of thinking, feeling, sensing, and intuition.

Kellogg (1977) suggests that the form of the square in mandalas can represent one's environment, the people and situations which comprise one's milieu. When the square fills the circle, as in the squaring of the circle, Kellogg finds the mandala takes on special meaning. It symbolizes the consolidation of energy necessary to empower the ego. Issues regarding the establishment of one's personal identity and relinquishing dependency ties to the parents may be shown when one's mandalas take this form. Kellogg suggests that mandalas of the squared circle indicate that

> symbolically, one is in touch with the maternal and paternal power within oneself. One can begin to incorporate straight lines as representative of the conscious planning ability. . . . one no longer feels acted upon but now gains a center of activity. One is linking up both the receptive and active halves of self. (1978:119)

Rationality, earthiness, and firm grounding in reality are suggested by the straight-lined square. Since the outer circle of the mandala suggests the psychological boundaries of the person, the presence of the square inside the mandala circle suggests that qualities symbolized by the square have been incorporated. These may include clear thinking, readiness to learn, and a desire to achieve. Squared-circle mandalas come at a time when we are closely aligned with the Self, often experienced in the guise of the archetypal parents. When you see squares in your mandalas, and when you square the circle, you may be gifted with a surge of energy that can be channeled into consciousness, enhanced self-esteem, and heroic endeavors.

STAR

Stars glitter in the dark night sky and guide the wanderer home. To those who know their patterns, they form a stately procession of fantastic creatures, deities, and archaic implements. Ancients considered stars symbols of heavenly favor and guidance. It was a star that led the wise men to Bethlehem and marked the spot where the Christ child lay.

Persians worshipped the morning star as a manifestation of the goddess Inanna, Queen of Heaven. Stars are found in the symbology of Christianity as well. The Virgin of the Immaculate conception is crowned with stars. "Stella Maris," or Star of the Sea, is one of the Virgin's titles. Christ is also symbolized by a luminous heavenly body: first as the child whose birth is marked by the appearance of a star and later when he says of himself, "I am the root and the offspring of David, the bright and the morning star" (Rev. 22:16).

A rising star is identified with something coming into being, such as the birth of an outstanding human being. In the Bible a star is associated with the appearance of the Jewish Messiah (Num. 24:17). A falling star speaks of that which is heavenly or spiritual coming to ground and impacting material existence. According to a Cherokee legend (Ywahoo, 1987), Star Woman falls from her abode in the Pleiades. Her arrival on earth brings about the awakening of torpid creatures who then become human beings.

Stars are also related to the soul. According to the ancient Greek philosophers the soul is not completely in the body. Part of the soul soars above the person like a star. The soul star generates the person's inspirations, creativity, and enthusiasm. A similar idea was put forward by the alchemist Paracelsus. He believed that, "The true man is the star in us. The star desires to drive man towards great wisdom" (cited in Jung, 1983:131).

Jung often saw stars in mandalas done by his patients. They were usually placed in the center and had four, eight, or twelve rays. In the work of one man, Jung identifies a four-rayed star as a symbol of the Self "appearing as a star out of chaos" (ibid., 1973b:90–91). The star represents "the transcendent totality" (ibid., 98) which subsumes disorder.

The five-pointed star may be based on natural plant forms, such as flowers and fruit considered attributes of the ancient goddesses. For example, the core of an apple is a star. The five-pointed star appears in Egyptian hieroglyphics where it has the meaning of "rising upward toward the point of origin" (Cirlot, 1962:295). This may refer to Nut, star-breasted goddess of the night sky. A five-pointed star inverted, on the other hand, has been used to symbolize forces of dissolution, the demonic, or the occult.

Kellogg (1977) finds in the five-pointed star a shape that resembles the human being standing firmly on two feet. She is in agreement with Jung, who considers the five-pointed star a symbol for "the material and bodily man" (1973b:89). Their work suggests that the five-pointed star in a mandala indicates a well-grounded sense of identity. Kellogg finds that the star may also give information about a person's interaction with the material world. According to her the appearance of a star in a mandala suggests the ability to bring inspiration into reality.

A sense of self-worth, identity, mission, and readiness to accomplish are conveyed by a star that fills the space in your mandala circle. Numerous smaller stars speak of potentials, competing goals, or generativity. Stars can have any number of points, of course. When studying the stars in your mandala, count the number of points they have. The number and its symbolism can be considered when you interpret the meaning. A star proclaims your identity as a singular being. You are unique in all the world. Stars in your mandala may also be a reminder that you are a creature with a soul. You are called to make a special connection with your true inner Self and live out the destiny that is yours alone.

TREE

 The tree is a symbol of life, ever-abundant and self-renewing. Trees were considered sacred at one time. Mesopotamian ziggurats were topped by a living tree, tribute to Inanna, goddess of all nourishment. The Druids worshipped their gods in sacred groves of trees. Certain trees have even been thought of as oracles whose voices could be interpreted only by a sage or priestess living beneath their branches (Walker, 1988). The Bible mentions Deborah, a wise woman who lived and ruled under a tree bearing her name (Judges 4:5).

The Tree of Life in the Garden of Eden yielded fruit that gave consciousness of good and evil. Its ripe offering introduced the original couple to a world of dualities. Tradition has it that the cross on which Jesus died was hewn from this tree. In medieval Christian art the cross is sometimes shown as a living tree bearing flowers and fruit as in the primordial garden.

The upward thrust of the tree's branches are balanced by the downward expansion of its roots. This makes the tree an apt symbol for the connection between different levels of reality: the underworld of the unconscious, the middle world of the earth and ordinary waking consciousness, and the upper world of heaven or transpersonal consciousness. The mythic world tree of Norse tradition, Yggdrasil is an example of a tree that creates and sustains life through its connections with different levels of existence. The mystical tree of the Kabbalah also grows through several levels as emanations descend to create the world, and, eventually, ascend along the same pathway to bring creation to an end.

A symbol, such as the tree, which connects different levels of reality is called an *axis mundi,* or world axis. Other axis mundi symbols include the cross, ladders, stairs, and mountains. The axis mundi marks the mystic center of the universe. It is the bridge or ladder by means of which the soul may reach God (Cirlot, 1962). The tree, then, can be a symbol of one's connection to God.

Jung considered the tree a symbol for the archetype of the Self. The Self might be thought of as the image of God existing within each person. He writes that "if the mandala may be described as a symbol of the self seen in cross section, then the tree would represent a profile view of it: the self depicted as a process of growth" (1983:253). Jung felt that the tree symbolized the urge in each of us to grow and fulfill an inner image of wholeness that mirrors the perfection of God.

The tree is rich with symbolism. Some of its more common associations are enumerated by Jung:

> . . . growth, life, unfolding of form in a physical and spiritual sense, development, growth from below upwards and from above down-wards, the maternal aspect (protection, shade, shelter, nourishing fruits, source of life, solidity, permanence, firm-rootedness, but also being "rooted to the spot"), old age, personality, and finally death and rebirth. (1983:272)

When you see a tree in your mandala, know that it is an image of yourself as well as a symbol of the Self. The tree that you draw may incorporate indications of "forgotten" injuries in broken branches or holes in the tree trunk (Hammer, 1975). Your capacity to interact well with others can be shown by an expansive canopy of tree branches. A leafless tree may indicate that you are in a dormant phase when, like the tree in wintertime, life-giving energy is withdrawn out of sight into deeply hidden roots.

Women who are mothers often draw trees with fruit or flowers. If the tree in your mandala goes outside the circle, you may be feeling an urge to grow beyond the familiar boundaries of identity which you have established for yourself. When the roots of your tree are exposed, you may be feeling insecure, uprooted, or vulnerable. You might even be experiencing problems with your feet. The trees you draw portray your whole self: the physical, emotional, and spiritual aspects of who you are.

TRIANGLE

 The triangle is a symbol of dynamism, an indicator of direction, and an attribute of deities both masculine and feminine. It is related to the number three. In Christianity the triangle is a symbol of the Trinity because, like the Trinity, its three equal parts are joined together in one. A more generalized spiritual meaning is found in the upward-pointing triangle by Jung (1974). For him it is a symbol of the tendency of the universe to converge toward a point of unity.

The downward-pointing triangle is a symbol of the feminine because of its resemblance to the female pubic area. It is called the *yoni yantra* in Indian tradition, where it is a religious symbol representing the feminine principle as the source of all things. The balancing principle of the masculine is represented by an upward-pointing triangle. Beautiful mandalas based on the intersection of upward- and downward-pointing triangles are used for meditation purposes in India.

A related form is found in the European symbol called Solomon's Seal, a favorite of medieval mystics. This six-pointed star, like the yoni yantra, is formed by overlapping triangles. For alchemists the upward-pointing triangle symbolizes fire (libido, life force, spirit, yang), while the downward-pointing triangle symbolizes water (unconscious, potential, natural man, yin). In the metaphorical language of these philosophers, the mixture of fire and water produces the human soul (the whole person). Solomon's Seal represents this confluence and also the soul itself. (Cirlot, 1962)

The poet Yeats (as described in Purce, 1974) performed a meditation derived from the ideas of the alchemists. He visualized two conical spirals spinning upward and downward through the body to meet near the heart. The lower spiral represents fire, the upper symbolizes water. The coming together and intersection of the two gyres in the heart was a vehicle to satisfy the mystic's longing for the conjunction of spirit and matter. It is symbolized by a six-pointed Seal of Solomon which, in Hindu tradition, is the symbol of the heart chakra itself.

The six-pointed star is important in Jewish tradition as the Star of David and a symbol of the Jewish religion. Jewish mystical tradition holds that the star represents a mythical couple in close embrace within the Ark of the Covenant. Walker (1988) contends that this concept was probably seeded by the influence of Indian religion.

A six-pointed Solomon's Seal in your mandala may be an indication that you have succeeded in bringing together opposing forces to create a new synthesis. In the view of Kellogg (1977), this symbol implies a perfect balance between the energies suggested by upward- and downward-pointing triangles. When you see the six-pointed star in your mandala, you may have recently completed an important body of work. Perhaps you are experiencing a feeling of harmony, fulfillment, and satisfaction.

The upward-pointing triangle in mandalas often announces the appearance of something new, a rebirth, or a burst of creativity. Kellogg finds that a triangle in the center of the mandala connotes aspiration, while a triangle whose peak is near the top reflects assertiveness. The triangle may also symbolize material pushing up from the unconscious (Jung, 1973b). Exactly what is coming to light can sometimes be learned through one's associations to the color of the triangle.

Triangles pointing downward seem to indicate ideas that are being released from consciousness. The downward-pointing triangle may also reflect an ending, or a time of change following the completion of something. According to Kellogg the downward-pointing triangle represents a "pull toward the earth or death and destruction" (1977:126). It suggests a time when one's awareness of life, death, and rebirth is heightened through experiences of loss. In ancient times this cycle was mediated by dark goddesses such as Hecate, Kali, and Tiamat.

Triangles are direction indicators in mandalas. They not only point up and down, they may point toward the center or away as well. One or more triangles pointed outward in a mandala may indicate the presence of aggressive energy or a felt need for self-protection (Jung, 1973b). One or more triangles directed toward the center of the mandala may reveal aggression directed inward against oneself.

You should consider carefully other symbols in your mandala to which the triangle seems to point. The triangle may be your unconscious telling you to pay attention to something specific. Associations to the symbol emphasized by the triangle may help you know what has true value for you. With this knowledge you can establish priorities that are in keeping with your psyche's deepest directives.

The triangles in your mandalas introduce change. They direct your attention to the timeless balance of rising and falling energies. A triangle can show you what you need to know in order to stay on the mark. Triangles can point you toward your soul's connection deep within the heart.

WEB

 The web is an archetypal symbol of the weaving that brings form into being. The spider in her web is considered an incarnation of the goddess by many peoples. The Greeks thought of her as Arachne, goddess of spinning. She was said to have the power to spin out the fate of human beings.

Native American legends tell of Spider Woman, the creator of the universe. Her work begins with the spinning of two threads, which she stretches north-south and east-west. As she spins, the day takes shape; with night she undoes what she has made during the day. The spider has a similar place in Indian culture. She is regarded as a symbol of Maya, the weaver who creates the illusory reality of the world of the senses.

The female spider has somewhat sinister connotations in our culture. She is associated with the negative aspects of the feminine that ensnare, devour, and destroy. Yet her beautiful web is a source of genuine amazement and admiration. According to Robert Johnson, the spider sitting in her web can be viewed as a mandala symbolizing the mother complex.

> The spider and her web (so often in people's dreams!) is a rudimentary mandala and represents the energy source from which an

evolved mandala springs. The shape of the spider is mandala-like in that it is a circle with legs reaching out in a symmetrical pattern. And the spider web is certainly a mandala in its own right.

The energy system in back of this is that mandala is always feminine (though it may contain masculine elements), and one's relationship to femininity is the crucial issue whether one has a system of pathology (the spider's bite) or the beginning of the healing symbol (the spider's web). No one except an expert studying the subject ever sees a male spider. They are minuscule in size and perish during mating. So every spider one sees is a female and thus a great symbol of the begining of the mandala energy. To evolve one's mother complex (spider in its stinging aspect) into the healing form of the mandala is a very large part of one's spiritual development. This is more difficult for a man that a woman but common to both. (Personal communication, 1990)

Kellogg also relates the web form in mandalas to one's experience of the feminine. She finds that it symbolizes a close connection with mother as the matrix of new growth. This may recall one's real life experience before birth, or it may relate to the beginning of a new cycle of personal growth. If the web in your mandala is complete and firmly attached to the circle of the mandala, you have the necessary resolve to carry through on your latest initiative. Kellogg suggests that a broken web may be a symbolic reliving of a prenatal existence when life was threatened owing to "lack of will to thrive" (1978:91) or an unwelcoming uterine environment. She finds that a precarious early life experience may even be related to drug addiction later on. Addicts, she states, may be "self-medicating themselves, in order to keep such memories out of awareness" (ibid.).

When you see the symbol of the web in your mandala, perhaps you are revisiting some of your earlier childhood memories. You may also be laying the foundation for a new cycle of growth. The symbolism of the spider with her web connects you with primal facts of creation and destruction, for as Cirlot explains, "spiders in their ceaseless weaving and killing—building and destroying—symbolize the ceaseless alternation of forces on which the stability of the universe depends" (1962:290).

The rhythms of the spider may also suggest the continuous death and rebirth of the ego as it passes through unending transformations orchestrated by the Self, the mysterious center of the web of life.

6 THE GREAT ROUND
OF MANDALA FORMS

To everything there is a season, and a time for every purpose under the
heaven.   —Eccles. 3:1

THE SEASONS TEACH US about the growth cycle: the planting of
the seed, the growing of the plant, the maturation of the plant, and
the harvest, followed by the thrashing, and the return of seed to the
earth to be grown for a new cycle. This experience of the seasons
leads us to the notion of cycles: a pattern of repetition. Seasonal
rhythms shape our thoughts by providing a model of how things
come to be and how they pass away.

For example, information about the seasonal rotation of the sun
and other heavenly bodies is expressed in the zodiac. The interplay
of these planetary cycles is elaborated into astrology, a philosophy
that gives life meaning in many cultures around the world. The
Chinese *I Ching* is another ancient system for assessing the natural
cyclical flow of events. Readings of the I Ching enable persons to
align their actions with the patterns of nature so as to live in
harmony.

What do systems such as these have in common? They illustrate
a general process by which primordial energy takes shape, grows to
fulfillment in embodiment, then releases embodiment, and returns
to the source from which it came. They express in more elaborate
terms the simple, yet awesome, lessons we learn from seed plants in
the fields. It is quite natural to see the stages of a human life in light
of such models.

Not only do the cycles of nature form our thoughts, but our
inner life, being a part of nature, is itself orderly and patterned,
even though sometimes it may not feel that way. For example,

consider the daily cycle of our consciousness. When we are asleep, we are not conscious. As we wake up, consciousness returns, and with it our sense of identity. By midday we are probably functioning at our best: we are alert, thinking clearly, and performing well. As the afternoon wears on, we grow tired and sleepy. With evening we experience a brief surge in energy with heightened awareness of tastes, smells, and sounds. By late evening our energy level falls and we are ready to surrender consciousness to sleep again. This is a natural cycle that repeats itself each day.

We also experience patterns of longer duration, some lasting throughout our lifetime. Individuation is such a pattern. It moves us from the simplicity of wholeness in childhood into an ever more complicated and complex differentiation. Through adulthood we strive to attain fullness, balance, and harmony in a complex pattern that is ourselves. As our lifetime fulfills itself, we are drawn toward an increasingly simple, resonant wholeness that subsumes our former complications. The archetype of the Self governs the natural cycle of individuation.

We find within the individuation process a dynamic relationship between Self and ego that displays a natural rhythm of alternating closeness and separation. The close alignment of ego and Self is revealed when young children create mandala drawings. Their mandalas reflect the fact that the ego is developing within the matrix of the Self. As we mature into young adults, the ego achieves a separation from the archetypal structure of the Self. We encounter the Self again in midlife, often as the urge to express our untapped potential, to live the life unlived, and to complete the pattern of wholeness ordained by the Self.

Within this larger pattern of ego-Self relationship there are many instances of approach and withdrawal. As adults we may become aware of the Self during times of crisis or transition when its imagery appears in our dreams, drawings, and ordinary daily encounters. This is because the Self stands not only as a center and a container of the psyche, but, as Edinger (1987) has explained, the Self also serves as a guarantor for the ego. It stands behind the ego, as it were, and supports the ego structure at times when its functioning is disturbed or challenged.

The Self is there always whether or not we are aware of it. There is a lifelong relationship between the ego and the Self. In fact, a healthy connection between the ego and Self is very important if one is to be a fully functioning person. It is this linkage that is forged by the individuation process.

Edinger conceptualizes the dance between ego and Self as a spiral along which the ego draws closer to the Self and then moves away into a position of separateness from the Self. During times of separation between ego and Self, the person often feels depressed and alienated. When the ego is closely identified with the Self, the person may experience a sense of power and inflation. Throughout a lifetime one circulates many times from one position to the other, and countless others in between.

Edinger illustrates the rhythmic relationship between Self and

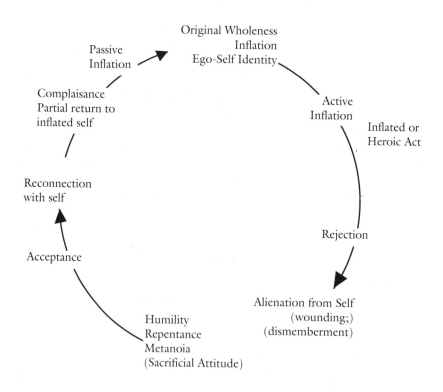

The psychic life cycle. (Edinger, 1972: 41)

ego with a circle. At the top of the circle we find a close alignment between ego and Self, as in the original wholeness experienced by children. Moving clockwise down the right side, the ego separates from the Self. The connection becomes more distant until at the bottom of the circle we find the ego experience of alienation from the Self. This marks the turning point when ego begins to move closer to Self once again. Moving in a clockwise direction upward along the left side of the circle, we notice that a reconnection with the Self is experienced, leading eventually to identity of ego with Self and the experience of inflation once more. The cycle then repeats itself.

Our inner life is expressed through images that we dream, imagine, and draw. The archetype of the Self, as we know, is often reflected in the mandala. Are particular mandala forms associated with individuation? If so, can we identify mandalas that give information about the relationship between ego and Self? The work of Jung, von Franz, Harding, and Kellogg suggests some interesting answers to these questions.

Jung frequently saw mandalas in the artwork of clients experiencing individuation. He compiled a list of the designs he observed, including the following:

1. *Circular, spherical,* or *egg-shaped* formation.
2. The circle is elaborated into a *flower* (rose, lotus) or a *wheel.*
3. A centre expressed by a *sun, star,* or *cross,* usually with four, eight, or twelve rays.
4. The circles, spheres, and cruciform figures are often represented in *rotation* (swastika).
5. The circle is represented by a *snake* coiled about a centre, either ring-shaped (uroboros) or spiral (Orphic egg).
6. *Squaring of the circle,* taking the form of a circle in a square or vice versa.
7. *Castle, city,* and *courtyard (temenos)* motifs, quadratic or circular.
8. *Eye* (pupil and iris).
9. Besides the tetradic figures (and multiples of four), there are also triadic and pentadic ones. . . . (1973b:77)

Jung mentions no particular order in which the forms evolve from one to another. They simply told him that the process of individuation was activated.

Von Franz defines the mandala in such a way as to suggest that mandala design motifs might repeat in a cyclical pattern. She explains that

> the mandala serves a conservative purpose—namely, to restore a previously existing order. But it also serves the creative purpose of giving expression and form to something that does not yet exist, something new and unique. . . . The process is that of the ascending spiral, which grows upward while simultaneously returning again and again to the same point. (Cited in Jung, 1964:225)

Von Franz describes the cyclical nature of the process that produces the mandala, but she does not mention particular designs associated with stages of growth. Harding, however, singles out three mandala forms and links them to successive steps in the individuation process.

She identifies these motifs as the "circle," the "mandala," and the "hermetic vessel." The circle suggests the totality of the psyche. The mandala, according to Harding's definition, is a circle that incorporates a square, cross, or triangle and performs the specialized function of reconciling the opposites. The hermetic vessel is suggested by a cooking pot, an egg, a womb symbol, a cauldron, a chalice, or any container in which a fundamental transformation takes place. Harding states that "although these symbols vary greatly as regards both the form and the order in which they occur in different individuals undergoing analysis, they do roughly correspond to stages in the development process" (1973:323). She suggests that while there are variations in the experiences of individuals and in their mandalas, a universal pattern reflecting the individuation process underlies these infinite forms.

The mandalas analysts see are usually done by clients without any suggestion from the analyst. The analysand has a compelling urge to create a circular mandala design. Such mandalas seem to appear most often when the person is in some sort of crisis. The ego is overwhelmed, or in a state of flux during reorientation, and the customary way of functioning is no longer possible for a person. When one's ego organization is temporarily disrupted, the creation of mandalas can be a soothing experience. The desire to draw mandalas seems to reveal the organizing capacity of the archetype of the Self, especially in its function as guarantor for the ego.

It is not necessary to wait until a crisis to draw mandalas. Indeed, we should cultivate our lifelong relationship with the archetype of the Self. We need to establish and maintain an appropriate connection with this primal source of energy within us. By drawing mandalas, we can allow the energies of the archetypal Self to enrich and influence our conscious existence appropriately. Mandalas allow us to receive information from the archetypal psyche through visual imagery that can be integrated.

As an art therapist, Joan Kellogg pioneered the use of mandalas for personal growth. In order to identify the forms of mandalas, she analyzed and interpreted thousands during the 1970s. Her attempt to find an orderly pattern underlying individual variations was at first unsuccessful. Then a breakthrough came in a dream: she saw a little man, staring intently at her while he walked backwards in a circle, drawing in the sand with a stick. This sparked the insight that led to her development of the Archetypal Stages of the Great Round of Mandala (personal communication, 1983).

The Great Round consists of twelve prototypical mandala forms which reflect a "spiraling path of psychological development" (Kellogg and DiLeo, 1982:38). Each form represents a significant stage along a continuous path of personal growth. The twelve stages encapsulate the unfolding of a cycle that is lived not once but many times. The mandalas of the Great Round reflect the dynamic relationship between ego and Self.

Individual mandalas seldom coincide neatly with a single prototypical mandala form. Combinations of the forms are more likely to occur in our mandalas. Yet, identifying the patterns most like our own mandala helps us understand our ego position in relationship to the Self. This knowledge can allow us to make choices that align our energies with the psychological growth process indicated.

To better understand the Great Round, let us take the example of a familiar activity through each of the twelve stages. This activity is the baking of a pie (adapted from Kellogg, 1986). The process begins at stage one at the bottom of the circle. Our pie maker here is in a deep dreamless sleep. At stage two our pie maker's sleep is not quite so deep. She is having a pleasant dream: cherries, apples, something fragrant, everything dancing together without identifiable form.

At stage three she wakes up and has a vague, undefined, but nonetheless compelling urge to begin something, she knows not

Making a pie on the Great Round.

what. In stage four our pie maker visits her mother at home, and learns how her mother bakes brownies. This is enjoyable, but with stage five, the pie maker stirs up her energy and leaves home, filled with hope and self-doubt, to find her own way. In stage six she realizes that what she wants to do is bake pies, and therefore she wants to become a pie maker. Her education begins. She develops skills and she becomes her own person, sorting out her own values, ideas, and desires from what her father and mother like.

Finally at stage seven her preparation is complete. She is trained, and she has the tools and ingredients she needs to begin work as a pie maker. At stage eight the pie maker is actually doing her work, baking a pie. She is bringing into reality what began as a dream in stage two.

With stage nine the work is complete. There is the satisfaction of a project fulfilled. But even as she basks in the glow of success, she knows her pie will not last forever. At stage ten the pleasure has faded and our pie maker is lost and uncertain what to do next.

In stage eleven she has the wisdom to realize that what she must do is cut up the pie, share it with friends, and consume it. In this way she gets nourishment from the whole process, and takes the essence of her experience with her to stage twelve. In stage twelve she looks back with satisfaction over all the events of her pie-making. She begins to get sleepy. Soon she will fall asleep again, dream another dream, and begin another passage through the Great Round.

As you can see from this example, each stage has its own tasks or challenges. It is characterized by a distinctive quality of consciousness and by certain feelings. Each stage has its own viewpoint or perspective on reality. When we find ourselves returning to a stage again, we resonate with all our previous experiences in this stage. We have an opportunity to rework and realign past experience in light of the present, and to weave the past and present into a harmonious pattern.

Take, for example, our pie maker. Perhaps when she went off to school the first time she had not completed all the growing necessary to make that departure from home a complete success. When she returns to school later in stage six to study pie-making, she is reminded of that earlier experience. She has the opportunity to put in a different perspective the memory of that time as she lives in the present. She can complete unfinished business and see her earlier experience in a new way as she lives with understanding in the present.

The example of the pie maker illustrates the twelve stages of the Great Round. The Great Round, like Edinger's conceptualization of the relationship between ego and Self, is a schema for describing a continuous, cyclical pattern of personal growth. Comparing the two approaches, we might find that the place of ego-Self alienation in Edinger's system is like stage one in Kellogg's Great Round. Ego-Self identity in Edinger's diagram would compare with stage seven in Kellogg's system. Other stages of the Great Round would fall between these two positions in Edinger's diagram.

Now that the concept of the stages of the Great Round has been introduced, I propose to discuss each stage in greater detail. I will describe the sorts of experiences associated with each stage, its developmental tasks, the quality of consciousness, and the feelings associated with it. The verbal description of each stage will be accompanied by a variation of the illustration of the mandala forms Kellogg has identified as typical for that stage. As you study the Great Round, please remember that your individual mandalas will rarely be exactly like those in the illustrations. You may find characteristics of mandalas from several stages in your own. Most likely your experience will be something like each of the stages your mandala resembles.

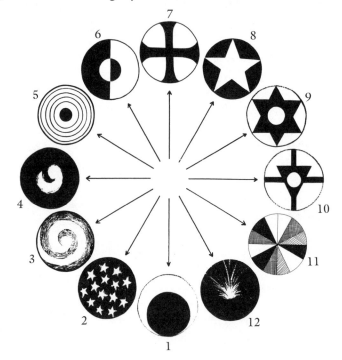

Archetypal stages of the Great Round of Mandala (Kellogg, 1978): (1) The Void, (2) Bliss, (3) Labyrinth / Spiral, (4) Beginning, (5) The Target, (6) Paradoxical Split / Dragon Fight, (7) Squaring the Circle, (8) The Functioning Ego, (9) Crystallization, (10) Gates of Death, (11) Fragmentation, (12) Transcendental Ecstasy. (Drawing © 1978 by Joan Kellogg)

STAGE ONE: THE VOID

 The Void is reminiscent of our very earliest memories, memories encoded at the cellular level prior to our birth. This stage recalls our experiences prior to the division of reality into the opposites. In mythological terms, stage one represents the moment when darkness and light, Good and Evil, or male and female are separated in the world. It marks the beginning of dualities which color human existence.

Mystics return to this state of mind, and then move beyond the forms and categories of mind to achieve a transcendent state of nonduality that, in psychological terms, resembles the mind-set of the fetus in its mother's womb. The state of formlessness and nonduality that precedes stage one may be known for fleeting moments as a peak experience when we move from the end of a cycle on the Great Round, and into stage one once again. Kellogg calls this stage the "white void." It represents the attainment of God-consciousness. When experiencing the white void one may have feelings of "salvation, redemption, joy, freedom, reconciliation, love and ecstasy" (Kellogg and DiLeo, 1982:40). The white void is indicated by mandalas that contain a lustrous white area, often in the center of the mandala.

Entry into stage one is sometimes experienced as a fall into darkness. Metaphorically speaking, this is the point at which consciousness enters matter. This stage compares with the dark prima materia with which the alchemists began their work. Kellogg and DiLeo describe this stage as the "dark void." It is "the transpersonal state of ignorance, darkness, confusion, alienation, pain, agony, oppression and constriction in which consciousness falls in the creation of matter" (ibid.). Stage one in some ways resembles sleep because motor functioning, mental processes, and emotions tend to be depressed. We have the feeling of being weighted down. We tend to be forgetful. Life is experienced as a waking dream and we are sleepwalkers.

With faith in an ultimate order some may take comfort here, but it is often a difficult stage. The world view of stage one might be thought of as something like that of a fish: underwater and looking up at shapes on the surface of the water that make little sense. The tasks for stage one are waiting, keeping faith, trusting the process, and being patient with our poor performance.

Mandalas created while experiencing this stage may be dark or completely black. Sometimes they are simply circles left white, or with very pale color. Mandalas here have little or no form. This is partly because the activity of drawing is difficult when experiencing The Void.

Stage one activates memories of one's intrauterine experience. If our early life in the womb was uncertain, either because we failed to thrive or the uterine environment was not supportive, we may create a particular mandala pattern when we reexperience The Void. Our mandala may resemble a spider's web, in black and white or shades of blue and yellow. The spider's web recalls the fetal connection to the walls of the womb.

It is interesting to note that the spider is prominent in the creation stories of India and numerous Native American tribes. It is said that she brings the world into being through her delicate, rhythmic weaving. Robert Johnson has pointed out that the spider and her web represent the energy source from which the evolved mandala springs. When we create a spider web mandala, perhaps we are reaching back to heal some of our earliest experiences, and recreate our view of reality as we begin our passage around the Great Round.

The Void is the primal beginning of our cycle of growth. It is our step from spirit into matter, the commencement of the process by which we balance the opposites of our human nature. Strange that our mandalas here should sometimes resemble the cool, distant spaces of an arctic snowfield. So much activity is taking place out of sight.

STAGE TWO: BLISS

Stage two is called Bliss. This stage corresponds to the intrauterine experience as a state of blissful union and containment of all things. Consciousness here is diffuse, dreamy, and lacking a clear sense of ego boundaries. Like the baby in its mother's womb, we do not know nor care what is self and other. What matters is the pleasure of the experience. Infinite possibilities exist in this stage, but it is a time of suspended action, passivity, and an almost dreamlike state of mind.

The perspective is somewhat impersonal, disengaged, and

marked by a passive enjoyment of the world and its pleasures. We identify with the nourishing, cosmic rhythms of the universe in a kind of *participation mystique*. Kellogg finds that experience in this stage reinforces belief in an immanent Godhead "who in a very real and comforting way inhabits all space equally" (1978:93). However, if one's intrauterine experience was not positive, returning to this stage may be unpleasant.

Bliss is characterized by images of water, "water that fertilizes, purifies and dissolves" (ibid.). Mythologically, this stage might be pictured as the spilling of divine spermatozoa, in the form of golden drops of sunlight, upon the passive blue waters of the primeval feminine. Bliss can also be symbolized by the uroboros, the legendary serpent which both creates and destroys itself.

The task here is to begin to discriminate among the countless possibilities. We must focus on just one, giving up all the others. This sometimes causes feelings of sadness as we mourn that which might have been. However, it is possible that something not chosen in one cycle of the Great Round will present itself to us again, and we will have the opportunity to develop it later.

Mandalas created by persons experiencing Bliss are characterized by a lack of form and a feeling of fluidity in the designs. We see numerous similar tiny forms scattered like stars within the mandala. Sometimes the mandala looks like an aquarium filled with fish eggs, miniscule creatures, or strange plants. There is the suggestion of fertility, but no clear sense of what is developing.

Artwork may spill over to the space surrounding the mandala as well. Colors tend to be blues and yellows, pale orchids, and pastel pinks. A touch of red in these mandalas may emphasize generativity, as in the yolk of a fertilized bird's egg. Dark shades of blue can reflect a negative experience in this stage, although Kellogg finds that "in a more mindful, intellectual experience without the sensation of diffusion, dark and light blue with white dots or stars will appear" in mandalas (1978:94).

Stage two, Bliss, is a place of sublime peace, where we are rocked upon the waters of a gentle world. Time moves slowly. We experience ourselves as all-loving and infinitely loved. In this drowsy predawn existence, we hardly notice that something important is missing: our individuality.

STAGE THREE: LABYRINTH OR SPIRAL

 Stage three exemplifies an experience like our intrauterine connection with the womb through the umbilical cord. It also recalls the severing of our umbilical connection during the birth process. The dreamy, passive state of stage two is quickened in stage three, just as the baby freed from blissful confinement in the womb begins to breathe, stretch, and move its arms and legs. A mythic metaphor for the quickening of life in the Labyrinth is the breath of God upon the waters, bringing life and motion to the world.

Consciousness in stage three is alert, intuitive, and focused. During stage three, individual consciousness or identity is beginning its separation from the *participation mystique* which characterizes stage two. As Kellogg and DiLeo explain:

> out of numerous stars and out of the many potential consciousnesses, one star, one individual consciousness, will finally emerge at stage eight of "The Functioning Ego." That point marks the completion of the first half of the journey. From Universal Consciousness we come to a single individualized consciousness. (1982:41)

The Labyrinth or Spiral marks the beginning of a process that culminates in an individualized consciousness. In stage three one experiences the activation or reactivation of life force within the psyche. This stage is the commencement of a journey, whose final goal is yet a mystery. It is a seeking without a clear idea of what is sought after.

The cosmos which was all of a piece in the previous stage is differentiated into a top and bottom in the Labyrinth. This layering of consciousness is represented in mythology as different worlds connected by mysterious passages, such as the road to the Grail Castle, the bowels of the behemoth, a stairway to heaven, or the Tree of Life. The worlds of myth reflect the experiences of shamans, artists, and mystics within different levels of consciousness. Initiation ceremonies bestow upon the young shaman a new umbilical cord linking him directly to the universe at some constant point such as a star. These mythic connections symbolize their movements from one state to another, and serve as images to assist their safe return from inner journeys.

When we are living in the Labyrinth, we become aware of the levels of consciousness. We may find that we are remembering our dreams, that we have a keen sense of the presence of absent loved ones, or a renewed awareness of the divine patterning of persons, relationships, and events in our lives. While we are capable of important insights into the nature of reality, we are unable to translate our knowledge into action because we lack a defined locus of power from which to act. Ego boundaries are diffused. We do not have a firmly defined sense of self.

While in the Labyrinth we feel a quickening. We sense that we are growing, and the rate at which we are changing here may actually cause us to experience dizziness. Our mood may shift quickly as a reflection of our ephemeral sense of identity. Life takes on meaning here with the feeling that something important has begun.

The challenge of the shaman who visits extraordinary levels of consciousness is to bring knowledge acquired there back to share with the tribe in a form that they will find useful. Our task for stage three is akin to the shaman's. We are to take the information we receive from various states of mind, and our dreams and inspirations, and shape them into a form that can be understood, appreciated, and used by others. With this arduous work we bring ourselves into being as well.

Mandalas of the Labyrinth exhibit a spiral pattern and often suggest depth or dimensionality. Colors are usually springtime pastels, especially light blues, lavender, and pinks, although bright, ethnic colors are not unusual. One often sees green spirals suggesting growing plants or vines. Curving lines are typical of Labyrinth mandalas. There is no pronounced center design in these mandalas. Kellogg finds that when the labyrinth mandala consists of black lines on white "it signifies the beginning of process in the space-time continuum, the spinning out of the soul or spirit and its descent into matter or maya" (1978:99).

The Labyrinth or Spiral is a time of heightened consciousness. We experience increasing energy and the desire to move, create, and become. It is a time of beginning something important. In Kellogg's words, "it is an abandonment in order to seek embodiment" (ibid., 100). The Labyrinth is a place of discovery where we wake up to find the world a strange, wonderful, and mysterious place.

STAGE FOUR: BEGINNING

 Stage Four is called Beginning. It signifies the choice of just one of the myriad possibilities in stage three, and shows that the development of the chosen one has begun. It recalls the infant dependent on its mother for nourishment. The child is separate, but contained within the mother's world.

Consciousness here reflects a dawning sense of self and the conviction that one is unique. The foundations of the ego are laid down or reworked when we pass through this stage. When in stage four we can take pleasure in nurturing something new, young, and tender in ourselves. It is normal to be narcissistic and self-absorbed during this stage. We may become passive and dependent in relationships as we seek to recapture for awhile the positive aspects of the mother-child relationship.

Religious traditions use our positive memories of early childhood to teach us about God as a loving parent who gives us the nourishment we need. It is interesting to notice that the circle with a dot in the center, an ancient symbol for God, can easily be seen as a breast. This mandala design is varied in the rose windows of Christian churches where an image of the Christ child is often placed in the center. Surrounding him is a flower like circle which symbolizes the mother Mary.

The task in Beginning is to honor the growth of the new, and to be a good parent to yourself. You may want to pay special attention to your diet, and be sure to get the rest and exercise that are good for your body. This is the psychological space of early childhood, and you may return here from time to time for renewal. Your challenge is not to cling to infantile behaviors longer than is necessary.

Mandalas created by persons living in Beginning have a center form such as a dot, a circle, a fetus, or an upward-pointing triangle. A small boat floating on a quiet sea is another design typical of this stage. Sometimes the figure eight appears in these mandalas, suggesting the close bond between a mother and baby. When the

center of your mandala contains a circle, perhaps you are symbolizing God within, from whom spills forth an experience that brings
you new life. Lines in the mandalas of stage four are typically
curved. Colors tend to be pale pinks, lavenders, and blues, especially
when you are nostalgic for your experience as an infant.

Beginning is a romantic time when it is easy to trust. This
pleasant stage recaptures the glow of infancy, when, like small
princes and princesses, we sat enthroned on our mother's lap. Some
of us may be seduced into wishing to spend our lives here. This is
a mistake, for our calling is to move on. If consciousness is to be
differentiated, we must separate from our parents. Only in this way
can we attain the individual consciousness of which human beings
are capable.

STAGE FIVE: THE TARGET

 Stage five is called the Target. It reflects a sharp change
from the pleasant containment of stage four. The Target
recalls the toddler's antagonism towards its mother. It
conveys the feeling of an even earlier encounter with the
"other," when the womb begins contractions that push the baby
out of its cozy existence. This is an unpleasant experience, but a
necessary one in order to begin the separation from paradise that
establishes our identity.

Consciousness here reflects an awareness of self as the one who
is suffering and does not know why. Obsessive thinking is not
unusual for people experiencing this stage. There is a sense of
struggling to maintain control in order to cope. Projection is typical
of this stage as we impute our own anger and aggression to others.

We feel vulnerable, angry, indignant, paranoid, and anxious. We
may feel as if we are targeted for unpleasant attention. Some of us
may resort to magical thinking in order to maintain a sense of
security. We may imagine that we have more power than we really
do. Ritual and routine become important to give us a sense of
order.

From the perspective of The Target, we see the world as a
dangerous place. We might characterize this stage as an experience
of the negative mother. It is the opposite of the previous stage. The
tasks here are to take courage, to confront our fears so as to reclaim

projections, and to surrender our claim on the blissful state of infancy. A great deal of energy is needed to leave this position because we must relinquish the dream of merging with the mother even though we have nothing to put in its place. Stage five might be compared to an alchemist vessel in which ingredients are tightly sealed and pressure is increased until a transformation is brought about.

Mandalas created by those experiencing stage five resemble a target. Concentric circles of colors and patterns radiate outward from the center. Sometimes we have to imagine that the mandala is a sphere in order to identify its target design. Colors tend to be bright. They are often placed side by side in combinations that clash.

While it is difficult to say anything positive about The Target, the pressures of this stage are often exactly what we need to grow. As Kellogg and DiLeo point out,

> it is in the very midst of opposition, paradoxes, anxiety, and conflicts that the human mind can transcend its limitations. To induce this gigantic cramp of consciousness the Zen chela is given a Koan by his master, "Show me the face before you were born!" By entering a seemingly impossible struggle, man eventually can go beyond it. (1982:42)

STAGE SIX: THE DRAGON FIGHT

Stage six is called the Dragon Fight. The dragon being fought is the uroboros which represents the archetypal parents. The influence of the archetypal parents resides in us as the internalized directives of our real life parents. Our struggle is the separation of the ego, as the carrier of individual consciousness, from the matrix of the parents' world of ideas.

The slaying of the dragon is a metaphor for freeing oneself from the collective values and drives imposed by and through the parents. We might think of the mother as a carrier of collective drives and instincts. The father transmits the values and traditions of his time. Once this heroic act is completed, then the archetypal parents wear a different aspect. As Neumann says, "they are no longer hostile, confining powers, but companions, bestowing their blessings on the life and work of the victorious hero-son [and heroine-daughter]" (1974:22). The accomplishment of this inner work eases the relationship with the real-life parents as well.

We develop a distinct sense of self through the Dragon Fight. This work is typically done in adolescence, although we return many times to this position and rework the experience. The world view here is the perspective of the young hero, the challenger who steals fire from the gods, David in his combat with Goliath. The tasks are to cease our childlike claims on the parents, to risk disobedience, and to take responsibility for our own life.

During the Dragon Fight it is not unusual to feel alienation, fear, loneliness, and depression alternating with elation, excitement, and happiness. We have here the experience of leaving paradise, and we feel sad about that. Yet we also have the sense of going forward to high adventure, and this pulls us forward. We feel ambivalence as we are forced to confront the paradoxes in our existence and endure the tension of the opposites within ourselves.

Mandalas created by persons experiencing stage six show a division into two halves. Often a third object or design motif appears superimposed upon the split between halves. Sometimes mandalas of the Dragon Fight will be landscapes. The earth symbolizes mother and the sky represents father. The sun rising in the center reflects the (re)birth of the ego.

Landscape mandalas are usually done with the colors seen in nature. Other Dragon Fight mandalas are characterized by bright colors. Complementary colors may appear side by side giving a sense of energetic confrontation. The split down the middle is usually the only straight line that appears in these mandalas. Most lines are curved. Sometimes even the center division is curved too, as in the yin-yang symbol of China.

Stage six is a time of inner conflict. Strife is sometimes experienced in our relationships as well. With the Dragon Fight we differentiate qualities within ourselves so as to give birth to a new sense of self. It is an exciting time full of energy, passion, and change.

STAGE SEVEN: THE SQUARING OF THE CIRCLE

 Stage seven is called the Squaring of the Circle. This stage marks the full-fledged establishment of the ego. There is a strong sense of autonomy at this time. One has the ability to learn, plan, and love. Because the ego is closely aligned with the Self, an experience of inflation is not uncommon during this stage.

The clash of the opposites is resolved with the Squaring of the Circle. There is no longer the tug-of-war that was experienced in stage six. Metaphorically speaking, one has given the parents back to each other. We have incorporated within ourselves the qualities of each that are necessary for a fully functioning adult identity. Sexuality that was diffuse in earlier stages is focused toward genital expression in stage seven. One is ready for a mate.

This is a place of balance between maternal and paternal power. We have access to both the active and receptive within ourselves. We no longer feel acted upon. We feel capable of initiating action instead of being the passive recipient of the actions of others. We are ready to "do," not just "be."

The perspective is that of being on top of the world. Consciousness is as bright and intense as the sun at high noon. Thinking is highlighted and rationality is much appreciated. The task here is to put our best efforts into a quest: to find our soul mate, to identify our life work, to make a commitment, and put our shoulder to the wheel.

Typical mandala forms of Squaring of the Circle display designs characterized by four. Crosses, squares, stars, and flowers with four petals are often seen. These forms represent the integration of the masculine (straight lines) with the feminine (curving line of the circle). We may sometimes produce mandalas that are completely gold or yellow like the sun. These seem stimulated by an experience of euphoria brought on by the close association between ego and Self. A negative response to the inflation common during this stage may cause us to descend to the opposite position on the Great Round, The Void.

Stage seven is the pivotal point in the Great Round. Stages up to Squaring of the Circle have been characterized by curved lines. Relatedness to the parents, especially the mother, has been quite important. We might describe the left side of the Great Round as the Matriarchy. We could then think of the right side of the Great Round as the Patriarchy. With the shift to the Patriarchy we reach the stages where skill and meshing with the real world are emphasized. Our mandalas in the stages seven through eleven tend to have more straight lines.

The Squaring of the Circle is the place where we take a stand on what we know within ourselves to be right. It is the beginning of life lived according to our own values. Behind the development of our individuality is the Self, the dynamism that compels us to become who we were meant to be. When at stage seven, our conscious attitudes are most strongly influenced by the archetype of the Self. Powered by the Self we have the courage to become truly heroic, putting our best efforts in the service of high ideals.

STAGE EIGHT: THE FUNCTIONING EGO

 Stage eight is called the Functioning Ego. This space represents individuals functioning effectively in their milieu. It is the culmination of the process begun in stage three: the attainment of individual consciousness. We have a clear sense of self firmly grounded in an accurate body image. When alone we no longer feel lonely. We are actively engaged with reality and take pleasure in work. When we experience stage eight we not only have the skills to do and to be, but we have the capacity to mesh with the real world, to work within a group, and to translate our ideals into action.

Despite an accurate understanding of reality, inflation is not uncommon during Functioning Ego because the ego remains closely aligned with the archetype of the Self. The realistic perspective of stage eight means that one is capable of effective work within organizations. We are occupied with putting our inspirations into a form that can be useful to others. The task is balancing individual goals with the structure of organization. Sometimes we must create ingenious camouflage to clothe personal projects in an appearance that complies with the standards of society.

This stage is an important indicator of the mobilization of will, and with it a sense of responsibility for directing one's own destiny. One commences an active role in the world, and accepts the burden of choice. The number five, associated with Functioning Ego, symbolizes the human figure, feet firmly planted and arms extended reaching out to contact the world. Kellogg and DiLeo write that stage eight "symbolizes the power of man" (1982:43). They are no doubt referring to the human capacity to develop an individual consciousness with the ability to will, think, create, and be self-aware.

Individuals experiencing Functioning Ego create mandalas with designs such as five-pointed stars and five-petaled flowers. The four-armed swastika is also seen here. Its center point, plus its four arms, add up to the five elements usually found in stage eight mandalas. Swastikas incorporate the principle of movement, and underscore one's sense of self as a center of power and effectiveness.

Stage eight is a time of much activity directed toward clearly defined goals. We know ourselves, what we want to do, and how to do it. Our efforts are well received because we offer the excitement of genuine creativity in a form that can be appreciated. The time we live in stage eight is our most productive in terms of the patriarchal world.

STAGE NINE: CRYSTALLIZATION

 Stage nine, Crystallization, reflects the completion of important creative endeavors. These might be something like launching a new business, creating a garden, or raising a family. The accomplishment might be some piece of inner work as well. The inspiration that energizes consciousness begins to slow a bit here because our creative activity is nearing completion.

There is a real coming together in Crystallization as we shape our place in the world by the work we do. During Crystallization our thoughts may be of such clarity that we achieve an intellectual understanding of the world and our place in it. This stage often brings a feeling of satisfaction, harmony, and fulfillment. Our self-esteem is enhanced by the pride of accomplishment. Crystallization is reminiscent of middle age.

It seems ironic, but it is quite true, that during the height of our achievement we begin to sense the inevitability of our destruction. After complying with the standards of the patriarchy to accomplish our work, we must then bow to the law of nature which decrees: all that is created must eventually be destroyed. Just as the rose begins to drop its petals moments after the height of its glory, so the accomplishments of humankind are bound to fade and lose the liveliness they once had. The task for Crystallization, then, is to enjoy our success to the fullest, without becoming attached to it, so that we can gracefully relinquish our position when the time comes.

Crystallization epitomizes the patriarchal world of rules. What began as an original creative act becomes standard procedure as the actions are repeated. A group established in the service of personal ideals evolves into an organization with a structure. The mystic's vision spilled out on paper becomes over time a liturgical form. Some of the most beautiful and graceful works of mankind are produced in this way.

Jung (1974) conjectured that the ritual mandalas of India and Tibet were derived in this manner from individual experiences. These mandalas have served generations as a guide for meditation. They consist of intricate geometric patterns that convey the idea of a cosmic order underlying the chaotic events of perceived reality. Rose windows in Christian cathedrals may have had similar beginnings as a mystic's vision of God in the exquisite pattern of a flower's petals. Contemplating these ritual mandalas is comforting.

Mandalas created by persons experiencing stage nine tend to be lovely, symmetrically balanced designs containing even numbers greater than four. They have a center and projections expanding outward to the circumference. A six-pointed star, or an eight-petaled flower are examples of designs seen here. These mandalas appear static, as if they capture a split second of time in a dazzling, motionless display. They suggest a feeling of "being" rather than "doing" that reflects the slowing of creative energy during the stage.

Creating the mandalas of Crystallization can be a pleasurable balance of rational thought and feeling-toned color choices. The intricate patterns require planning, measurement, and careful drawing for successful execution. A wide variety of colors is seen here with special emphasis given to the dark and bright contrasts of autumn. Perhaps more than in any other stage, our use of colors brings a personal depth of meaning to the project that can be truly revealing. Our associations to the colors we use can tell us about our state of mind poised at the pinnacle of success, soon to begin a descent.

STAGE TEN: GATES OF DEATH

 Stage ten, called Gates of Death, marks the onset of entropy in our Great Round cycle of life, death, and rebirth. This stage signifies the end of a cycle. For example, it might indicate the fulfillment of parenting responsibilities, the completion of a project, or the arrival of retirement. Gates of Death may also reveal an end, at least temporarily, to the enthronement of ego as the center of the psyche. Stage ten can disclose a shift toward the Self as the real center of psychic life.

During Gates of Death, ways of being that are customary become dead, empty, and meaningless. What once was perfect simply does not feel right anymore. There is a sense of deflation as the connection between ego and Self grows more distant. Kellogg writes that "Gates of Death represents the death of outmoded conscious contents and the pain of change" (1978:129).

The midlife crisis typifies stage ten. Feelings of loss, depression, and helplessness are not uncommon here. The perspective in Gates of Death is characterized by a feeling of being bound, helpless, and forced to make a sacrifice. We may knowingly or unknowingly adopt masochistic behaviors while enduring this stage. The tasks are to reassess our life goals, surrender outmoded ideas about who we are, and bear the pain of surrender.

Mandala designs created by persons experiencing Gates of Death often suggest the cross of crucifixion. Each quadrant of the mandala may be a different color, symbolizing fragmentation. One looks for a fifth element to appear in these designs, as a symbol of the unifying nucleus. Kellogg has found that when stage ten mandalas have the fifth element: "the suffering becomes ecstatic and a peak experience ensues" (ibid., 130). The wheel motif appears, suggesting martyrdom and the relentless turning of the wheel of life. Designs with an X convey the sense that one is at a crossroads, pulled in both directions. The downward-pointing triangle is seen also, indicating "the descent into the unconscious domain in search of renewal" (ibid., 129). Colors typical of this stage are dark indigo blue and shades of red.

During Gates of Death our interest shifts away from the group to focus more on ourselves. We become increasingly aware of our inner world. We are conscious of the relentless cycles of nature, especially decay and the inevitable approach of death. The task here in the words of Meister Eckhart is to "Let go and let God."

STAGE ELEVEN: FRAGMENTATION

Stage eleven, Fragmentation, is a time of fear, confusion, loss of meaning, and disorientation. One's world has fallen apart. The psychological disturbance during Fragmentation may create physical symptoms such as nausea, diarrhea, or an aversion to light. During this stage we may find ourselves in an altered state of consciousness where intuition becomes prominent and synchronicities are commonplace.

Fragmentation is truly the dark night of the soul. The world does not make sense anymore when we are in this stage. We experience ourselves moved around by inexorable forces over which we have no control. We are visited by strange, frightening, and disreputable messengers uninvited. Kellogg and DiLeo have found that "transpersonal experiences, dreams and fantasies of mutilation, death, contortion, decapitation, humiliation, disintegration, [and] castration abound at this stage" (1982:45). The task is to surrender, to face the shadows, to listen to the trickster, and, in short, to let the former order disintegrate.

Fragmentation can be experienced as a time of purification. Kellogg and DiLeo explain that "various issues encountered in the previous stages of conscious development are now to be experienced once again, this time however, so that we can be freed of them, rather than to be conditioned by them" (ibid.). In stage eleven we must enter once again the experience of profound loss and tearing separation from our original state of blissful unity. We reenact within ourselves this act of violence and aggression so that we become freed from its memory.

Typical mandala forms look like a pie sliced up, with each slice a different color. Mandalas sometimes look like a crazy quilt that has no sense of order or harmony. These mandalas do not have a center. The sense of disintegration is sometimes shown in mandalas by colors that have been layered, with the result being messy, disorderly, and unpleasant to look at. Colors in mandalas of stage eleven tend to be either dark and muddy or overly bright and psychedelic.

Through Fragmentation we descend into the Matriarchy once

again. Mythologically this passage is mediated by dark, powerful monsters who devour and tear apart that which has form in order to reduce it once again to formlessness. Only in this way can it be received by the Great Mother. It may be comforting to remember that this is a necessary, natural process that makes possible the miraculous regeneration of the new. Our faith in a deeper order may blossom to sustain us through this time of transition.

STAGE TWELVE: TRANSCENDENT ECSTASY

 Stage twelve, Transcendent Ecstasy, marks the blissful return home, the coming together of a fragmented ego in a new alignment. In stage twelve the ego is a transparent locus of consciousness. We are aware, but sense the importance of our relationship to a higher power, the Self. Our psychic life organizes around the Self as its true center. The ego functions as an expression of the dynamism of the Self. Powerful energy channeled by the ego in Transcendent Ecstasy often results in a peak experience.

During Transcendent Ecstasy we are blessed with feelings of joy, harmony, and reverence. Instead of feeling invaded by light as in stage eleven, we may experience ourselves as suffused by light. Paradoxes that were once disturbing are resolved through nonrational means, by grace. The world radiates perfection, and we are both an all-important and infinitesimal element within it. This stage is reminiscent of the alchemical quintessence, a highly refined synthesis resulting from many complicated procedures.

The energy of Transcendent Ecstasy might be conceptualized as the awakening of the kundalini serpent lodged at the base of the spine. Its release can be pictured as an uncoiling upward through the spine to become poised as a beautiful flower above the head. As energy pulses through the chakras along the spine, restrictions which diminish the free flow of energy are cleared. Consciousness is alert, active, and diffuse.

Mandalas produced during Transcendent Ecstasy suggest a fountain of light. One often sees mandalas with a chalice or other vessel receiving an infusion of light from above. Human figures with arms outstretched and birds in flight are also common symbols. While there may be a central symbol, there tends to be a focal point implied near the top of these mandalas.

Designs may go beyond the boundaries of the circle. Colors are a combination of dark and light, such as midnight blue and pale yellow. The lustrous pearlized effects associated with numinous experiences are often seen. The mandalas of Transcendent Ecstasy create an impression that is luminous, uplifting, and awe-inspiring.

The tasks of Transcendent Ecstasy are to accept the gift of grace gratefully, humbly, as the fruit of life fully lived. We are to carry the memory of the experiences like a glowing seed into the darkness. There we will plant it for a new cycle. The seed of Transcendent Ecstasy carries us forward to a new beginning on the Great Round.

The mandalas of the Great Round are typical forms related to the experiences associated with each stage. One's own personal growth pattern will not follow neatly from one stage to the next in clockwise order. You may skip stages and move backwards as well as forward in the process. It is not unusual to move from one stage to its opposite across the Great Round.

If you draw mandalas over a period of years, looking at all your mandalas at once helps you identify the progression of forms that reveals your movement along the path of individuation. Sometimes one stage appears much more often than others. Perhaps this stage is the one in which you feel most comfortable. The stage that never appears in your mandalas may be one which is especially difficult for you.

Looking at mandalas and their cyclical changes reminds me of climbing to the top of an old brick lighthouse. The lighthouse is tall and slender with a spiral staircase. At each level there is a window. As I climb the stairs, I can look out the windows and see how far above the ground I am, what the sky looks like, and where the sun is shining. With each turn the windows help me keep my bearings. Your mandalas are like windows on your inner world. They help you get your bearings as you spiral along the path of individuation. With what you see in your mandalas, you can live your life with greater awareness, understanding, and appreciation.

7 DANCING THE ROUND

Mandalas are magic, moments captured, mirrors of our path
Adding colour and form to the awesome inner dance;
Never ending as eternity swings nearer and away along the circle's
    edge,
Drawn in and out, moving delicately over our souls,
Asking only openness and space to see the
Light that shines, the wheel that turns
Again.
                                      —Maureen Ritchie

PREVIOUS CHAPTERS HAVE GIVEN information about the mandala and how to use it. This chapter is devoted to the stories of people who have found the mandala a meaningful pathway to self-discovery. Their experiences show how the mandala can be used for seeking one's inner truth, for balancing energy, for personal growth, and for healing. Let us begin with Debbie.

Debbie, a married woman in her early thirties, was the mother of two young children. She was an understanding mother who intuitively provided her children with many opportunities for learning. As the children grew older Debbie began to ponder her plans for the future. What to do? Then one summer day, her choice became clear. Here is Debbie's description of her experience.

Moment of Decision

I was on vacation in the Poconos with my family. I had to make a decision that summer about a career. I had the opportunity to train with a court reporter. It was a lucrative field. I had typing skills and the ability to learn the other skills, but something told me it would not be fulfilling. It was a technical job.

All my life I had enjoyed working with children. Although my degree was not in education, I thought about becoming a teacher. But I felt I lacked the necessary organizational skills and I was put off by the thoughts of working within the structure of the school system. Still, I had thought a lot about teaching.

On the day I drew my mandala I had gotten pastels out for the children. They were laid out on a table under a tree outside. I looked down from an upstairs window on the children below. I suddenly had an overwhelming feeling that teaching was the work for me. I was filled with a warmth, and I felt the urge to draw a mandala.

I rushed downstairs and drew a free hand circle and filled it in with color. I felt an incredible surge of energy. I knew then that teaching was an organic expression of who I was. Drawing the mandala was an affirmation of that being the direction I wanted to follow. The energy I felt overpowered my doubts, bringing the realization that working within the system was possible without compromising my own teaching goals and ideas.

Drawing the mandala was a powerful, transcendent experience. The mandala itself is a tangible memory of that experience. It brings back the feeling I had when I made it. It was inspired. The mandala sustains me as I look at it. I am now teaching with the plan to get the courses I need to become certified.

Debbie's mandala (Plate 3) is full of yellow, the color that often suggests intuitive insights, new understanding, or a readiness to learn. The jewel-like colors of the triangles surrounding the yellow center come in sets of five. Five is a number associated with bringing into realization one's dreams and ambitions. The triangular form is repeated, symbolizing dynamic movement. The triangles point toward the center of the mandala, indicating an intense focus on self-identity.

The colors appearing in the triangles—red, purple, and blue—can indicate a freeing of energy once bound in loyalty to the mother. A similar trend is revealed in the yellow, orange, and magneta splash in the center of the mandala. These colors are often seen in the work of women achieving a connection with their own inner masculine, and releasing self-imposed limitations once maintained out of dedication to the father. These colors suggest a release of psychic energy for the pursuit of individual goals.

The jagged edge of the yellow, sunlike shape conveys a feeling of challenge. Altogether this mandala is reminiscent of an ancient battle shield. Such mandalas speak of the hero's or heroine's quest in the service of noble ideals. Debbie's mandala appears to be an invocation of her own deep resources of power, drawn up from within and directed outward into activity. Her mandala stands as a firm-footed statement of her calling to bring to light her unique abilities in the teaching of young children.

Nita Sue discovered the mandala at an art therapy workshop, and it seized her imagination. Her youngest child had departed for college. Her husband's work required that she pull up roots and move to another city. Nita Sue's life was in a transition that had activated her unconscious. Pressure to expand her awareness of herself challenged her desire for stability. By creating mandalas she was able to give herself an anchor during a year of change.

Year of Change

Until I was 30, I considered myself an artist working in painting and drawing. About that time, I vividly remember looking at a book of Van Gogh's work, admiring his passionate color, and making a conscious decision to give up painting. I thought, "I can't handle color." I know now I was right. Color unlocks emotion in a way I was unable to tolerate. At that time, though, being able to handle color meant learning a set of rules and applying them in ways that would win approval. As a child, I had been part of a family in chaos. Avoiding conflict, finding approval, and maintaining control whenever possible ruled my life. Any time I failed in those three areas, I escaped into fantasy through books or television. As my two daughters grew older, the complexities of family life dispelled even the illusion of control and freedom from conflict.

I first began to work with mandalas at a Journey Into Wholeness workshop when I was 46. I had been in therapy with a counselor named Mike for several years, both with my family and as an individual. For someone like me, traditional counseling can be a long, slow process. I spent more time trying to figure out the "right" feelings and responses I thought my counselor wanted from me than in confronting myself with honesty. Still, we worked and I learned. At last, I was ready for a major breakthrough. When I saw a conference on Carl Jung was to be offered at one of my favorite places, Mo-Ranch Presbyterian Assembly, I knew I was supposed to go.

I attended the small group mandala workshop led by Susanne Fincher. Her only instruction was to draw a circle and fill it in with color, but my inner authority voice told me the design should have a center and symmetry. As I drew, I wanted a bright sunburst breaking out. Instead, the yellow turned dirty and looked tainted. When Susanne asked if anyone felt worse after doing the mandala than before, I was the only one in the group who raised my hand. I felt I was separating myself from a group whose approval I wanted badly. I was demonstrating my inability to have the appropriate feelings. The only true rule, I learned, was my inability to control either the mandala or my feelings while I drew one.

When the conference ended, I began to do at least one mandala a day. My plan was to work for the entire year and return to the next conference with a full portfolio, so to speak. In time, I did just that. At first, I seemed to be constitutionally incapable of setting the color free. My conscious mind tried to impose some kind of order—not objective order, but trying to make this "picture of my soul" show all the right symbols for a tidy inside—boundaries not too thick or too thin, colors balanced and not dominated by any single one, shapes not too many and/or fragmented. All in all, it is a testimony to the power of the mandala that I couldn't turn out perfect little reproductions of some conscious plan. And after a short while, I forgot any "rules" I thought I knew and let the colors do whatever they wanted.

For me, working with the individual mandala was progressive. Using oil pastels, I would start with certain shapes and colors and add more, sometimes vigorously obliterating entire areas. I scraped away colors and even used colored pencils and oil pastels together. I was doing several mandalas every day. I dated, numbered, and titled each one. With some, I took on the role of each shape or color and described myself. The results seemed to have a certain revelatory function. I was uncovering things about myself in a very diffuse way, symbolic, not tied to particular incidents or insights I had in any verbal sense of "knowing," but rather in a dream-like sense of interaction between the conscious and the unconscious.

In my journals and in therapy at the time, I was dealing with a negative internal voice criticizing or mocking me whenever I felt good about some achievement. Challenging a voice that seemed to me to be speaking the truth was difficult. I used mandalas, prayer, meditation, as well as therapy to do so. I also used the technique of active imagination. In one active imagination session when I tried to confront the voice within that so often stopped me with a negative comment, I wrote, "A big room. I have done three mandalas. People say, 'Oh, how beautiful.' 'I really connect when I look at them.' The Master of Ceremonies takes me up on stage so everyone can praise me. They applaud. I'm smiling—feeling good, happy about what I'm doing. But the Voice on the left says, 'Who do you think you're kidding?' I turn, ANGRY, but can't see anyone. I say, 'No! I won't have it!' even though there was nobody to confront. The M.C. gives me a box—a big box like a gift, all wrapped up. I take it. The Voice says, 'Yes, that's it! It's in the box!' It is a good, excited tone of voice. I say, 'What's in the box?' The Voice says, 'You won't know until you unwrap it.' But it's not time to unwrap it."

That experience was the first time I could see my Shadow side turn from negative to positive. Encouraged, I continued to push myself deeper and deeper. Only a few days later, I did four mandalas that took me over the edge.

As always, I began work on the mandala with a confusion of feelings. The first one contained a small white flower compressed by black. The second one [not shown] I named from a section of Tennyson's poem, "The Lady of Shalott" and said, "The Lady's doom came when she looked at life face to face, not through a mirror." I also saw in this one a reference to Robert Johnson's story of the "Silver-Handed Maiden," as well as references to a dream I had at Mo-Ranch in which I had silver feet. I saw silver hands and feet interacting with a splitting-open egg shape.

I knew I was in emotional trouble by that time, but I kept on pushing myself to go deeper. While I was working on the next one, I was overcome by futility and rage, and ripped the center of the mandala. I wrote on it, "I'm afraid of the core." In my journal, I said, "I am defeated. No more. I quit. Every time I stop reading or T.V., I cry. I feel like I've always been crying. All my life. All I remember is crying—or trying not to—or trying to behave. No more. I quit." When I talked to Mike later, he and I agreed this was a kind of suicide. For me to destroy my work, to rip what I understood to be a picture of my soul, was a cry of pain. Robert Johnson says when you decide to commit suicide, "Good! Now make sure you don't hurt yourself when you do it." For me, this was a symbolic suicide. Something old had died.

After I was calm enough, I immediately drew another mandala. At the time, it seemed necessary. Now, it seems to me a supreme act of courage. The circle was, I wrote, "diminished, small, but power-ful." This total collapse of the ego had left something solid and enduring behind. The next day, as I titled my mandala, I was still in "A Not-Good Place." The boundaries had dissolved completely. Fortunately, I talked to Mike several times during this experience. His support helped me continue an extremely painful process. The mandalas were a nonverbal focus which, I believe, helped me deal with preverbal feelings. Something in the process peeled away layer after layer of hidden feelings. My symbolic suicide was the break-through I needed to see that avoiding my feelings was far more painful in the long run than any confrontation. I accepted it. I don't understand it in any verbal sense of being able to explain. I only know it's true. A few months later, I ended my therapy. I allowed myself to explore art again, not only as a therapy tool, but also as an expression of who I am. And I'm OK.

The first mandala of the series (Plate 4) described by Nita Sue predicts an intensification of feelings of conflict. The design is comprised of four areas. Four is usually associated with wholeness, balance, and harmony, but this is not shown in Nita Sue's mandala. Each area is full of movement and seems to oppose the other three, like so many armies marching against one another into battle. Most of her colors are dark and muddy, suggesting the disintegration of form near the end of a circuit on the Great Round of Mandalas. The arrows and knives directed toward the center of the mandala speak of self-critical thoughts.

Nita Sue's associations to the black in her first mandala are "shadow, power, cloud." In Jungian thought the shadow is those qualities which do not fit in with our idea of who we are. The pressure of these forgotten qualities to be known creates conflict with our preferred conscious identity, the ego. Nita Sue describes the black arrows in her mandala as "strong, pushing . . . breaking out of the brown triangle." It appears that Nita Sue is called upon to acknowledge some truths about herself that have been kept hidden in her unconscious.

In her next mandala (Plate 5), we see the black has formed a box that holds a red, white, and gold flower on a blue background. These colors so tightly held by the black suggest the sealing of an alchemical vessel for the work of transformation. Nita Sue sees a pink question mark surrounding the box. She does not know what will come next, an uncomfortable feeling for someone accustomed to a predictable way of life.

The inner pressures of the transformation process continue as shown in the next mandala (Plate 6). Forms are shattered and brightly colored, showing powerful emotions. The black has penetrated to the center. Here heavy drawing pressure, prompted by anger and frustration, causes Nita Sue to tear through the paper. Damage to one's creation is like an attack on oneself. However, in order for Nita Sue to construct a more flexible identity for herself, the old identity must be dismantled. The tear in the paper is like a ritual act that accompanies the destruction of the old way of being. She reveals to herself a more genuine identity in her next, smaller mandala. This sense of a new self is described in the poem accompanying the mandala:

> There is a face in the darkness
> Could we but see, and to see
> We have only to look.

She presses fearlessly onward, carried along by her growth process. The depth of reorganization Nita Sue is experiencing is revealed by her next mandala (Plate 7). The circle of the mandala, which often reflects the ego boundaries, is missing. In its place are streams of color that flow around the black box, as if washing away old residues. The black box is now empty of everything but a black dot. It is no doubt related to the box Nita Sue is tempted to open during her active imagination.

Colors frame the box in a way that resembles an eye. The formation of a new ego, or "I," is suggested by this eye motif subtly woven into the design. Before the new organization of her ego is accomplished, however, Nita Sue's mandalas reveal that she experiences more upheaval. About a week later she creates a rainbow experience mandala, indicating a profound reordering of psychic energy (Plate 8).

Nita Sue's exploration of a new identity continues through her drawings. A mandala done six weeks later (Plate 9) shows the consolidation of her inner work. A blue boxlike shape occupies the center. It appears to be open, allowing the dark inside to be seen. The box has a three-dimensionality not seen in similar box designs of earlier mandalas. Her design suggests that some of the darkness of the shadow has been assimilated. It appears that Nita Sue has expanded her conscious identity into a personality organization with more depth and openness.

The box is surrounded by a geometric yellow and red form that might be a flower. The six petals of this flowerlike form suggest the coming together of spirit and body in a dynamic connection. It recalls the golden flower described as the ultimate goal in alchemical writings. This mandala is an affirmation of the rewards to be gained by staying open to the unconscious during a difficult period of growth. It reflects Nita Sue's discovery of a new way of being that allows her to have feelings, free herself from needless limitations, and accept her value as a unique, gifted, and loving person.

Marilyn was a busy music therapist. She traveled all over the country teaching classes about the use of music and guided imagery. Her teaching activities included the drawing of mandalas. On one occasion the mandala she drew during a class proved to be very instructive for her. Her story shows how she used drawing mandalas to focus her energy.

Choosing Balance

I was just beginning to teach an extended training session that demands a great deal of energy through five 14-hour days. One of my staff was leading the group of twelve or so persons in an exercise to draw the mandala. I participated with the group and drew my own mandala. I thoroughly enjoyed the drawing. I chose vibrant colors: red, orange, yellow. I added some blue for contrast and interest. The strokes were quick and lively, a profusion of lines exploded from a center which was not clearly defined. The mandala was full of life and vitality. A dancing form or a flower in the middle of the mandala was suggested, but it was not clear enough to be a focus. It was playful and fun.

We put the mandalas on the walls so we could all enjoy the colors and forms which had found their way onto each paper. After everyone had left the room for the night, I began to arrange things for the next day. I looked at my mandala on the wall and was suddenly struck by what I had drawn. My mandala with its profusion of color expanding out from a center was energetic and joyful. If I took this drawing as a reflection of myself, this was indeed a positive state to be in. But this was only the first day of a five-day course in which I had major responsibility. I needed to garner my energy so that I would not become exhausted early in the course. As I looked at the mandala, I felt that I needed to contain this energy; bring it into form and order.

I sat down with another piece of paper and began to compose a mandala which could reflect containment rather than expansion. I began with a soft blue and made a small spiral in the center. I added some lavender to the spiral. Then feeling that structure was needed, I drew a six-pointed star. I associate the six-pointed star with a melding of the human being's upward aspiration to God and God's extending to humanity. It seemed an appropriate symbol for the task at hand. I wanted to maintain a sense of the expansiveness of the first mandala, yet I wanted it to be contained in form. The blue star came into shape. Then I added lavender and purple to the star. With each layering of color, I reinforced within myself the structure of the six-pointed star. I felt my focus coming into a center within myself. The mandala was meditating me. After the star was completed, I added the border, beginning with blue, then adding yellow, coral, and white. This border was a way of remembering the vitality of the first mandala.

When I completed the mandala, I added it to the gallery, placing it above the first mandala I had drawn. I was fascinated to look at them both because they were such contrasts. I liked the first one very much. It was fun and vivacious. The second one was calm and restful in comparison. These mandalas were reminders of the balance that I wanted to strike in my role as teacher in this setting. There was room for both within me. Throughout the week, I would glance at these mandalas and smile with gratitude at the important lesson they had taught me. I was able to use the drawing of the mandala as a behavioral corrective by consciously creating a form which symbolized the balance I wanted to maintain. I had learned a new way of centering using the mandala. It is indeed a magical circle.

Marilyn's first mandala (Plate 10) looks like fire. It suggests the intensity of the noonday sun. The center flowerlike form appears to have four petals, with perhaps the suggestion of a fifth petal, or possibly even a sixth. The outer circle of Marilyn's first mandala is penetrated by the flamelike dashes of color, suggesting her ego boundaries were diffused by the powerful charge of energy she was experiencing.

The open boundary of the mandala together with the hot, fiery colors and the numbers four, five, and six in her design suggest that Marilyn's ego was closely aligned with the archetype of the Self. Inflation, resulting in a feeling of power, energy, and aliveness, is not unusual during such times. However, the person cannot tolerate this level of energy for long without becoming quite tired.

Marilyn was wise enough to recognize the necessity to contain this archetypal energy to meet the demands of her responsibilities as a teacher. Even though the six-pointed star form of her second mandala (Plate 11) was consciously chosen, we see its form foreshadowed in the flower like center of her first mandala. The same colors appear in both mandalas, except that the second mandala has no red. It has lavender. Where has the red gone in the second mandala? It is probably deep in the unconscious, as indicated by the empty space inside the mandala. Red is also contained in lavender, and so we might consider lavender the channel through which the great energy of the previous mandala still moves.

Lavender is thought of as a spiritual color. It is associated with the seventh chakra which mediates spiritual realization. We can see in Marilyn's mandalas a successful shift of energy from lower chakras related to concerns of preservation, autonomy, and mastery to higher chakras having to do with caring, intuition, and spirituality. In her second mandala the very soft colors of the boundary applied over a clearly defined pencil line show us that Marilyn probably revealed to others in her group a personal warmth modulated by a clear sense of her own limits.

Marilyn's first mandala drawing helped her see what her inner reality was. She then chose to contain her psychic energy by drawing a second mandala. In this way Marilyn brought forward latent potentials within her psyche to accomplish the goals she set for herself. Marilyn has shown us that drawing consciously chosen mandala forms can serve as a vehicle to express our emotions, alter our mood, or focus our energy.

Laurie was an active tennis player, jogger, and sports enthusiast. She worked her way through college, and she was the first member of her family to earn a degree. At the age of twenty-one Laurie had just been accepted to medical school when she learned that she had cancer. In an effort to cope with her illness, she joined an art therapy group. It was here that she learned about drawing mandalas. The mandala became her companion on a personal quest that led to self-discovery, renewed spirituality, and healing. This is Laurie's story.

Healing from Within

I was introduced to the mandala in an art therapy group in 1982. My primary reason for joining the group was to deal with issues around living with cancer which had been diagnosed in 1978 and was metastatic. The art therapist had suggested that we all start a journal which could be visual and written word. She also suggested that the mandala was a good way to center oneself in journalling. I immediately got the drawing pad and drew several circles through-out the book. I decided then that the mandala was probably a safe way to start this art therapy process I was now engaged in.

I began drawing mandalas in the journal at night, which had been my most difficult time. The ritual act itself became an important part of ending my days. I enjoyed sitting in my bed producing "windows into my soul," as they often felt to me. I sometimes knew their meanings and other times I could only guess. I was certain that there was importance in whatever I put in the circle because it had come to me without forethought or contriving. The spontaneous delivery of images in the mandala would feel almost magical. Every mandala I drew or eventually painted became a discovery about who I am.

I found that the circle itself offered a sense of safety that I had never felt. The boundaries of the mandala gave me a certain freedom to do whatever I wanted in the sacred center. Cancer seemed to rape freedom at times, but not in the circle. It was mine, and within its walls I was free.

I started with a single line within the circle and from there I created visions and images that seemed for me to be mirrors of what I was feeling and thinking at the time. I hesitated to venture out of the lines of the circle. Eventually, because I had experienced the inner safety, I was able to explore what it felt like to "leave the circle." As I first began to step outside the boundaries, I felt as if I had betrayed the mandala, somewhat like the betrayal I had felt in leaving my mother as I had grown of age. I then knew that a lot of my process had been working through "leaving the womb." As I experimented with the exploration outside of the circle, I began to feel better and stronger about leaving. It also felt important to leave and then retreat again to the safety in the circle.

The individual mandalas became processes within a process. I went through many series of different images. Sometimes the images seemed to have meaning on several levels. I could find my emotional, physical, and spiritual self in the mandalas.

I drew many versions of a dead, lifeless tree with roots clinging in the ground. I knew that I was clinging to life every day in my struggle to beat cancer. The trees were powerful and ever-changing. They began as dark, shadowy figures silhouetted by moonlight. They appeared later as flaming red figures filled with rage, and finally became beautiful green leafed giants. Their branches reached high into the sky as if trying to pull from the heavens.

I drew many ocean waves that seemed to speak of the overwhelming sadness that had come through looking at death. Because I was in chemotherapy treatment, my body fluids were often imbalanced. I felt the ocean waves were also a picture of my bloated body tissues.

I felt that each time I drew a mandala I was having a conversation with different parts of myself. Dealing with cancer had been a lonely experience. Reaching out was difficult because of the enormous sense of not wanting to burden. The experience of learning about myself through the art helped me to feel stronger in my relationships with other people. I drew many images of a lonely person in a boat, way out on the horizon. As I began to experience the richness of my own inner life and reach out, I was able to draw two people in the boats.

The sun became an important image. It seemed to help me in making a positive visualization of the radiation that was destroying cancer cells. I often took mandalas with me to treatments and looked at them as the work was being done. The sun also seemed to be positive masculine energy for me as I struggled with my own inner masculine and the reality of growing up with abusive, violent men.

Drawing as I listened to music late at night became a spiritual time for me. The emotional satisfaction of finding magic in the circle was changing my life on a daily basis. Seeing the images and feeling the power of their messages brought out feelings that had been dead or festering beneath the surface. I knew that even though it became painful at times, I would have to continue with this extraction of feelings so that I could heal.

I drew a mandala daily for two years as I struggled to beat the cancer and find out more of who I was and where I came from. The mandala gave me many new insights. I learned about my true self which, in turn, helped me to find strength, hope, and courage to believe that I had what it took to survive.

Today, several years later, I still draw or paint mandalas, still finding new facets of my inner self. The art of making the mandala bears a special power for me and brings many gifts as I journey through. My cancer is in remission now. I have a firm knowing that through the concentrated effort of looking into the mandala and committing myself to my inner healing, I am alive.

Laurie's tree mandala (Plate 12) seems to be a vivid reflection of her deeply felt determination to live. Perhaps her tenacious hold on life was first learned in a womb that was less than welcoming. Her association of the mandala with a womb seems to verify that she was reworking some of these very early memories at the same time she coped with her current life-threatening situation.

Although the tree in her second mandala (Plate 13) is leafless, it is far from lifeless. Its roots and branches appear to undulate and push outward in all directions. Looking at the image one feels an effort by the tree to reach out, touch, and explore all the space available within the circle. This suggests a powerful will to live.

The landscape surrounding the striving tree is muted in color, and yet the hills are gently sloped, suggesting, perhaps, a woman's body. The sky is empty, and yet we know that the sky is traditionally associated with masculine deities. We could look upon Laurie's mandala as symbolizing her discovery of identity, represented by the tree, as separate from the parents, represented by the earth and the sky. This suggests a reworking of adolescent issues related to leaving the childhood home.

Laurie's boat mandala (Plate 14) portrays her feelings of loneliness. However, the sturdiness of the boat speaks of her buoyant ability to ride the ups and downs of life. A calm sea contrasts with a towering wave that appears to threaten the tiny craft. The reality of death seems suggested by the wave. It appears frozen in a graceful curve that both invites and repels. The sun brings warmth into the mandala. Its rays touch the small boat, but do not penetrate the wave. Perhaps the sun is a symbol for Laurie's increasing self-awareness, bringing light to that which is deep, dark, and powerful within her: the long-buried emotions attached to traumas she worked hard to forget.

Laurie's fifth mandala (Plate 15) shows a figure bathing in sunlight framed by a upward-pointing triangle. The upward-pointing triangle reveals something coming into being, energy on the rise, or unconscious contents pushing into consciousness. All of these meanings seem relevant, for Laurie draws on deep healing resources within herself which allow her to be open to the pain of her past. Her willingness to experience her emotions enables her to claim her power and take responsibility for her own life. The green that surrounds the triangle, being a combination of masculine yellow and feminine blue, suggests the coming together of masculine and feminine energies in a sacred inner marriage. Green is associated with love, harmony, and living things. It is an apt symbol of the healing that brings new life.

Laurie's last mandala (Plate 16) shows us a tree that is covered with leaves. Its form suggests new growth from the roots of a tree once cut down. Birds and butterflies hover near the tree. This mandala shows in symbols Laurie's resurrection from a state very near death.

Magic circle, sacred ritual, reflection of self: the mandala is all these and more. This ancient symbol is a living reality in the lives of modern men and women. As the outward and visible sign of the archetypal Self, it guides, directs, protects, and challenges us to become the persons we truly are meant to be. The stories of Debbie, Marilyn, Nita Sue, and Laurie tell how deeply meaningful the creation of mandalas can be in one's life. It is my hope that with what has been given in this book you will be inspired to walk the path of the mandala when the time is right.

8 MANDALAS AND GROUPS

THE HISTORY OF the relationship between mandalas and groups begins, most likely, with the taming of fire. Gathering round and facing toward a fire at the center of the circle, one's familiars can be seen and recognized visually. As the group, family, or tribe circles around, equally sharing the benefits of the fire's warmth and light, survival is enhanced. Whatever is outside the circle is left in darkness, and difficult to see in the dancing firelight's shadows. The unknown outside the circle naturally stirs feelings of anxiety and dread, and further reinforces the bonds of interdependence among those in the fire circle. Therefore, by its very nature as boundary between inner and outer, the circle creates group feeling, and bestows a sense of belonging on members of the circle. We can see in this scenario the primal elements of a mandala: center (fire) and circle (those gathered around). The circle defines a valued space, set apart from the otherness of space outside the circle.

Through the ages, experiences, meanings, and finally symbolism accrued to this basic formulation of mandalas and groups. Connections were generated between fire and sun, light, consciousness, and self-awareness. Cognates for the circle were found in mountains, caves, horizon lines, solar and lunar pathways, seasonal cycles, and personal boundaries giving rise to a sense of self.

Our focus for this chapter is on mandalas and groups. Growing from the primal fire circle mandala, it seems that there are a number of ways mandalas affirm group identity, and enhance members' feelings of belonging. Mandalas created by groups can provide a matrix for personal growth and self-awareness. Also, viewing groups themselves as mandalas can help members relate to deeper and wider realities in ways that are personally meaningful. We will explore group possibilities along a continuum from mandalas in groups to groups as mandalas. Each section suggests mandala-making activities for groups, arranged from least to most challenging.

GROUPS ARE CIRCLES OF SELF-AWARENESS

Babies are born into the family circle, and are trained in the ways of the tribe by parents, grandparents, aunts, uncles, and other important elders. As it was then, so it is now. Even in contemporary societies the process of introducing young ones into the ways of the culture remains largely the responsibility of family. As George Herbert Mead opines, a child's sense of self develops first "in relation to the selves of the other members of his social group" ([1934] 1962:164). More than just acceptable behavior is taught; patterns of thought, interpretations of reality, and models for relating to self and others are imprinted as what Mead called "the generalized other" ([1934] 1962:154). So we can truly say that the family circle is a mandala that gives birth to the individual; in this sense, a group can be considered a type of mandala that supports individual growth and self-awareness.

Throughout our lives, human beings naturally live in groups where important learning takes place. As we enter new groups, apart from our families, each new group functions in the present, yet also resonates with the birth family, childhood playgroups, and peer social groups. Groups intentionally formed for personal growth provide opportunities to explore personal identity, try new behaviors, and change in ways that are healthy, appropriate, and freeing. This is where the concept of group therapy has come from, as pioneered by Jacob L. Moreno (1966)—awareness of the significance of interpersonal connections and interactions among group members as a source of personal insight and self-awareness.

Forming a group based on mandala-making for personal growth can create opportunities for personal insight, healing, and wholeness. It is generally agreed upon that in order for a group to encourage personal growth it must provide an atmosphere of safety. A carefully formed group envelops members in a circle of support that allows each to pursue their individual self-expression. Groups can benefit from agreeing on their ground rules in the beginning.

The guidelines for a mandala group with a goal of personal growth might include these:

GROUP GUIDELINES

There is no right or wrong way to create a mandala

Emphasize the process, not the product

Respect the artist as the authority about their own work

Avoid analyzing or interpreting other's creative expression by preceding responses to another's mandala with the statement, "If this were my mandala . . ."

Sharing one's work is always optional

Once the group itself is established as a safe container, mandala activities that increase self-awareness can take many forms.

Suggested Activities to Encourage Individual Growth within a Group

Group members are instructed in the creation and interpretation of their own personal mandalas. Group time is used to create and interpret personal mandalas. When they are completed, group members have an opportunity to share their mandalas.

Group members create their own mandalas, and arrange them inside a circle drawn on a large piece of paper, along with mandalas created by other group members. While witnessing this mandala of mandalas, group members respond by personal journaling or group sharing. Let these questions guide the reflection: What do I like/dislike about seeing my mandala joined with others in the circle? Where do I prefer my mandala to be? Why? Whose mandala do I want mine to be near? Why? Whose mandala do I like best? Least? Why? Finally, complete this sentence, addressing your mandala: "I like you (mandala) because you are ____." Now, in order to integrate your mandala as a reflection of your own positive qualities, rewrite your sentence substituting "I am" for the statement, "I like you because you are ____." Read the new sentence silently or aloud to the group.

Group members work as a team to create a large mandala together (see the instructions for drawing a large mandala below). While working on the mandala, increase your self-awareness by noticing and discussing your behaviors. For example: Did you take the lead? How much of the space in the mandala did you claim? Did you share art materials? Did you strive to create consensus in the group? Did you challenge and stir things up? Did you prefer to work with others or work alone? How did this activity affect your sense of belonging in the group? Please verbalize your answers in the group.

Group members each choose a partner and create a mandala together. Decide with your partner what you will do, and who will do what. (Examples: circle drawer, designer, colorist, materials procurer, starter, finisher). When your mandala is completed, talk with your partner, then with the group, about how it was to work together fulfilling these roles, and how you feel about the mandala you created together. Did having specific roles help or hinder you and your partner? Why? Why not?

Drawing a Large Mandala

Drawing a large mandala (on paper 24 inches or wider) can make for a good format for group mandala work. To make a large mandala, tape together pieces of paper to make a square a bit larger than the mandala you wish to create (2-inch-wide cello tape or masking tape works best). Turn the paper over so the tape is on the back. Stretch a string or lay a stick from one corner of the paper to the opposite corner and make a light line a few inches long near the center of the paper. Repeat this procedure between the remaining two corners, drawing a second line that crosses the first. The intersection of these two lines marks the center point of your mandala.

Tie a piece of string to a pencil. Establish the radius of your mandala by holding your string (or having a partner hold it) anchored at the center, and lengthening or shortening the string until the pencil marks fall inside the four straight edges of the square paper and create the size circle you want. Now have your partner firmly press the end of the measured string down on the center point. Swing the pencil around the center point, keeping the string taut as you mark the circle.

Tip: The partner anchoring the string in the center will need to pivot the anchor point of the string while keeping it over the center as the circle is being drawn. This assures that the string stays the same length all around the circle. Keep the pencil perpendicular to the surface of the paper for a perfect circle.

MANDALAS AFFIRM GROUP IDENTITY

While making mandalas in a group can be a powerful way to strengthen the individual, it is also a dynamic way to foster group identity. Some groups are brought together through a spiritual connection that is expressed in the creation of mandalas. Examples of mandalas produced by such groups include Tibetan sand mandalas, Navaho dry paintings, and Gothic cathedral labyrinths. These mandalas are created according to traditional guidelines that express the shared beliefs of a community of people. Their creation is a ritual that brings into the present moment, enlivens, and affirms the group's belief system. Members of the community witness, participate in, and support the mandala work. They partake of the special atmosphere, share sacred foods that may be part of the event, sing prayers, and may be present for the ceremonial destruction of the mandala. These actions reinforce the identity of the community within which the mandala is created.

Groups without official religious affiliations may also make use of mandalas to enhance group identity. The mandala construction grows out of deeply shared values that may or may not be spiritually based. The mandala making provides a way to help new members feel a part of the group, and reinforces ties among members.

Suggested Activities to Foster Group Identity

For groups that meet regularly, members agree to color pre-drawn mandalas during one of their meetings. When completed, the mandalas are displayed on a bulletin board and members have an opportunity to look at them all together.

A group of people convene with the purpose of building a labyrinth. Members design and create the labyrinth, marking the path with string. After the time of building, viewing, and walking the labyrinth, the group deconstructs the labyrinth. This activity can be taken further by lining the labyrinth path with cans of healthy foods that are later donated to a local food bank.

For group members separated geographically, each member draws individual mandalas. Members then share their mandalas with others in the group by either mailing or e-mailing their mandalas to one or all of the members. Alternatively, if possible, members can log on to an

Internet video conferencing service at a mutually agreed upon time and take turns showing and talking about their mandalas.

For a group of friends, the group creates a summer solstice mandala each year around June 21. The mandala making becomes a celebration of summer, of life's abundance, and of the beauty of the sun. It is also an observance marking the group's continuity from one year to the next.

For participants at a professional conference, the group collaborates to create a large mandala in memory of the association members who have died since the last conference. The mandala is exhibited in a place of honor in the main meeting room during the conference.

For a group completing a class, workshop, or retreat, the group marks the ending of their group by creating a mandala together. After viewing their mandala, they cut it into pieces so each can take a bit of it as a reminder of their shared experience together.

For a family, the members hold a discussion about their values. After reaching agreement, all family members contribute to creating a mandala together. The family then takes time to witness and comment on their mandala. Finally, they decide together what to do with their completed mandala.

WHAT ARE THE SEASONS OF A GROUP?

Groups, like all natural phenomena, are subject to natural cycles. They are governed by patterns of forming, functioning, and dissolving. Every group is unique. Its members contribute past experiences, skills, assumptions, and expectations to the fabric of each group experience. However, groups are more than the sum of the individual members. Beneath the qualities that distinguish a particular group from all others lie similarities all groups share. The most important is this: no group lasts forever. Therefore, groups are shaped by the inevitability that they will have a beginning, middle, and an end—in other words, a group is a process.

Irvin D. Yalom offers a model of group process that describes stages in therapeutic group development. Yalom concedes that "there exists no empirical proof that stages in group therapy do or do not exist" (1995:303). Yet group leaders find his stage theory useful. The initial stage has to do with orientation to the group, hesitant participation, dependency, and an attempt to find meaning. The second stage is characterized by a struggle for power that leads to conflict and the establishment of group order. During the third stage, according to Yalom, a group develops cohesiveness and experiences intimacy. He emphasizes that stages can occur in any order, and can be experienced by group members more than once. Yalom, however, does not include in his group process theory a stage describing the ending of a group. This gap is filled by another theorist.

Earlier in this book I described Joan Kellogg's paradigm of the Archetypal Stages of the Great Round of Mandala, or Great Round (see pages 144–169). Kellogg presents the Great Round as a representation of natural stages of change. Hers is a formulation useful for understanding individual cycles of personal growth. The Great Round is also useful as a theory of group process. Kellogg's conception of the stages of change is similar to Yalom's stages, with one important difference: Kellogg addresses the ending stages not included in Yalom's theory of groups. Let us compare Kellogg's Great Round stage theory with the stages of group process identified by Yalom.

The Great Round is comprised of twelve archetypal stages that together describe a wide array of human experiences. Stage One has the quality of resting in the darkness. It is a time of withdrawal from active social interaction. Group members experiencing this stage may be silent, distracted, or excuse themselves for various reasons from the group room. Stage Two is characterized by a dreamy, unfocused consciousness and diffuse personal boundaries. Group members experiencing this stage might express an impersonal love for all in the group. They might claim an ability to get along with anybody.

Stage Three is a time of increased energy and a sense of adventure. It is like committing to take a journey without a clear destination. Group members become interested in each other and express excitement about the possibilities of the group experience. Stage Four highlights comfortable dependency. A sense of entitlement is experienced here. Group members may guilelessly demand special attention during group or request adjustment of group boundaries for their convenience. These four stages align with Yalom's initial stage.

Stage Five is significant as a time of claiming selfhood. It is characterized by an ambivalent struggle for independence. Group members may register dissatisfaction yet fail to articulate their desires clearly. Stage Six is characterized by a struggle with authority that empowers and defines personal boundaries clearly. Challenges to the leader can be overt, hostile, and legalistic. These two stages recall Yalom's second stage.

Stage Seven is a time of experiencing clarity, balance, and self-awareness. Group members show increased appreciation of each other and the leader as unique individuals. Stage Eight is a time when creativity, productivity, and cooperation are experienced through successful functioning in the world. Group members are actively exploring the potentials of themselves and the group. Stage Nine is a time of reaping rewards. Group members may share a mellow sense of satisfaction, appreciation, and accomplishment about the group experience. Their personal growth in the group is openly acknowledged. These two stages seem aligned with Yalom's third and final stage.

Kellogg's stages continue. Stage Ten is a realization that the end of the group process is approaching. Group members may express sadness about the ending of the group, and anxiously bargain to forestall the ending, or raise painful reminders of differences as a way to disengage from one another. Stage Eleven has the quality of things falling apart. It is a time when the feeling of safety is lost. Anxiety in the group increases. Group members may resort to withdrawal, conflict, or hopelessness in order to cope. Stage Twelve is the experience of accepting impermanence and discovering a renewed commitment to life. Members cease their attempts to control or bargain for security. They move to a deeper level of intimacy, opening to the gifts of companionship that come with the final stage of shared group experience, and generalizing their group connections to create a sense of oneness with those beyond the group.

It seems that the natural evolution of a group is well described by Kellogg's stages of the Great Round. The process of the group through time gives momentum to the progression from stage one through stage twelve. This underlying dynamic of the group carries individuals into personal experiences of the stages. However, the stages do not determine individual behavior. Each person encounters stages in their unique way, based on past experience, their repertoire of social roles, and their potentials for creativity and self-awareness in the present moment.

Individuals may have several "home stages" where they tend to feel most comfortable. These are usually ways of being and behaving that come most naturally because of one's abilities, one's level of psychosocial development, or rewards given by family of origin for particular behaviors. For example, a very quiet, immature young woman might be most at home in stage two where she can dream life away with few demands. Yet an accident in which she is seriously injured might catapult her into experiencing stage ten where anxiety, loss, and fear of dying must be confronted. For her and the group this would be a challenging opportunity for growth.

Stage theory can provide useful language for processing group interactions. When individuals in the group are in conflict, referring to Kellogg's Great Round stage theory could normalize the feelings and give the group a context for understanding their impasse. Highlighting a stage during a turning point in the group dynamics can help individuals connect the present experience in the group with their own previous experiences of the stage. Knowing about Kellogg's stages ten through twelve can support members through a constructive termination with the group.

When applying the stages of the Great Round to group process, stages can be tracked in at least three ways: 1) by referring to the time frame of the group; 2) by noting members' behaviors during group; 3) by comparing mandalas created during the group with the Archetypal Stages of the Great Round of Mandala. In a time-limited group, early meetings will exhibit qualities of stages one through four. As the group nears the halfway mark, behaviors typical of stages five through eight will appear. During the second half of the group, members may exhibit qualities of stages nine through twelve. In an art-making group, the mandalas created by group members can be an indicator of the stage of the group. When several mandalas resemble the forms associated with a particular stage, the group is probably experiencing that stage. Also, tracking the behaviors of group members can give information about the group's movement through the stages.

Suggested Activities to Develop an Understanding of a Group's Cycle

After an introduction to the Great Round, group members receive a copy of the Archetypal Stages of the Great Round of Mandala (page 152). Working individually, members mark the stage(s) of the Great Round they and fellow group members are experiencing in the present. Members compare and discuss responses with each other in the group.

The group arranges itself in a circle (works best with a group of twelve or more). Everyone draws individual mandalas. Assuming the group leader occupies stage seven, group members are designated positions on the Great Round with reference to the leader's position. In other words, the person seated opposite the leader will be in the stage one position, and so on around the circle for stages one through twelve. The group then explores similarities and differences between their mandalas and the Great Round stage where the mandala's creator is seated.

Group members draw individual mandalas and identify the stage of the Great Round to which their mandala seems most related. Group members then share personal insights from their mandalas and relate these to the stage(s) they are currently experiencing in the group.

A group convenes for thirteen meetings. At the first meeting, the Archetypal Stages of the Great Round of Mandala is explained; each subsequent meeting focuses on one stage: the second meeting focuses on stage one of the Great Round, the next meeting explores stage two, and so on throughout the remainder of the group meetings. Members are asked to read about each stage before coming to the group meeting. During group, members create a mandala that represents their experience and understanding of the stage. (Mandalas may or may not resemble the mandala designs on page 152.) Group members share their mandalas and insights related to the stage.

GROUPS AS MANDALAS

Jung had much to say about the relationship between the therapist and client. He conceptualized their meetings as generating a transformative field which protects and sets apart both in the intense encounter.

> The therapist is no longer the agent of treatment but a fellow participant in a process of individual development. (1954:8)

Jung referred to this interpersonal encounter as a *temenos* or "sacred space." According to Jung, part of a therapist's role is "the drawing of a spellbinding circle" (1968:53), a container in which personal growth can be realized. He believed that this space was ultimately generated by the Self, a transpersonal pattern of wholeness that is the source of an urge to fulfill one's potentials. Since Jung describes the Self as the origin of mandala symbolism as well as the temenos enveloping client and therapist, we can then conclude that the temenos itself is a sort of mandala. So Jung conceptualized the analytical relationship as a mandala containing the encounter of two human beings.

Jung's work preceded the development of group therapy. Nevertheless, something of the quality of temenos is found in Zerka T. Moreno's description of a group's potential to

> develop and share an unconscious life, from which its members draw their strength, knowledge, and security. This co-unconscious network is the river bed to which the individual histories act as contributories, their "stream" of co-consciousness and co-unconsciousness. (1966:80–81)

Like the temenos of analyst and patient, the group itself generates a field of profound meaning. Therefore, we are justified in taking the view that the group and its myriad connections between members can also be considered a mandala. The group as mandala resembles the mandala created by an individual: a work of art expressing the attempt to fulfill a unique pattern of wholeness.

How does a group mandala come into being? The group mandala is a group of people set apart, individually defined, and bound together in a particular time and place. The group mandala arises from the common interactional matrix and is comprised of the shared consciousness and unconsciousness of group members. Each particular group constellation has implicit within it what is needed to actualize wholeness. The Archetypal Stages of the Great Round comprise aspects of the group mandala that work at the level of group process, both holding and shaping the experiences of group members. The stages also function as potential roles for group members.

The natural urge to complete the gestalt of wholeness, which is potential in the group mandala, means there is a tendency for the group members to actualize as many stages as possible. Thus, in the example earlier of the unfortunate young woman suddenly shifted from stage two to stage ten, the group members would shift stages in response to the personal disturbance that unequivocally takes her to an experience of stage ten. Another member would likely shift to fill stage two vacated by her, perhaps even a member who exited stage ten when she entered it.

More than a group working to foster a group identity, the group as a mandala works as a complete system, with each individual playing a critical role in actualizing the potential wholeness of the group.

Suggested Activities to Establish the Group as a Mandala

A group's leader draws a large circle on paper and cuts it into puzzle pieces. The leader mails a puzzle piece to each person in a group soon to gather (family reunion, casual wedding rehearsal dinner, first meeting of a group or class), and invites them to decorate their piece and bring it with them to the meeting. When together, the group assembles the pieces to create a group mandala.

A group adopts the practice of creating individual mandalas as a response to their group experience. As a group ending activity, members hold up their mandalas all together. Group members witness each other's mandalas without verbal commentary.

A group sits in silence together in a circle before beginning their group activities. Each member tunes in to their sense of the group as a whole. Each member carries this impression into creating a mandala. Everyone then shares their mandala with the group.

When away from a group, members can spend time in solitary reflection and visualize their group. Members then draw the group as a mandala. Members personally respond to their mandala by journaling about it and their group. At the group's next meeting, members can share their mandala and journaling.

Members of a group can reflect on themselves as both individuals and as part of a group. Each member considers what role(s) they are playing in the group, and how they are contributing to the wholeness of the group mandala. Members then draw a mandala expressing their thoughts and share it with their group.

Together the group creates a deck of cards representing the twelve stages of the Great Round. The cards are placed in the center of the group. Taking turns, each member selects one card, and speaks of what they are bringing to the group mandala related to this stage. At the close of the group, cards are collected and the deck stored in a safe place.

During a group meeting, members tune in to their experience of the group in the present moment. This awareness becomes the starting point for a mandala. Members' mandalas are displayed all together. Members consider their mandalas as a reflection of the mandala that is the group.

Each member draws their group as a circle filled with symbols representing each group member. Members draw lines connecting the symbols to reflect their perception of interpersonal relationships among members of the group, including themselves. The mandala is then shared with the group.

During a meeting, members pay attention to the group as mandala. Each consider if they are aware of any areas of the group mandala that need tending. Each member finds a way to share their awareness within the structure of the group mandala.

GROUP MANDALAS AS WORKS OF ART

Viewing a group as a mandala is an aesthetic as well as a psychological approach. Nicolas Bourriaud, the art critic and philosopher, posits a new aesthetic for appreciating conceptual art, that is, art that does not present itself as a product but rather as an experience involving individuals at a particular time and place.

> The role of artworks is no longer to form imaginary and utopian realities, but to actually be ways of living and models of action within the existing real, whatever the scale chosen by the artist. (2002:13)

It is a small step from this concept of art making to viewing a group as art-in-process. Taking this approach, group members become primary constituents within, as well as co-creators of, the artform that is the group mandala.

Suggested Activities to Enhance the Group Mandala as a Form of Art

> A group attends a performance of the choral work "Spem in alium" by Thomas Tallis, staged as originally presented in 1611: eight choirs of five voices each, arranged in an octagon around the audience. Alternately, a group listens to a recording of the piece in surround sound.
>
> A group comes together for circle dancing. They choose dances that range from traditional folk dances to contemporary dances such as those of Dances of Universal Peace, Circle of Peace Dances, or Taize. Their dancing creates the most ephemeral of group mandalas.
>
> A group arranges itself in an open circle holding hands to establish the form of a mandala. The leader drops the hand of the person on her/his right and leads the group in a slow spiraling walk counterclockwise

into a tight formation where all are standing close. After a brief silence, the group begins to randomly tone or sing together, continuing to stand close so all are immersed in the sound. After a few minutes, everyone joins hands and follows the leader in a slow clockwise spiral, singing or in silence, ending in a circle holding hands facing toward the center of the circle. The group lets the mandala dissolve by dropping hands.

A group signs up to join a neighborhood festival parade. Wearing bright colored t-shirts with hoods or matching hats, they move along the parade route while continually reconfiguring themselves in different color combinations and interconnections with hands and arms, like a human kaleidoscope. Movements may be choreographed and synchronized or spontaneous with the goal to maintain a mandala formation. Bystanders with shirts matching the group's, and therefore "the right color," might be invited to join as the mandala moves along.

In a large gathering in relative darkness (prior to an outdoor film showing, sports, or music performance) group members arrive, each carrying a flashlight, and scatter throughout the crowd. At an agreed time, group members turn on their flashlights and slowly move toward a designated area where they converge and stand close together to create a solid disk of light. Gently shaking their flashlights could produce a sparkle effect. Group members hold the form of their group mandala of light for a few moments, then turn off their flashlights all at once and disperse into the crowd, handing their flashlights to strangers.

In this chapter some possibilities for working with mandalas in groups have been offered. Some functions of mandalas in groups have been described. Ways to apply the mandala theory of the Archetypal Stages of the Great Round of Mandala to group process have been suggested. Activities generated by the view that groups are mandalas have been introduced. May this addition to *Creating Mandalas* inspire your own creative thinking about groups and mandalas.

REFERENCES

Argüelles, José, and Miriam Argüelles. 1972. *Mandala*. Boulder and London: Shambhala Publications.

Bahti, Tom. 1966. *Southwestern Indian Art and Crafts*. Flagstaff, Ariz.: KC Publications.

Birren, Faber. 1988. *The Symbolism of Color*. Secaucus, N.J.: Citadel Press.

Bourriaud, Nicolas. 2002. *Relational Aesthetics*. Paris: Les Presses du Réel.

Campbell, Joseph. 1971. *The Hero with a Thousand Faces*. New York: World Publishing Co.

Chicago, Judy. 1979. *The Dinner Party: A Symbol of Our Heritage*. Garden City, N.Y.: Anchor Press.

————. 1982. *Through the Flower: My Struggle As a Woman Artist*. Garden City, N.Y.: Doubleday.

Cirlot, J. E. 1962. *A Dictionary of Symbols*. New York: Philosophical Library.

The Complete Grimm's Fairy Tales. 1972. New York: Pantheon Books.

Craven, Roy C. 1976. *A Concise History of Indian Art*. New York: Oxford University Press.

de Vries, Ad. 1976. *Dictionary of Symbols and Imagery*. Amsterdam: North-Holland Publishing Company.

Di Leo, Francesco, Stanislav Graf, and Joan Kellogg. 1977. "The Use of a Mind Revealing Drug (D.P.T.), Music, and Mandalas in Psychotherapy: A Case Presentation." *Proceedings of the Eighth Annual Conference of the American Art Therapy Association*, pp. 78–86.

Edinger, Edward F. 1987. *Ego and Archetype*. New York: Viking Penguin.

————. 1990. *Anatomy of the Psyche: Alchemical Symbolism in Psychotherapy*. La Salle, Ill.: Open Court.

Elsen, Albert E. 1962. *Purposes of Art*. New York: Holt, Rinehart and Winston.

Ferguson, George. 1961. *Signs and Symbols in Christian Art*. London: Oxford University Press.

Fincher, Susanne F., and Diana Gregory. 2008. "Mandala: An Experiential Group Process Model." *The American Art Therapy Association Conference*, November 19–23, in Cleveland, Ohio.

Fisher, Sally. 1980. *The Tale of the Shining Princess*. New York: Viking Press.

Fox, Matthew (ed.). 1985. *Illuminations of Hildegard of Bingen*. Santa Fe: Bear and Company.

Gelling, Peter, and Hilda Ellis Davidson. 1969. *The Chariot of the Sun*. New York: Frederick A. Praeger.

Goethe, Johann Wolfgang von. [1840] 1970. *Theory of Colours*. Cambridge, Mass.: M.I.T. Press.

Graves, Robert. 1981. *Greek Myths*. Vol. 2. New York: Penguin Books.

Griggs, C. Wilfred (ed.). 1985. *Ramses II*. Provo, Utah: Brigham Young University Print Services.

Hammer, Emanuel F. 1975. *The Clinical Application of Projective Drawings*. Springfield, Ill.: Charles C. Thomas.

Harding, M. Esther. 1973. *Psychic Energy: Its Source and Its Transformation*. 2nd ed. Princeton N.J.: Princeton University Press.

Jacobi, Jolande. 1979. *The Psychology of C. G. Jung: An Introduction with Illustrations*. New Haven, Conn.: Yale University Press.

John of the Cross. 1959. *Dark Night of the Soul*. Garden City, N.Y.: Image Books, Doubleday.

Johnson, Robert A. 1987. *Ecstasy: Understanding the Psychology of Joy*. San Francisco: Harper & Row.

Jung, C. G. 1954. *The Practice of Psychotherapy*. Princeton, N.J.: Princeton University Press.

———. 1964. *Man and His Symbols*. Garden City, N.Y.: Doubleday.

———. 1965. *Memories, Dreams, Reflections*. Ed. Aniela Jaffé. Trans. Richard and Clara Winston. New York: Random House.

———. 1968. *Psychology and Alchemy*. Princeton, N.J.: Princeton University Press.

———. 1969. *Archetypes of the Collective Unconscious*. Princeton, N.J.: Princeton University Press.

———. 1973a. *Four Archetypes*. Princeton, N.J.: Princeton University Press.

———. 1973b. *Mandala Symbolism*. Princeton, N.J.: Princeton University Press.

———. 1974. *Dreams*. Princeton, N.J.: Princeton University Press.

———. 1976a. *Mysterium Coniunctionis: An Inquiry into the Separation and Synthesis of Psychic Opposites in Alchemy*. Princeton, N.J.: Princeton University Press.

———. 1976b. "Psychological Commentary on Kundalini Yoga." *Spring: An Annual of Archetypal Psychology and Jungian Thought*, pp. 1–34.

———. 1976c. *Symbols of Transformation*. 2nd ed. Princeton, N.J.: Princeton University Press.

———. 1979. *Aion*. 2nd ed. Princeton, N.J.: Princeton University Press.

———. 1983. *Alchemical Studies*. Princeton, N.J.: Princeton University Press.

Kaufman, Walter (ed.). 1961. *Philosophic Classics: Thales to St. Thomas*. Englewood Cliffs, N.J.: PrenticeHall.

Kellogg, Joan. 1977. "The Meaning of Color and Shape in Mandalas." *American Journal of Art Therapy* 16: 123–126.

———. 1983. Lecture at Atlanta Art Therapy Institute, Atlanta, Georgia.

———. 1986. "Color Theory from the Perspective of the Great Round of Mandala." Unpublished manuscript.

———. 2002. *Mandala: Path of Beauty*. Raleigh, N.C.: MARI Creative Resources.

———, and F. B. Di Leo. 1982. "Archetypal Stages of the Great Round of Mandala." *Journal of Religion and Psychical Research* 5: 38–49.

Kellogg, Rhoda. 1967. *Psychology of Children's Art*. San Diego: CRM.

———. 1970. *Analyzing Children's Art*. Palo Alto, Calif.: National Press Books.

Langer, Susanne K. 1976. *Philosophy in a New Key: A Study in the Symbolism of Reason, Rite, and Art*. 3rd ed. Cambridge, Mass.: Harvard University Press.

Lüscher, Max. 1969. *The Lüscher Color Test*. New York: Random House.

Luzzatto, Paola, and Bonnie Gabriel. 2000. "The Creative Journey: A Model for Short-term Group Art Therapy with Posttreatment Cancer Patients." *Art Therapy: Journal of the American Art Therapy Association* 17: 265–269.

Moody, Raymond. 1975. *Life after Life*. New York: Bantam Books.

Moreno, Jacob L. (ed.). 1966. *The International Handbook of Group Psychotherapy*. New York: Philosophical Library.

Moreno, Zerka T. 1966. "Evolution and Dynamics of the Group Psychotherapy Movement." In *The International Handbook of Group Psychotherapy*, ed. Jacob L. Moreno. New York: Philosophical Library.

Morris, Charles W. (ed.). [1934] 1962. *Mind, Self, and Society*. Vol. 1 of *Works of George Herbert Mead*. Chicago and London: The University of Chicago Press.

Neihardt, John (ed). 1961. *Black Elk Speaks*. Lincoln, Neb.: University of Nebraska Press.

Neumann, Erich. 1974. *Art and the Creative Unconscious*. Princeton, N.J.: Princeton University Press.

————. 1973. *The Origins and History of Consciousness.* Princeton, N.J.: Princeton University Press.

Ornstein, Robert. 1975. *Psychology of Consciousness.* New York: Penguin Books.

Purce, Jill. 1974. *The Mystic Spiral: Journey of the Soul.* New York: Thames and Hudson.

Radha, Swami Sivananda. 1978. *Kundalini Yoga for the West.* Spokane, Wash.: Timeless Books.

Storm, Hyemeyohsts. 1973. *Seven Arrows.* New York: Ballantine Books.

Teresa of Ávila. 1961. *Interior Castle.* Garden City, N.Y.: Image Books, Doubleday.

Tucci, Giuseppe. 1961. *Theory and Practice of the Mandala.* London: Rider and Company.

Villaseñor, David. 1963. *Indian Sandpainting of the Greater Southwest.* Healdsburg, Calif.: Naturegraph Company.

von Franz, Marie-Louise. 1986. *Number and Time.* Evanston, Ill.: Northwestern University Press.

————. 1974. *Shadow and Evil in Fairy Tales.* Zurich: Spring Publications.

Wagner, Richard. [1876] 1960. *The Ring of the Nibelung.* New York: E. P. Dutton & Co.

Walker, Barbara G. 1988. *The Woman's Dictionary of Symbols and Sacred Objects.* San Francisco: Harper & Row.

Williamson, Ray. 1978. "Native Americans Were Continent's First Astronomers." *Smithsonian* 10: 78–85.

Yalom, Irvin D. 1995. *The Theory and Practice of Group Psychotherapy.* 4th ed. New York: Basic Books.

Ywahoo, Dhyani. 1987. *Voices of Our Ancestors: Cherokee Teachings from the Wisdom Fire.* Boston: Shambhala Publications.

Zaslavsky, Claudia. 1973. *Africa Counts: Number and Pattern in African Culture.* Boston: Prindle, Weber, and Schmidt.

INDEX

on red, 48, 49
on turquoise, 70
on yellow, 53, 55
kivas, 11
Kuan Yin, 42
kundalini, 133, 168

labyrinths, 188
lamb, 113–114
Langer, Susanne, 5
Last Supper, the, 111
Laveau, Marie, 122
lavender, 63–64
Lent, 61, 70
Leo, 54
Libra, 57
lightning, 129–130
lion, 113
Lucifer, 95
Lüscher, Max
    on black, 38
    on blue, 51, 52
    on brown, 68
    on purple, 61
    on red, 49
    on yellow, 55

Maat, 124
Madonna, 37. *See also* Virgin Mary
magenta, 66–67
mandalas, 1, 13, 19
    children's, 20–21, 145
    group processes, 184–197
    line quality in, 91, 92, 162
    meditation with, 13, 15, 18
    orientation with, 7, 8, 12, 21
    pearly effect in, 45, 168
    placement of design elements in,
        34–35, 92
    rainbow experience, 82, 132, 176
    symbol for Self, 2, 19, 20
    Tibetan, 12, 17–18, 47, 50, 165

mandorla, 120
Maori, legends, 5, 36
marriage, 66, 108, 182. *See also coniunctio*
Mars, 48
Maryland Psychiatric Research Center, 24
Maya, 142
Mead, George Herbert, 185
medicine wheel, 77–79
    East, 55
    North, 43
    South, 56
    West, 39
Mercury, 63
"Miss X," 110
Mithra, 130
moon
    legends, 5, 41
    as natural symbol, 3, 5, 42
moon time, 123
Moreno, Zerka T., 194
Mother Earth, 38
Mother Nature, 37, 59
mysticism, 108, 116, 153, 156, 165

Navaho sandpainting, 10
near-death experience, 43, 52
Neumann, Erich, 21
New Jerusalem, 14
nigredo, 37, 86, 113
nirvana, 16
numbers
    one, 93–94
    two, 94–96
    three, 96–98
    four, 98–100
    five, 100–101
    six, 101–103
    seven, 103–105
    eight, 105–106
    nine, 106–107
    ten, 107–108
    eleven, 108–109